# THE INVENTION OF SCOTLAND

The late Hugh Trevor-Roper (Lord Dacre of Glanton) was Regius Professor of History at the University of Oxford, and a prolific scholar. His posthumous book, *Europe's Physician: The Various Life of Sir Theodore de Mayerne*, was published by Yale University Press in 2006. For thirty years Trevor-Roper, who was married to a Scot, spent university vacations at Chiefswood, his home outside Melrose.

# THE INVENTION OF
# SCOTLAND

*Myth and History*

HUGH TREVOR-ROPER

YALE UNIVERSITY PRESS
NEW HAVEN AND LONDON

Editor's foreword © Jeremy J. Cater

First printed in paperback 2009

Published with assistance from the Annie Burr Lewis Fund

For information about this and other Yale University Press publications, please contact:
U.S. Office:      sales.press@yale.edu    www.yalebooks.com
Europe Office:    sales@yaleup.co.uk      www.yaleup.co.uk

Set in Minion by J&L Composition Ltd, Filey, North Yorkshire
Printed in Great Britain by TJ International Ltd, Padstow, Cornwall

Library of Congress Cataloguing-in-Publication Data

Trevor-Roper, H. R. (Hugh Redwald), 1914–2003.
    The invention of Scotland: myth and history/Hugh Trevor-Roper.
        p. cm.
    Includes bibliographical references and index.
    ISBN 978–0–300–13686–9 (alk. paper)
    1. Scotland—Historiography.    2. National    characteristics,    Scottish—
Historiography.    3. Scotland—Civilization—Historiography.    4. Scotland—
History   I. Title.
    DA759.T74 2008
    941.10072—dc22

                                                                    2007032173
A catalogue record for this book is available from the British Library.

ISBN 978-0-300-158298 (pbk)

10 9 8 7 6 5 4 3 2 1

The publishers and Estate of Lord Dacre of Glanton thank the Past and Present Society for kind permission to reproduce material from Trevor-Roper's essay 'The Invention of Tradition: the Highland Tradition of Scotland' in *The Invention of Tradition*, ed. Eric Hobsbawm and Terence Ranger (Cambridge University Press, 1983).

# Contents

# Illustrations

# Editor's Foreword

Jeremy J. Cater

The recovery and publication of a book which was left unfinished by its author over twenty years earlier requires some explanation. The decision depends on who the author was, how far and why the book was not completed, and what it can contribute to the present. Hugh Trevor-Roper was a master historian; and even in this short work his many talents are amply displayed – as, indeed, they were so often in his collections of essays. Here, as elsewhere, we see the imaginative insight into characters; the awareness of social and intellectual context; the broad and deep vision across space and through time which allowed the drawing-in of illuminating parallels or differences; the determination to drive all interpretation as far as it would go, to arrange all explanation in a large and satisfying synthesis; the delight in the dramatic and the ridiculous; the varied and ingenious syntax; the clear, elegant and witty choice of words and metaphors that would stimulate and amuse the reader.

Trevor-Roper left this book incomplete only in a restricted sense of the word. He had not, it is true, given any of the text its final polish, preparatory to publication. Phrasing needed to be tightened, repetitions eliminated, fuller notes supplied, linking passages written: but these are matters of detail, which I shall touch on later in describing my editorial work. The eight chapters of the book now published were there in structure and in essence as they stand now. What is missing is the beginning and the end of the book as he envisaged it. Those eight chapters describe three types of myth – political, literary and sartorial – which he located in the context of several centuries of

Scottish history. He intended to write a preliminary chapter on myth in general. Such a chapter – from his pen – would undoubtedly have been valuable. All that I could find of it, however, is the fragment which stands now in place of an introduction. Concerning the conclusion of the book I am less certain. In describing his project to a friend in December 1979 he hinted at a fourth myth, which would carry the analysis further down in time. The suggestion was tentative, and may even have been playful. At any rate, so far as I can find, nothing further was done in that direction. Two years later he seems to have stopped working on this book, with the present eight chapters written; other projects, other work, took over. He continued to think, talk, and correspond on this subject for several years more; but he never went back to write the larger book on it which he had once intended.

Trevor-Roper's interest in the subject was of long standing; and parts of this book are revised versions of essays already published elsewhere. In particular, chapters two and three – on George Buchanan and his critics – constitute a reconsidered and rewritten version of work which he published as a separate supplement to the *English Historical Review* in 1966. Chapters seven and eight – on the rise of the tartan and the kilt – first appeared in a collection entitled *The Invention of Tradition*, edited by Eric Hobsbawm and Terence Ranger, which was issued in 1983 by Cambridge University Press on behalf of the Past and Present Society. A very brief summary of chapters four to six – on James Macpherson and 'Ossian' – appeared as an article in *The Spectator* magazine in March 1985. All three main sections of the book were based on a good deal of research; and they sustain challenging, and still relevant interpretations of their specific topics. Indeed, I believe that the chapters on James Macpherson and 'Ossian' will be found to present ideas and information which are still new, despite the efforts of other writers during the twenty-five years since Trevor-Roper was at work on this area. The whole book, moreover, is greater than the sum of its individual parts. Taken together, its three sections add up to a profound and coherent interpretation of the rôle of mythic feeling and mythic thinking in the cultural development of Scotland over many centuries. Considerable depth of perspective on this theme is added by the first chapter, though it is based rather on a fresh reading of the obvious sources than on the kind of detailed and original research which underlies what comes later. For that first chapter shows the construction, during the middle ages, of that mythic mould of historical self-consciousness in the Scots which was to shape their understandings and imaginings for centuries thereafter – and still does, to some extent, even today.

It may be helpful to know something of when and why Trevor-Roper chose to write this book about the historical identity of the Scots. He always felt himself to be an Englishman; but the Scots were far more to him than merely his neighbour nation. His engagement with the Scots began early and was long lasting. Born and brought up in the north of Northumberland, on the English side of the historic border between the two nations, his sense of the past was awakened in childhood by the physical remains of the frontier: the Roman wall, the peel-towers, Bamburgh castle. In later youth, his historical imagination was stimulated by reading the poetry and novels of Sir Walter Scott, reflecting the other side of the border. Indeed, his contact with the Scots – or the Scotch, as he preferred to call them, following what he regarded as good historical precedents – was substantially closer and more personal than these relatively abstract considerations might imply. Later in life he would some- times tell people that he had had a Scotch nanny, followed by a Scotch governess, and had then been sent to a Scotch school (in Dunbar). After an interval, he would continue, he had married a Scotch wife (Lady Alexandra, daughter of Earl Haig of Bemersyde), and had a Scotch home (Chiefswood just outside Melrose, a house built by Sir Walter Scott for his daughter and son-in-law, J.G. Lockhart, his future biographer). For twenty-eight years after 1959, Trevor-Roper would spend part of each university vacation in the peace and beauty of Chiefswood, reading, reflecting, writing, exchanging hospitality with his Scotch neighbours; going occasion- ally to Edinburgh to work in the National Library, or to attend events at the Festival.

That personal background produced an intellectual foreground. Trevor-Roper was always a believer in, and a practitioner of, a comparative approach to history. In a series of essays which he wrote during the 1960s Scotland became one of his comparators.

Sometimes this was in European-wide sweeps which drew in Scottish examples: as in his essays on the European witch-craze of the sixteenth and seventeenth centuries, and on the religious origins of the Enlightenment. Sometimes he focussed more specifically on situations, trends or individuals in Scottish history: as in his essays on George Buchanan, on David Hume, on the impact of Cromwellian rule in Scotland, and on the Scottish Enlightenment. That series of essays came to an end with the two short works which he wrote in 1971 to commemorate the bicentenary of the birth of Sir Walter Scott: his essay on 'Sir Walter Scott and History', broadcast on radio and published in *The Listener* for 19 August 1971, and his more general address (in March) as president of the Sir Walter Scott Club of Edinburgh – published in *Sir Walter Scott, 1771–1832: an Edinburgh Keepsake* (ed. Allan Frazer, Edinburgh, 1971).

For five years after 1971 Trevor-Roper wrote nothing more on Scottish history, other than a handful of brief book reviews in newspapers. He had turned his attention elsewhere. In those years he was, as usual, writing several books at the same time. He wrote two books on very different subjects, both of which appeared in 1976: a book on Habsburg patronage of art in the sixteenth and early seventeenth centuries; and a study of the extraordinary Anglo-Chinese forger and fraud of the late nineteenth and twentieth centuries, Sir Edmund Backhouse. At the same time he was continuing his long-term research, begun at the start of this decade, into the life of the great Huguenot doctor, Sir Theodore Mayerne, which would not be published for another thirty years.

Then, at the very end of 1976, Trevor-Roper revealed that his interest in Scottish history had only been dormant, or smouldering, and was now rekindled. In December he delivered a lecture at University College London on 'The Anglo-Scottish Union', which appeared in print in *The New Review* in February 1977 (republished in his last collection of essays, *From Counter-Reformation to Glorious Revolution*, London, 1992). That year, 1977, saw several more items on Scottish history flow from his pen. He contributed a piece on 'British Civil Wars: the Jacobite Rebellions of 1715 and 1745' to the *Sunday Telegraph* on 3 April. During the summer he gave a paper on Scottish history to a conference in Oxford, organised by the historical journal *Past and Present*. In August he delivered a lecture at Edinburgh on 'The Scottish Enlightenment', which was published in *Blackwoods Magazine* in November. He wrote a major review of William Ferguson's book, *Scotland's Relations with England: a Survey to 1707*, which appeared in the *Times Literary Supplement* on 9 September. The subject of the *Past and Present* conference in Oxford in the summer of 1977 had been 'The Invention of Tradition'; and the paper which Trevor-Roper contributed to it was the germ of this book.

What was it that brought Trevor-Roper back to writing on Scottish history at that time? The answer can hardly be in doubt. It was the prospect, or the spectre, of 'Scottish devolution': the proposal to set up a legislative assembly at Edinburgh, with some powers devolved down from Westminster, which threatened sooner or later, in his opinion, a dissolution of the Union of 1707. As a committed unionist, Trevor-Roper opposed this proposal; as an active citizen, he took up his pen to explain to the public what he saw as its disadvantages. In 1976 he published three articles in the newspaper press on different aspects of this topic: 'Scotching the Myth of Devolution' in *The Times* on 28 April; 'Fief in our Time' in *The Scotsman* on 23 August; and 'The English Assembly: a Cautionary Tale' in *The Times* on 23 September. In that year, and in the three following years, he continued his efforts, in various ways and at different levels, to discredit the Labour government's devolution project, which he believed was based on fallacious arguments and would engender serious adverse consequences. He gave a talk on 'The Unity of the Kingdom' to a group of prominent Tory MPs. He contributed a foreword to the book against Scottish devolution written by the rebel Scottish Labour MP, Tam Dalyell (his neighbour in the Lothian counties). He corresponded with many private individuals all over the United Kingdom. It is against this background of political contest that we must envisage the initiation and early continuation of this book on the rôle played by myth in Scottish history.

Trevor-Roper did not deny that Scotland had real problems: the decline of heavy industry, for instance; the endemic corruption of local government monopolised by a single set of people; and the persistent emigration of men and women of talent. What he did deny was that legislative devolution was the proper answer to these problems. Proper answers of a pragmatic kind lay elsewhere: in administrative decentralisation, in an alteration of economic and educational policies, etc. But to set up in Edinburgh a separate Parliament for Scotland, with some of the emblems but a limited supply of the substance of sovereignty, seemed to him a recipe for political instability, the fomenting of discontent, and ultimately a probable re-separation of Scotland from England. This last he opposed because, as a historian, he believed that both countries had derived great benefits from being joined together in the Union.

Rational argument, of a pragmatic kind, about the merits or demerits of a devolved Scottish assembly – and even about the merits and demerits of the Union – was one thing. Quite another was the attempt by Scottish nationalists to rouse atavistic tribal loyalties in support of their cause through appeal to a fraudulent romantic version of the country's history. Though quite happy to accept the maintenance of national identities, Trevor-Roper was strongly averse from nationalism, whether Scottish or English. In his lifetime, he had seen enough of the effects of nationalism in practice to loathe it on principle.

In the early 1960s Trevor-Roper had remarked on the apparent addiction of the Scots to historical myth (as in the matter of the kilt). He had blamed the professional historians of the country for doing too little to educate their compatriots into more self-critical habits of thought. And he had said that, if native historians were reluctant to de-mythologise, he would lend his own pen to assist the process. One of the early fruits of this de-mythologising agenda was his essay of 1966, in which he revealed George Buchanan as the conscious perpetrator of a politically convenient myth about the country's ancient constitution, even after being forced (by an outsider) to recognise it as fiction. In his essays of 1971, Trevor-Roper moved on to address the mythologising activities of Sir Walter Scott. He showed how Scott had sought to cement the Union of 1707, with its benefits of economic advance and civil freedom, by creating a new identity for Scotsmen within the broader British community; and how, in order to reconcile his people to the pain of losing their old historical identity, he had created, through the magic of his imaginative fantasy (though a very rational man himself in other ways), a healing myth about old Scotland. Scott's myth had obliterated all the historic animosities between Highlanders and Lowlanders, Celts and Saxons; and had brought into being, instead, a modern 'synthetic Scotsman', with a Lowland head and Highland dress, willing and able to face the future constructively.

In the mid-1970s Trevor-Roper saw romantic nationalists at work in Scotland again, busily re-creating the image of the past in order to suit their present purposes. They were seeking to harness the real discontents within Scottish society in order to drive forward a political programme which aimed at the re-creation of an independent Scotland, freed from the supposedly contaminating and oppressive influence of England. Trevor-Roper's objection to this movement was both practical and historical. For, on the one hand, he believed that Scotland and England (and Wales) would be safer and more progressive in character together within the United Kingdom than they would be separately. On the other hand, he considered that the versions of the past which the romantic nationalists found usable were constructions which owed more to myth than to reality. It was to warn the public about the difference between reality and myth in history that he took up the task of writing this book.

For the polemical origin of the impulse to write the book, no apology is surely necessary. Once the research and the writing began, the normal controls of objective historical scholarship were applied. The evidence collected had to be weighed, and was weighed, in fairness of interpretation, and then made available with accuracy of presentation. As for the subject itself, it illustrates very well Trevor-Roper's constant insistence that history should be written to inform the general public as widely as possible on questions that mattered to the present; and that good history should drive out bad.

Little need be said of the stages through which Trevor-Roper progressed once he had decided to write the book. Aside from quiet reading in various libraries, there was some visiting of places associated with the subjects which he would be describing – an approach which he had learned, indeed, from the practice of Sir Walter Scott.

Thus we find him, in 1978, visiting Windsor Castle to view a book on tartans illustrated by one of the Sobieski Stuart brothers and later donated to the royal library; in 1979, visiting the Highland Museum at Comrie in Perthshire; in 1980, visiting Macpherson territory in the Spey valley of Badenoch. By the beginning of December 1979, at the latest, he had settled in his mind the division of the book into three myths (or perhaps four). He had accepted an invitation to deliver three lectures in the following spring at Emory University, Atlanta, Georgia; and those lectures were to be entitled 'Myth and History in Scotland'. The lectures (the Walter Turner Candler Lectures) were duly given in Atlanta in the last week of March 1980. During the remainder of that year the three lectures were expanded into eight chapters. By early 1981 he was ready to air various parts of the book in public – mostly the parts on James Macpherson and 'Ossian' – at venues in Oxford, Cambridge and Edinburgh. Some adjustment – some rethinking, additional research and rewriting – followed thereafter, as it usually did subsequent to his delivery of talks or seminar papers. But then, at some point, he ceased to work on it actively, though discussion continued for a while longer.

Why then did Trevor-Roper, having written so much of this book, stop working on it? Several factors may have been involved. During this time he became busier than ever; and new opportunities and directions opened to him. In June 1979, as he was lecturing in Boulder, Colorado, he heard that he had been made a peer by Mrs Thatcher, the new prime minister following the general election in May. On his return to Britain he would take the title of Lord Dacre and begin to attend debates in the upper house of Parliament. As a member of the Board of Directors of Times Newspapers, he was of course involved in extra meetings and grave decision-making during the bitter and protracted battle which then raged over the future of that newspaper. In December 1979 he heard that he had been elected Master of Peterhouse college in Cambridge: a post which he would take up in October of the following year. He calculated that he would gain seven years of office at Cambridge for the one remaining year he would relinquish at Oxford; and that he would enjoy more time for his own research and writing as the head of a college than he had had as Regius Professor. He was disagreeably surprised to discover, on the latter calculation, that the opposite was true. At Peterhouse he found a great deal of work to do. In November 1981 he lamented to an Oxford friend that his migration to Cambridge had proved a terrible interruption to the orderly pursuit of his historical projects.

Meanwhile, engagements entered into previously for the production of more essays, mostly on English history, pressed upon him. Chief among them at that time were *Renaissance Essays*, which appeared in 1985, and *Catholics, Anglicans and Puritans: Seventeenth-Century Essays*, which followed in 1987. Always he continued, intermittently and when he could find the time, his long-drawn-out research on Sir Theodore Mayerne, which would only be published in 2006, three years after his death. Among these other interests and activities, his book on Scottish history was crowded out.

There were at least two other reasons why he did not complete that book within the time frame which he had originally allotted to it. One of the main driving forces behind the book, as we have seen, was Trevor-Roper's opposition to a legislative devolution for Scotland. When the Conservative party under Mrs Thatcher won the general election of 1979, the previous government's proposals for Scottish devolution were shelved for an indefinite period. For Trevor-Roper that removed a spur to action, though he continued to be carried forward for a time by the momentum which he had already accumulated.

Secondly, there had always been a secret obstruction to his research for this book. He had learned in the summer of 1974 that an important collection of letters written by James Macpherson had survived, and was in private hands. The holder of that collection, who himself possessed no legal right to it, was a historian placed in a prominent public position; and, when other scholars applied to him for access to this collection, he allowed or denied it, according to his personal whim. Regarding this situation as extraordinary and intolerable, Trevor-Roper began at that time, at first by polite enquiry and diplomacy, to try and open up this collection to scholars more generally. Three years later he redoubled his efforts; for by now, engaged on the writing of this book, he wished to see that collection of letters himself. During the next five years he kept up the pressure through correspondence with the principal personage involved, and many others. He was met by resistance, evasion, half-promises, denial. He found a way to offset the problem partially; but, to him, this was an unsatisfactory solution. Eventually, in May 1982, he was informed that his campaign had succeeded at last: for the collection of Macpherson manuscripts had been handed over to the India Office Library, there to be sorted and calendared, and made available to the public at some time in the future.[1] But this would be too late for Trevor-Roper. One month afterwards, he told an Oxford friend who enquired about the progress of his Scottish book that he could not, at present, realistically foresee its completion as a whole; but that, in the meantime, he would make parts of it available separately.

We may also wonder what part may have been played in the discontinuance of this book in 1982 by that mysterious fourth myth, at which he had hinted in 1979, when he was full of enthusiasm about the whole project. If the elaboration of that fourth myth was ever a serious proposition, he must presumably have concluded by 1982 that he was unlikely to get back to it within the foreseeable future.

So far, this book has been presented as if it were concerned solely with the history and culture of Scotland. But that would be too narrow a view. For myth has played a vital part in the historical development of many communities. Ancient Greek city-states, great churches, modern nations: all have had their roots in, or have absorbed, or been encrusted by, collective mythologies. Some have been harmless, even benign; others malignant. Consider the contrast, touched on explicitly in this book, between the Scottish myths, which ended in reconciling Highlanders and Lowlanders into the acceptable form of a modern 'synthetic Scotsman', and the German myths, which, building on the barbaric heroes of the *Nibelungenlied*, ended in the destructive horrors of the Third Reich. Thus the book, exploring its theme in the local context of Scotland, reverberates more widely.

I must now describe the process by which Trevor-Roper's book has been made ready for publication. It was contained in two box-files. The first box contained various drafts of the text: from the initial

---

[1] A little more of this story is revealed in footnote 43 to chapter five.

handwritten lectures, as delivered at Emory University in March 1980, through various stages of typescript, added to and amended in manuscript, until they had reached a final, or almost final state. The second box, whose existence I discovered several months after the first, contained a mass of notes from Trevor-Roper's reading of the sources, some of his reflections on what he had found, and a quantity of correspondence connected with the writing of the book. As now published, the book consists primarily of the most complete text found in the first box, but with additions drawn from the contents of the second box, when materials appeared there which had not yet been fully incorporated or assimilated into the typescript drafts.

The chapters in which this transfer of materials has occurred from the 'notes box' to the 'text box' are numbers three to six. In chapter one there was some confusion in the first pages, indeed some contradiction between the two versions available: the initial handwritten lecture version and a subsequent typescript draft. In the absence of any typescript draft of this chapter which is marked as 'corrected' (unlike some of the others), I have had to straighten out the confusion as best I could – with external help, for which I am extremely grateful. There was also, later in this chapter, a clear but unexplained gap in the text, with no notes left to fill it, other than an indication of the subject matter required. I therefore wrote a short linking passage to cover that gap myself. Chapters two, seven and eight appear in print in a form virtually identical with their final typescript versions.

Readers will notice, in fact, that the beginning of chapter seven contains some recapitulation of what had gone before. That is because these two chapters were cut off from the book, and published separately as an essay in *The Invention of Tradition*. A brief introduction was added by Trevor-Roper for that format. I have chosen to leave that passage standing in the text of the book, although in purely literary terms it constitutes a blemish. For it contains, along with a little repetition, some of those general reflections from the mind of the author which, had he finished the writing of the book himself, would have been reorganised in order to reveal fully the widest significance of his theme, charged with its deepest meaning.

It only remains for me to thank those persons who have given me help, either concerning problems in the text, or with information for this foreword: Alan Bell, Ronald Black, Dauvit Broun, Judith Curthoys, Anthony Grafton, Nicholas Phillipson, Terence Ranger. I am especially grateful to Blair Worden, Trevor-Roper's literary executor, for entrusting to me the task of editing this book for publication: thus enabling me to repay, in some small measure, the great kindness which Hugh Trevor-Roper showed to me at an early stage in my career, as he did to so many other young scholars and would-be scholars.

# Introduction

At different times, and in various places, myth has played an important part in history. For what people believe is true is a force, even if it is not true. Myth may be a driving force: such as the myth of inevitability, encountered in Calvin, or of invincibility, as at Sparta. Myth may also be the *soul* of history, engendering imaginative literature in poetry or prose.

Some races, it seems, are more mythopoeic than others. The myths of ancient Greece are as inseparable from Greek history as they are from Greek literature. The Anglo-Saxons, on the other hand, have been the least mythopoeic of peoples. The English have created one of the great literatures of the world. Yet, have they a single myth that they can call their own? Almost all peoples have a myth of their own origin: a heroic age; divine descent; the discovery and colonisation of their land. The Anglo-Saxons have no such thing: no halo of romance surrounds the misty figures of their alleged leaders, Hengist and Horsa. All the myths of England come not from the Anglo-Saxons, but from the Celts. It was from Celtic Britain that Shakespeare and Spenser drew their native heroes. It was in the Celtic cycle of King Arthur and his court that Milton sought, and Malory and Tennyson found inspiration. It was in Celtic Scotland and Celtic Ireland that Romanticism re-created its mythology in the nineteenth century. The defeat of the Celts in England, in Wales, in Scotland, has inspired mythology. Neither in prosperity, nor in defeat, did the Anglo-Saxons, in their six-hundred-year rule in England, inspire a single work of myth or romance, then or thereafter – unless we allow that

title to the Augustan poet laureate Henry Pye, who published *Alfred,
an Epic Poem in Six Books* in 1801.

The creation, and re-creation, of myth requires a continuing
capacity for invention; and its formalisation can be seen as a ritual
adjustment, a formal accommodation of barbarism to civility. The
process therefore entails a necessary element of fantasy, often indistinguishable from fraud. Some of the heroes of this book will appear
as frauds, artists in fraud. But let it not be thought that I criticise
them for such artistry. Rather, let us praise them for having domesticated a dangerous process: a process which, in some countries, has
been far less innocent. In Germany, the ancient barbarians of the race
were revived in all their savagery, during the later nineteenth century
and the first half of the twentieth, as models for modern politics.
Ritualisation would have been better.

In this book I attempt to explore the interaction of myth and
history in Scotland. For in Scotland, it seems to me, myth has played
a far more important part in history than it has in England. Indeed, I
believe that the whole history of Scotland has been coloured by myth;
and that myth, in Scotland, is never driven out by reality, or by
reason, but lingers on until another myth has been discovered, or
elaborated, to replace it.

In what follows, I propose to illustrate this thesis by studying three
consecutive myths which have successively filled the four hundred
years of Scottish history from the sixteenth century to the twentieth.
They are (1) the political myth, the myth of the ancient constitution
of Scotland, which prevailed from the sixteenth century till the eighteenth; (2) the literary myth, the myth of the ancient poetry of
Scotland, which lasted from 1760 till the 1820s – if not beyond; and
(3) the sartorial myth, the myth of the ancient Scottish costume,
which began in the 1820s and is with us still. All these alleged legacies
of ancient Scotland are mythological: there was no ancient constitution, no ancient poetry, and no distinctive ancient dress – or at least,
whatever there was of them bears very little resemblance to what the
world was, for a long time, persuaded to believe. But these myths,
though they may explode on contact with the evidence, are nevertheless historically important. The myth of the ancient constitution was
the beginning of a political theory which, in the hands of English

whigs and French Huguenots, would become a political force in Europe. The myth of the ancient poetry was the beginning of an ideological current which, channelled by Goethe and Napoleon, would swell the European romantic movement. The myth of the ancient Highland dress supplied a distinctive feature by which Scots, and supposed Scots, could identify each other and be identified, at home and across the globe: in other words, it served as a communal integrator. Incidentally, it supported a significant textile industry and added to the gaiety of nations. All these myths, I shall suggest, were imported into Scotland from abroad: the first from France, the second from Ireland, the third from England; but in Scotland they were denizened, and it became a part of the national honour to maintain them – at least until a new myth should be imported to drive them out. And these three myths, which made Scotland known in the world, are connected with three famous names in literature: George Buchanan, James Macpherson, and Sir Walter Scott.

*Part I*

# THE POLITICAL MYTH

# 1

# Scotia's Rise to Glory?

The early history of all countries is obscure; but the mist which envelops the early history of Scotland is unique, both in density and duration. It was both thickened and prolonged by national pride and deliberate myth-making. As late as the end of the eighteenth century, the racial origins of the Scots and their relationship with the Irish was a matter of learned dispute; and the ablest scholars were led, by blind or interested guides, and by deliberate forgeries, into the grossest errors. In 1729, the first and greatest of Scottish antiquaries, Father Thomas Innes – an exiled Catholic priest and Jacobite who stood outside the interested intellectual establishment of Scotland – had destroyed the basis of the Scottish myths. But his work was barely noticed; and in 1776 even Edward Gibbon, misled by 'two learned and ingenious Highlanders', would be totally wrong about the origin of the Scots. A few years later Gibbon would discover another and better guide. John Pinkerton, whom he would patronise and encourage, would prove to be the ablest Scottish antiquary after Innes. Like Innes, he too would be a thorn in the side of the Scottish establishment. But he too would fall into error when he came to the origin of the Picts. It was not till the late nineteenth century that the mists of myth would be scientifically cleared away; and at least the outline of early Scottish history would become visible.

Since we are concerned here with the formation and accumulation of the myth, rather than with its ultimate dissipation, it will be convenient to begin by sketching the true outline of early Scottish history, as it has been established during the last century and a half.

We shall then be able to watch, with clearer understanding, the process by which it was gradually, over several centuries, obscured.

When the Romans established their power in Britain in the first century AD, they found the country occupied by a large number of different Celtic tribes. These tribes all spoke, apparently, what modern linguists term the P-Celtic branch of the language, of which variants would afterwards survive in Wales and Cornwall – and Brittany as well. In the northern part of the island, where the Romans did not succeed in establishing their power, the British tribes probably spoke the same sort of Celtic language as their southern counterparts. The Romans called the land that lay north of their *limes*, or frontier – that is, north of the wall of Antoninus which ran from the Firth of Forth to the Firth of Clyde – *Caledonia*; and they tended to refer to the tribes that lived in Caledonia as *Picts*: that is, people who painted their bodies. Several centuries after the Romans left Britain around AD 410, the Picts, as we shall see, came to be submerged so completely that very little can really be known about them: hardly anything has survived of their language except for some place and personal names, and perhaps a couple of dozen inscriptions carved on stones. Nevertheless, it seems clear enough from this evidence that the language spoken by the Picts belonged to the P-Celtic branch. In short, in so far as their language is a guide, the Pictish tribes belonged by cultural origin to the same group of peoples as the south Britons – though, of course, the Picts had not been Romanised subsequently.

In this last respect, the Picts were on a par with the Celtic tribes of Ireland, who were equally beyond the Roman Pale. But the tribes of Ireland spoke the Q-Celtic branch of the language, subsequently known as Gaelic; and in that respect, the Caledonians and the Irish were different peoples. The significance of this difference became apparent as Roman imperial power receded. During the fourth century the Romans became aware of a new people, or at least of a new name, the Scots. The Scottish tribe lived in north-east Ireland. They were certainly wild; and they were alleged to be cannibals.[1] They first appear as casual raiders on the western coasts of Roman Britain. They came to stay only after the Roman departure, and beyond the Roman *limes*, in Caledonia. At the beginning of the sixth century, while the Romanised Britons in the south were being pushed back towards the west by Anglo-Saxon invaders from the European continent, Scottish invaders from Ireland occupied the underpopulated coastline of what is now Argyllshire. There they set up their petty kingdom of Dalriada – so called from the name of their kingdom in Ulster, of which this colony in Argyll was an extension. The Scots had by now been Christianised, and were presumably no longer cannibals. The colony's leader, its first 'king', who had brought his band of Scots from Ireland to Caledonia, was Fergus, the son of Erc, who is said to have died in 503, three years after crossing the sea.

For almost 250 years, the Scots maintained, with varying fortunes, their kingdom of Dalriada. During all that time they remained as settlers in the wild country of Argyll, compressed between the sea and Drumalbyn, the dorsal mountain range which runs through Scotland from north to south. East of that range, the whole country north of the old Roman *limes* still belonged to the ancient people of Caledonia, the Picts. But the new kingdom of the Scots, though cramped in space and periodically falling into civil war or temporary subjection to the Picts, or to the Britons of Strathclyde, retained its hold and could rely on periodic refreshment and support from Ulster, of which it was naturally a part: for the sea, in so wild and mountainous an archipelago, unites rather than divides; and western Scotland was an extension of Ulster long before Ulster became an extension of western Scotland. Besides, the Scots of Dalriada had a claim to cultural superiority. They were Irish: and Ireland was the cultural centre of Britain in that dark age. It was through them that Irish Christianity came, with St Columba, to north Britain; and it was from their territory, from the island of Iona, that the new religion was spread by Scottish missionaries to the Picts of Caledonia and the Angles of Northumbria.

However, in about 740, the long period of coexistence between Picts and Scots seemed to enter a new phase. What little evidence there is has been interpreted by some historians as indicating a growing Pictish predominance. In 741 the Picts delivered a crushing blow in a decisive battle; and for some considerable time thereafter the kingdom of Dalriada lay subdued. The Scots recovered enough to break out of their own territory and launch a raid across Drumalbyn in 768. But the raids of Viking fleets down the western seas of northern Britain began to isolate Dalriada from Ireland, thereby sapping Scottish strength. The last man to be specifically identified by contemporary chronicles as king of Dalriada died in 792. The Picts, the ancient peoples of Caledonia, appeared to be still the dominant grouping in all the country north of the former Roman *limes*.

Thus the age of Charlemagne in continental Europe, the latter part of the eighth century, was also, it seemed, an age of continued and perhaps even increasing Pictish dominion in Caledonia. Neither in state nor in church did any significant dependence on Ireland remain. The settlement of the Scots in Dalriada still existed, of course; but it seems to have been politically fragmented and subjected to the Picts. The capital, or chief place, of Caledonia was the Pictish centre at Scone, or perhaps Forteviot nearby. The Church in Caledonia was the Pictish Church which, by now, like the Church in Anglian Northumbria, had disowned its Irish origins and transferred its loyalty to Rome. Early in the ninth century, Iona itself was destroyed by the terrible Norsemen, and its monks slaughtered; so Pictish kings took over the patronage of the Church throughout Caledonia. The names *Scotia* and *Scotus* were still used in Europe in that century, but they meant 'Ireland' and 'Irish'. The most famous bearer of that name was the philosopher John Scotus, who taught Greek at the court of the Emperor Charles the Bald. He was an Irishman: indeed, wrote under the name of Erigena, 'Irish-born'.[2]

In the year 800 the Scots looked set to disappear from north Britain: they would presumably merge, and be submerged, in the greater body of their neighbours. Outside Ireland they no longer had an independent identity. In Caledonia the future, like the past, appeared to belong to the Picts. In fact it did not. Half a century after the apparent end of the independent Scottish kingdom of Dalriada, Kenneth mac Alpin, a Scot, or partial Scot, took over the Pictish territories and declared himself King of the Picts and the Scots. Later, he would be known retrospectively as the first king of all 'Scotland'. For later, the very name of the Picts would be dropped; 'Pictavia', the name of their kingdom, would disappear; and the names of Scotia and Scotus would be quietly transferred from Ireland and the Irish to their modern signification. The Church would be the Church of the Scots. Even the Pictish language would disappear. In the end, the only Celtic language to survive in the Scoticised kingdom of Alba – as Caledonia was renamed – was the Irish branch: Gaelic, or 'Erse' as it came to be called for a time much later, the language of the Scots of Dalriada.

How had it happened? It seems that marriage alliances had taken place between the royal families of Picts and Scots in the years following the apparent extinction of Dalriada's independent existence in the late eighth century; and that Kenneth, as a Scot of Dalriada, may have been able to assert a claim to the Pictish throne through his mother at a time when male Pictish claimants were lacking or were weak. Recently, too, there had been increasing signs of military co-operation between Scots and Picts against a deadly common enemy: the invading Norsemen, then at the height of their destructive power. Kenneth took over the throne in Dalriada in the year following a disastrous defeat of a combined Scottish and Pictish army by the Norsemen in 839, in which many members of both the Scottish and the Pictish royal families had been killed. Force and fraud were then dextrously applied to secure his ascent from the Dalriadan to the Pictish throne a few years later. Whispers have reached us of a temporary tactical alliance with the Norse against the Picts, followed by a treacherous slaughter of the remaining Pictish leaders at a drunken banquet.

Having secured royal power in both kingdoms, Kenneth then set about the task of Scoticising the Picts: altering the inheritance laws in the state and appointment procedures in the Church, for instance. The process of transforming the character of Alba was probably assisted by the continuing devastation of the north and east of the country by the Norsemen: for Picts killed, carried away into slavery, or merely impoverished, could be replaced by Scottish settlers and Scottish lords brought in from the west. More generally, the influence of clerics drawn from the Irish Church, whose sway in north Britain was restored and extended by the mac Alpin dynasty, must surely have played an important part in the cultural remoulding of the country. The process of Scoticisation continued, in stages and in different ways, under Kenneth's successors during the next two centuries. The result, in the end, was that the Irish Scots, from a small original colony in a corner of Argyll, succeeded in imposing their name, their customs, and their language upon the more ancient and numerous people inhabiting the rest of the country.

After the construction of a unitary royal power, and a *Gleichshaltung*, or enforced amalgamation, of the Picts with the Scots, there came expansion of territory to the south. The new state pushed past the old Roman wall of Antoninus, between the Forth and the Clyde, to the Tweed–Solway line beyond. This was to prove the final frontier, though it was not seen that way then.

By the time the Normans conquered England in the second half of the eleventh century, and came up against that frontier, the northern kingdom had acquired a clear identity: it was not Caledonia, nor Pictavia, nor Alba; it was Scotland. It was not a racially united society; indeed it was now more diverse than before. To the Picts and the Scots there had now been added the English, the Angles of the Lothians and the Borders, and the Britons, the 'Welsh' of Strathclyde, in the south-west. More English, Anglo-Saxon émigrés, filtered across the frontier, and would take up positions at court and in the Church. Soon Norman barons and Norman monks would pour into the country, transforming its structure, establishing new forms of power, creating a modern feudal monarchy and a modern diocesan Church. These new influences would destroy the last relics of the Pictish inheritance, and would push Gaelic civilisation back into the Highlands and islands: there to remain cut off, static and primitive. But still the monarchy, Anglicised and Normanised though it was, would declare itself to be Scotch; and would look back, for its origin and history, not to these recent incomers from more civilised lands, nor to the ancient native people who must still, presumably, have provided a large proportion of its subjects, but to the Scots of Dalriada, who had acquired the kingdom from the Picts in the AD 840s, and who traced their remoter pedigree back to the leader of their original invasion in the early sixth century: the Irish adventurer, Fergus the son of Erc.

Such is the outline of early Scottish history, as it has been patiently re-established by modern scholars. Until the late eleventh century, at least, it was preserved, with reasonable accuracy, in record or memory, and commemorated by the bards who recited royal succession lists on ceremonial occasions. But from that time the mists began to gather; and that outline was gradually obscured and distorted by an ever-thickening cloud of mythology: a cloud which would not be effectively dispersed till another seven centuries had passed. The process began, it seems, spontaneously among the Scots: as a bid to capture history, like everything else, from the Picts. It was quickened by an external force: the national struggle with England for independence. It was consecrated, in the sixteenth century, by the most advanced thinkers of the time: the cultivated, cosmopolitan Scottish humanists of the Renaissance.

For the two hundred years between Kenneth mac Alpin in the mid-ninth century and Malcolm III in the later eleventh century we have, essentially, two kinds of sources that tell us something of how the Scots recorded and interpreted their history. Lists of kings in the royal succession were preserved: these would be recited publicly at enthronements, and no doubt on other important occasions. The length and continuity of the royal succession, thus proclaimed, would emphasise the crucial role played by the monarchy in the fortunes of its people. There were also folk memories, stories about the origin and character of the people itself, which crystallised occasionally as fragments embedded in the chronicles kept by monks, but which might also appear in connection with the king-lists. The information in the king-lists is narrow; that in the folk stories wider, but also woollier. These two kinds of sources, exiguous as they are, reveal, separately or in conjunction, at least an outline of the Scottish self-image as it developed.

Of the king-lists there are several versions,[3] reflecting the periodic need to revise and update them, and also their copying and deposit in different parts of the country – not to mention their diffusion outside Scotland itself – and, of course, the hazards of their survival or destruction. The process of copying and revision always entailed a risk of scribal error: through misreading, mis-spelling, or accidental omission or intrusion of names, etc. Another technical problem was just how to display, for the unified monarchy of later times, its inheritance from the dual monarchies of earlier times: from the parallel monarchies of the Picts and the Scots, which had coexisted for some three hundred years. The problem could be dealt with in different ways: there were separate lists of Pictish kings and of Dalriadan kings, and lists which attempted a combination. It is by tracing the changes made to these king-lists over time that we can observe the gradually developing current that was, in the end, to sweep the Picts out of the historical record, and produce, instead, an ever-longer and more glorious past for the Scots.

The memory of the Picts survived, more or less intact, into the reign of Malcolm III in the second half of the eleventh century. In two separate lists, Malcolm III was represented, on the one hand, as successor to a long line of Pictish kings and, on the other, to a slightly less long line of Scottish kings. The list of the kings of Dalriada ran back through Kenneth mac Alpin to Fergus son of Erc; and it recognised that the Pictish kingdom was already in existence before Fergus arrived from Ireland. About a century later, in the reign of William I, a small but significant alteration was made in the Scottish list. A scribe making out a list of the kings of Dalriada noticed a gap in the record, hitherto passed over in silence, between the death of a king in the late eighth century and the coming of his successor, Kenneth mac Alpin, about sixty years later. This gap had occurred in the latter part of the century of presumed Pictish overlordship; when, if there had been kings in Dalriada, they had presumably been 'under-kings', not worthy of being recorded. Having noticed this gap, our later twelfth-century scribe, whether because he was tidy-minded, or because his Scottish pride was piqued, we do not know, promptly filled it. Into those sixty years went four new kings: drawn, it is said, from the genealogy of the royal family of Dalriada, which had somehow been kept separately from the king-lists. The effect of this revision of the king-list was to obliterate evidence of the period of Pictish predominance, and to strengthen the claims of the Scottish dynasty to an unbroken succession and splendid independence.

What was needed next was the assertion of a Scottish claim to priority in time vis-à-vis the Picts. This need was duly filled, though not very neatly at first. It was filled in the next half-century, the first half of the thirteenth century, by the addition to a king-list, currently being revised, of a nugget of information derived from Scottish folk-memory. There was an ancient tradition among the Scots, perhaps reflecting a historical truth, that their race had come to Ireland from Spain. It now appeared that the famous Stone of Scone had participated in that journey. It had been taken from Spain to Ireland by someone called Simon Brecc; and, after resting many generations in Ireland, had been carried on to Caledonia by one of Simon's descendants, called Fergus son of Ferchar. This great event was said to have occurred in the fourth century BC. The first Scot to arrive in north Britain, Fergus son of Ferchar, had thus pipped Fergus son of Erc to the post by some seven centuries, as it turned out. Not surprisingly, in view of this stunning new historical revelation, the revised king-list, for the very first time, set down the line of the kings of Dalriada first, followed by the line of the Pictish kings.

True, this great Scottish leap backwards in time by seven centuries caused a few problems in its turn. The leap was so vertiginous that it left bystanders feeling somewhat dizzy and perplexed. No records had yet been discovered relating to those seven centuries. What were the names of the kings, people wondered, who must have followed each other in unbroken succession through that vast tract of time? And what notable things had they done? For the moment, these matters could be treated as mere details: deferred to later chroniclers in a mopping-up operation. The essential task, at least, had been achieved. The Picts had been comprehensively outplayed. The Scots had already wiped out evidence of Pictish domination over Dalriada, which had been too painful to be remembered. Now they had overtrumped the Picts in the matter of antiquity as well: 'Scotland', it was clear, had existed before 'Pictland'.

But the Scots could not afford to rest on their laurels. For in the business of story-telling, of pre-historical reconstruction, they now faced some stiff competition: and it was Celtic competition, from those other, no less imaginative Celts south of the Border, the Welsh, backed up by their patrons, the Anglo-Norman monarchs of England.

For let us not suppose that the Gaels of Scotland had a monopoly of the mythopoeic faculty. Early in the twelfth century, an imaginative Welshman, Geoffrey of Monmouth, had compiled the history of the kings of Britain, and had succeeded in pushing back the ancient British monarchy into heroic centuries and the best classical company. In fact, he declared, the kingdom of Britain had been founded and named by Brutus, the first 'Briton': the younger son of the Trojan Aeneas, who had come to Britain after the fall of Troy, and from whom the royal line had been continuous to the present day. Indeed (said Geoffrey) he could recount all the names and deeds of all these kings: for they had been recorded 'in continuous series, with most elegant speeches' in 'a very ancient book, in the British language' – that is, in Welsh – which had been given to him by his good friend Walter, archdeacon of Oxford; and as earnest of the contents of that important manuscript, he gave detailed accounts of such hitherto unrecorded kings of ancient Britain as Gogmagog, Hudibras, Bladud the founder of Bath and first aviator, Lear, Gorboduc, Ferrex and Porrex, and Lud, the builder of London. Geoffrey's History, a masterpiece of ingenious forgery, with its parade of apparent documentation and its virtuosity of mystification, was completed round about 1140; and it became immediately famous. It was circulated in hundreds of copies, and it generated a massive secondary literature, including the cycle of Arthurian romances.

Naturally, in an environment of competitive story-telling, the Scottish chroniclers did not wish to get left behind. Faced with the challenge of Geoffrey of Monmouth, they could not afford to leave the origins of the Scottish monarchy even in the fourth century BC. That might be enough to overtake the local Picts, encumbered as they were by the weight of their own historical failure. To overtake the more agile Welsh, the Scots had to carry their dynasty back beyond Brutus, and discover an eponymous hero earlier even than the Trojan war.

They found him in the days of Moses. Long ago, when the Scots had resided temporarily, for a few hundred years, in Ireland, their men of learning had been struck, with the zeal of converts to a new religion, by the opportunities for self-enhancement offered by the story of the Old Testament, which came in the baggage-train of Christianity. They had decided that they themselves were just as good as the Jews, and that God must certainly have intended them also to be a chosen people: a people parallel to the people of Israel. Their wanderings and their fortunes, past and future, could thus all be seen as a part of the divine purpose. This was the seed of the story, carried along in the folk-memory for many hundreds of years, which was to precipitate now, just as it was needed, in an account of the origins of the Scottish people that was attached to a current revision of the king-list.

The eponymous hero of the Scots, their equivalent of Brutus, was named Gaedil Glas – the name indicating that he was a Gael. Gaedil Glas was translated into something approaching a classical form: he was Gaythelos in Greek, or Gathelus in Latin. Gaythelos, said the learned men of Scotland, had been a Greek prince, the son of a king of Athens; and he had married Scota, the daughter of Pharaoh, king of Egypt – the same who had persecuted the children of Israel, and had been punished by plagues. Luckily Gaythelos had fallen out with his royal father-in-law, and had been exiled by him, just in time to escape the final denouement of that story: the drowning of the Egyptian royal house in the Red Sea. By the time of that famous catastrophe, Gaythelos and Scota had departed, with their followers, to Spain; from Spain, in due course, their descendants had passed to Ireland; and thence, in 333 BC, the newly discovered Fergus son of Ferchar had led them to their final home in Scotland. This history was established by 1249, when it formed the base of the royal succession, as recited by a *senachie*, or Gaelic bard, at the enthronement of Alexander III.[4] The bard recited backwards in Gaelic all the names of the young king's ancestors in the Scottish line: thirteen back to Kenneth mac Alpin; twenty-three to Fergus mac Erc; fifty-six to Fergus mac Ferchar; followed by an indefinite number, unrecorded by the chronicler, all the way to the Egyptian princess Scota and her Greek husband Gaythelos.

The official establishment of this history came not a moment too soon. For Alexander III was the last undisputed king of Scotland of the royal line of Kenneth mac Alpin; and when he perished, falling in the dark, with his horse, over a cliff on the Firth of Forth, the king of England moved in. The hundred-year-old English aim of securing the overlordship of Scotland entered a new phase; and the newly established history of the Scottish monarchy, devised to dish the Picts and outbid the Welsh, would be exploited, and confirmed, as an ideological weapon in the war of independence against the English.

From the beginning, that struggle was a war of propaganda as well as of arms. Against the English claim that the kingdom of Scotland was an English – or rather, Anglo-Norman – fief, the Scots insisted that it was an ancient independent monarchy; indeed, more ancient than that of England. In 1301 the rival myths were trotted out before the Pope – the Roman Pope Boniface VIII. In 1320, when the Avignon Pope John XXII refused to accept the verdict of the battle of Bannockburn, the Scottish leaders in arms drew up the famous Declaration of Arbroath – the Scottish Declaration of Independence. There the (mostly Norman) barons described to the Pope, in detail, the travels and exploits of their 'Scottish' ancestors: how they had passed from greater Scythia over the Tyrrhenian sea, and beyond the Pillars of Hercules; how they had stayed, for long tracts of time, in Spain, unconquered among the fiercest of warriors; and how, 'twelve hundred years after the setting forth of the people of Israel', by victory after victory and travail after travail, they had won for themselves the abodes in the west which they now held in continuous freedom and independence. They had expelled the Britons and utterly destroyed the Picts; they had been assailed again and again by Norseman, Dane and Saxon; but they had never been subdued. 'Within this realm', they added confidently, 'there have reigned one hundred and thirteen kings of native royal stock, *nullo aliengena interveniente*', without a single outsider among them. How had the figure of 113 kings of Scotland been arrived at? Under the pressure of events, the barons had evidently taken a quick look at the latest king-list and done a rough count of the kings that they had found there. They had read the list as a direct line: starting with Fergus son of Ferchar and all his successors of Dalriada until they petered out, then going next through the line of Pictish kings (without adverting to the fact), before coming back on the home straight with Kenneth mac Alpin and his successors of the 'amalgamated' monarchy.

The replacement of history by myth, largely completed by the early fourteenth century, was consolidated thereafter by a convenient documentary vacuum. In 1291, at the beginning of the contest for the succession to the Scottish throne, Edward I of England, intervening as umpire, had required that all the public records of Scotland relating to the monarchy since the time of Kenneth III (when the law of succession had been regulated) should be placed in his hands. Having delivered his judgment in favour of John Balliol, he returned these documents to the new king. But four years later, when Balliol renounced the homage which he had paid to the English king, the enraged sovereign entered Scotland, not this time as an umpire but as an avenger, with an army. He seized the royal fortresses, sent his puppet king back to England as a prisoner, and set out systematically to remove or destroy the symbols and evidence of Scottish independence. The coronation-stone of Scone and the regalia of Scotland were carried off to England; and the public records, so recently returned, were easily retaken. They were carried off into England, and disappeared into the English archives: there to be buried for centuries. According to the Scots, many of them were destroyed. How many such documents were taken, and how complete was the destruction (if indeed any of them were really destroyed), is a matter of historical doubt. Perhaps the story of the destruction is yet another Scottish myth.[5] However, true or false, it was believed by the Scots. In any case, some of the evidence of their history was now withheld from them; and Scottish patriots, while lamenting the infamous plunder, were enabled thereby to reconstruct their past more freely on the surviving basis of myth.

The opportunity for such reconstruction came in the subsequent century. The wars of English aggression and Scottish resistance went on, fiercely though intermittently, for six decades. At last, in 1357, the English king, by then Edward III, recognising that it was more urgent to defend his beleaguered territories in France than to try and extend his sway in the north, agreed by the treaty of Berwick to end hostilities – for the time being, at least. During the period of relative peace which followed, a chantry priest of Aberdeen set out to supply Scottish patriots with a continuous narrative history of their country. His name was John of Fordun.

John of Fordun is the first historian of Scotland, the pioneer beyond whose work no later historian, for four hundred years, would presume to look. Growing up in the later years of the wars of independence, he could look back with pride on that struggle, but with dismay on the loss of those documents which might have illustrated and explained it. He had some connection with the church of St Andrews, the great repository (and manufactory) of Scottish records – now sadly depleted. Like the great Elizabethan antiquaries whom the destruction of the monastic libraries by the Reformers would inspire to recover the English past, he resolved to repair, as far as possible, the damage done by 'that bloody oppressor' Edward I, and to be the restorer of Scottish history. So, after searching his own devastated country for what remained of its records, he set out on a journey of research abroad. He is said to have spent some years travelling, always on foot, through the neighbour kingdoms. From one of his continuators we have a description of him, wandering 'like a curious bee, through the meadows of England and the oracles of Ireland, carrying his manuscript in his bosom'. Pausing in towns and colleges, churches and abbeys, he conversed with historians and chronologers, listened to their gossip, and then stored it away 'like sweet honey in the hive of his folded notebook'. In England he found, in addition to manuscripts of Roman writers and of Gildas, Bede, etc., the fascinating new chronicles now being copied in so many monasteries; and, in particular, the works of those two garrulous Welshmen, Geoffrey of Monmouth and Gerald of Wales. In Ireland he found long pedigrees of Irish kings, who were described, in the language of the past, as 'Scotorum reges' reigning in 'Scotia'.

On his return to Scotland, Fordun wrote it all up. First, he described the modern period, from the time of Malcolm III, called Canmore, and his Saxon wife, Saint Margaret, until more recent times. Then, groping backwards in time, he pushed his way back through the dark ages until history disappeared in myth. For this early period, one of his sources was evidently a History of the Kings of Scotland from the very beginning till the time of Malcolm Canmore, which he had found in the Registry of the church of St Andrews: a mysterious work, now lost. Later, this lost work would become, in retrospect, even more mysterious.

John of Fordun did not complete his work. He died some time in the later fourteenth century, leaving the more modern part of his chronicle in the form of rough notes. It was completed in the next century by Walter Bower, abbot of Inchcolm; and, in that form, it came to be known as the *Scotichronicon*. But the part which concerns us is Fordun's own work: in particular the first five books, which include the earliest centuries: the centuries of myth.

Fordun was not a critical historian. He was described by one who knew him as 'a simple man, and not a graduate of any school'. He was a busy collector, and no doubt an honest man, who naively put together the material which he found; and the early material which he found consisted largely of the fabrications constructed or collected in the 150 years before his birth, padded out with history and gossip borrowed from English monks and Irish *senachies*, or bards – for that, presumably, is the meaning of 'the oracles of Ireland'. He also used English chronicles and some Irish manuscripts; but these last, he constantly misinterpreted. Whenever he came upon the word 'Scotus' or 'Scotia', he interpreted it as 'Scotch' or 'Scotland'. In this way he appropriated to Scotland much that was Irish; which greatly assisted the accomplishment of his intention. He was not the last Scottish writer to do this.

The result was predictable. Out of the ancient genealogies and king-lists, and the propaganda and the chronologies of the previous two centuries into which they had been subsumed, Fordun created, for the now clearly independent kingdom of Scotland, the first continuous, literary narrative history of its past. He did not invent: he merely covered the dry bones with flesh – or rather, perhaps, for he was neither a vivid nor an elegant writer, with dry, continuous skin. He described the romance of Gaythelos and Scota; their expulsion from Egypt by Pharaoh; their arrival in Spain; and their early discovery and annexation, through their son Hyber, of Hibernia, or Ireland. That annexation was not, indeed, very effective in international law, for it was not followed up for 250 years; but ultimately Fordun shows us the Scots landing in Ireland and peopling it. Long afterwards we are introduced to the Picts, who cast up in Ireland, having come from Pictavia: that is, from Poitou in France. The Scots, says Fordun, declined to admit the Picts into Ireland, but generously allowed them to go, with Scottish wives, to the unoccupied land of Caledonia. This occurred, we are told, about the time of the first capture of Rome – presumably its capture by the Gauls in 390 BC. However, the Picts behaved badly to those Scottish men who came over from Ireland to accompany, or to visit, the Scottish ladies; and so, their patience being exhausted, the Scots, under Fergus son of Ferchar, set out to colonise Caledonia for themselves; and to establish there, in 333 BC, a Scottish monarchy. For five centuries thereafter, while forty-five Scottish kings reigned in Dalriada, the Scots and the Picts remained the best of friends. Together they collaborated in writing a magnificent letter to Julius Caesar, telling him to get off the island. But alas, one day on a joint hunting party the Picts stole a Scottish dog, and refused to give it back to its indignant owners. Tempers flared; battle ensued; and the Picts, as light-minded as they were light-fingered, drove their former friends clean out of the country and back into Ireland. The Picts lived to regret their folly. Forty-three years later, hard pressed by a Roman tyrant called Maximus, they begged the Scots to return from Ireland and help them in their struggles. Naturally the Scots responded nobly to the Pictish plea. They returned to Dalriada; and there Fergus, son of Erc, refounded the Scottish monarchy a second time.

After the bridging of that brief chasm, the race of the Scottish kings was continuous: for by the device of throwing in a few extra Scottish kings thereafter, Fordun contrives, like some of the record keepers (or makers) before him, to suppress the memory of a period of Pictish domination. If we look closely at Fordun's text we can also observe another part of that process of royal inflation which was so intimately linked to the flattering extension of Scottish antiquity. In 1249, at the enthronement of Alexander III, the *senachie* had proclaimed the names of thirty-three kings in direct descent from Fergus son of Ferchar to Fergus son of Erc. By the time Fordun wrote his Chronicle, something over a century later, the list of kings had lengthened to forty-five; though Fordun disclaimed knowledge of the names, let alone the dates, of the extra members of the royal cast.[6]

From the time of their second coming to Dalriada, under Fergus son of Erc, the Scots always knew that the Picts could be a nasty people. They were 'prone to harm their neighbours', and were never to be fully trusted, even when they were allies against common enemies: Romans, Britons, Saxons, etc. Scottish bards and *senachies*, whose recitations and retroactive prophecies lay behind and were periodically quoted in Fordun's Chronicle, proclaimed the need for a final day of reckoning, in which the Picts would be utterly overthrown and eliminated. Fordun, indeed, provided his readers with a list of sixty-five Pictish kings, running from their origins down to that overthrow: a list which, he said, he had found in an old catalogue. But for over three hundred years he gave the Pictish kings remarkably little to do, except to serve as a foil to the busy doings of their Scottish contemporaries. Almost the only exceptions were where Fordun recorded the foundation, under three separate Pictish kings, of the important churches of St Andrews, Abernethy and Dunkeld: an aspect of the Pictish past in which Fordun, as a cleric, had a special interest.

At last the time came for the Picts to go to their doom, and for the Scots to accomplish their manifest destiny. For fifty years, under a king whom Fordun described as 'lazy', the Scots had ceased to struggle against the Picts. Then arose Alpin, father of Kenneth, who took up again the historic mission of the Scots. He pointed the way; but he was captured by the Picts, and had his head cut off. It was his son who would inherit the kingdom. Young Kenneth, mighty in his wisdom, succeeded. By a supernatural trick he persuaded the chieftains of his army, fearful of the Picts, to cross Drumalbyn and continue the struggle. Even more magical was Kenneth's military prowess. Seven battles in one day did he fight and win. Picts innumerable were slaughtered, and all the provinces of their kingdom overrun. The mopping-up of further Pictish resistance took time, of course. Under new leaders the Pictish forces regrouped in the wilderness. They lived by raiding. They intrigued with outside enemies: the English and the Norse. Thirty-five years after the triumph of the Scottish messiah Kenneth, his successor Constantine would be undone and slain in battle through Pictish treachery. But the Scots kept grinding the Picts down. At last the great work was finished. In the end, Fordun tells us with much satisfaction, not only were the kings and leaders of the Pictish nation eliminated; the whole race, along with its language, was wiped out. Indeed, so complete was the wiping-out of the Picts that they had virtually vanished from all Scottish remembrance by the time that Fordun wrote his Chronicle. Fordun says that few of his countrymen in the later fourteenth century believed that the Picts had had a real existence. Most Scots by then, hearing mention of the Picts, believed that they were mere phantoms: ghosts dreamed up by ancient Scottish imaginations to frighten children into good behaviour.[7]

This version of Scottish history, built up in the thirteenth and fourteenth centuries to dish the Picts and overtrump the Welsh, was thus finally established in consecutive narrative form. In the fifteenth century Fordun's narrative, as encapsulated in Bower's *Scotichronicon*, was disseminated throughout Scotland. Copies were made, and commented on, in every Scottish monastery or church to replace the records carried away, and allegedly destroyed, by Edward I. By the end of the fifteenth century it was the orthodoxy of Scotland, not to be doubted or disputed – any more than the people of England and Wales would doubt the myth of Brutus, to which it was, in part at least, a justified rejoinder. For in the fifteenth century we are still in the pre-critical age. None of the nations north of the Alps had yet dared to look critically at its own history; and the mythical kings of Scotland were no more absurd, and belief in them no more culpable, than the received legends of neighbouring countries. It was only in the sixteenth century that the antiquaries of England, Wales and Ireland began to cast doubt on these fabulous stories. Only in Scotland would such doubts not be entertained. Long after Geoffrey of Monmouth – 'lying Geoffrey' as Milton would call him – had been dismissed with ridicule in England, the fabulous history of John of Fordun, made even more fabulous by his successors, was authenticated by the greatest of Scottish scholars, and was enshrined in the official text books of Scotland.

How did this happen? Why did no Scottish scholar dismantle these medieval fabrications as Camden, in England, dismantled those of Geoffrey? On the face of it, this is surprising. For sixteenth-century Scotland was not a backwater, cut off from European movements of thought. Its best scholars studied regularly in France, at the university of Paris, one of the intellectual capitals of Europe. They travelled in England. They were masters of the Latin language. And if the Protestant Reformation severed them from Catholic Europe, it made them members of an even more closely knit and intellectually active movement, international Calvinism. Prima facie, there is every reason to suppose that criticism would prevail over myth in Scotland as in England; and indeed, we find, it attempted to do so. If it failed, that was not because Scottish critics did not exist: it is because Scottish society would not listen to them.

The first attempt to reopen the problems of early Scottish history was made at the beginning of the sixteenth century. It was made by the most interesting intellectual figure – and the most radical social and political thinker – who had yet appeared in Scotland: John Mair, or, as he was known internationally in the Latin-speaking world, Major.

Major was a man of cosmopolitan education and wide learning. After his school days in Haddington, he had gone, first, to England: to study at Christ's College in Cambridge; and then to France, to the university of Paris. Much of his life was spent teaching in Paris; but he remained grateful to his English teachers, was an admirer of England, and was respected there: he would be invited by Cardinal Wolsey to become one of the foundation members of his new college at Oxford. Major had an encyclopaedic mind, and wrote on all subjects, in the tradition of the medieval Schoolmen. He wrote in the style of the Schoolmen too, which enabled fashionable young humanists to sneer at his 'Sorbonnic' Latin; but his scholastic latinity expressed powerful ideas, while their new classicism of style was often empty of thought. If Major was the last of the Scottish Schoolmen, he was also the first Scottish critical historian.

One event which no doubt affected Major's thinking, and increased his respect for England, was the revolution which had happened in Scotland when he was about twenty years old. In 1488, three years after the defeat and death of Richard III in England, and the establishment of the Tudor dynasty, King James III of Scotland had similarly been defeated and killed in a civil war. But the results of these two comparable revolts had been very different. Whereas Henry Tudor's victory at Bosworth established a new dynasty in England which reduced over-mighty subjects to order, the battle at Stirling had exactly the opposite effect. The victorious barons promptly summoned a parliament to legalise their revolt and absolve them-selves of the murder of the king. From that time onward, till it moved in 1603 to the safety of England, the Scottish monarchy would be all too often at the mercy of a turbulent baronage. Thus the same years which marked the downfall of armed aristocratic faction in England marked its intensification in Scotland. Throughout his political and historical writings, Major shows a hatred and distrust of the nobility: of the Scottish barons who, for their own interest, opposed the usurpation of Edward I, even of Bruce himself. His hero, in the Scottish struggle for independence, is the supposedly plebeian William Wallace. The Scotch nobles, said Major, were worse enemies to Scottish independence than the king of England; they preferred English rule to that of the upstart Wallace; ultimately, he believed, they probably wished to see each protagonist weaken the other, in order that 'the kingdom would revert to them'. Here speaks the commentator on the events, not only of 1297, but also of 1488. Major's preferred solution to the problems of Scotland was to seek an equal union with England; so that the nobility of Scotland, like that of England, could be brought under the crown and used to advance, not retard, the social progress of his country. So, in writing his History, he did not confine himself to Scotland. His book was entitled *A History of Greater Britain, both England and Scotland.* It was published in Paris in 1521.

A man who looked critically at every institution – who denied divine authority to monarchy or nobility, or prescriptive right to common law – was not likely to leave historical myth unquestioned; and when Major turned to the earliest history of England and Scotland, he gave short shrift to the legendary origins of both countries. He dismissed the story of Brutus with contempt. He declared the story of Gaythelos and Scota a 'figment'. Ignoring all the intermediate chronicles, he went back to the oldest certain authority, the Englishman Bede, and allowed nothing that was not accepted by him. All that was certain in early Scottish history, he wrote, was that the Scots came from Ireland, and the Irish, originally, from Spain: 'the rest of the story I dismiss as doubtful and, in my own opinion, silly'. As for the Picts, they, he believed (again following Bede), had come to Britain following the Britons but before the Scots. On the arrival of the Scots in Dalriada, he is cautious. He quotes Bede, who describes them as a third race, arriving after the Britons and the Picts; then he adds that 'our annals' – that is, Fordun and the *Scotichronicon* – 'say that Fergus the son of Ferchar had come previously', bringing with him the stone on which the Scottish kings were later crowned at Scone. As this is not wholly incompatible with Bede's account, he does not altogether reject it; but he lays no emphasis on it. Even if the story is true, he says, it is historically unimportant: this first Fergus can have laid only 'a weak foundation' on which the later invaders built.[8]

Such was the historical criticism of John Major. It was the beginning of wisdom, the first attempt to look behind the accumulated myths of the Middle Ages, and to relate history to evidence. But how was it received in Scotland? The answer is, with complete indifference. The educated Scotchmen of the next generation were not interested in critical history. They ridiculed Major's unfashionable style. Why did he write in that crabbed Latin? Why did he not write like Cicero, and themselves? For the next two centuries the Scotch literati would pride themselves on the purity of their Latin – a characteristic that would be noticed by Dr Johnson – at the expense, often, of its content. So Major's work dropped unnoticed from the Paris press. It was not reprinted for 220 years, or translated into English for 370.

Besides, they soon had an alternative History of Scotland more to their taste. Only six years after the publication of Major's work, there appeared, from the same Paris press, a truly 'humanist' History of Scotland. This was the work of Hector Boece, known in Latin as Boethius.

What is 'humanist' history? To most people today, humanism is a word of praise, around which all the intellectual virtues have gathered. It implies, or is held to imply, scholarship, reason, progress, enlightenment. Whether that signification is justified today or not, it does not apply retrospectively to the sixteenth century. The greatest thinkers of that time knew well that the term 'humanism' meant something else. Humanism might entail criticism and philosophy; but it did not necessarily entail them, or indeed any specific content. It was a quality of form only. It meant a perfect Latin style such as Cicero might have owned. What was uttered in that style was irrelevant. And humanist history was, in fact, generally uncritical. To the humanists who, as Machiavelli would say, prized the forms of Antiquity without seeking to understand the lessons of Antiquity;

and who, as Bodin would say, were grammarians, not philosophers: history was 'philosophy teaching by examples': a pageant of events in which the great men of the past, through their lives, taught moral lessons. History's value lay not in its intrinsic truth – the humanists were not interested in historical truth for its own sake – or in its philosophical penetration in the explanation of causes and effects. Its value was rated by its 'exemplary portraits', its patriotism, and its rhetoric: its correct and fluent Latin prose. The classical model for humanist historians was Livy, whose rich and orotund prose portrayed, not the social and political, or even accidental, causes of the rise of Rome to greatness, but rather the virtues of individual humans displayed therein. Against this canon, John Major had sinned; and therefore his criticism and philosophy were rejected. By this canon, Hector Boece was guided; and therefore he could not fail.

Hector Boece came from Dundee; and, from his local school, went to the university of Paris, where he became first a student, then a professor, at the Collège de Montaigu. There he became acquainted with Erasmus, with whom he would afterward correspond occasionally. In Paris he also knew John Major, with whom he had so little in common, and William Elphinstone, bishop of Aberdeen, whom he would help to found King's College, Aberdeen. He himself became the first Principal of the college; and it was at Aberdeen, and with the encouragement of Bishop Elphinstone – himself a scholar and patron of learning – that he would write the book which was to make him famous in Scotland, ridiculous abroad: his *History of the Scots*.

Boece's *History* was a perfect example of humanist history. It contained no philosophy, no criticism, no real thought. But it was written in flowing classical Latin. As he himself wrote, in his dedication to the archbishop of St Andrews, his precursors had written in a barbarous style, and were therefore unreadable today; but he would use a correct and elegant latinity. He would also provide edifying moral examples, to show vice punished and virtue rewarded; and he would flatter the vanity of the Scots by showing that they were not only the heirs to the most ancient of European monarchies but also the possessors of the most ancient continuous civilisation. The Scots, in Boece's presentation, were a *Kulturvolk* who, in the centuries before Christ, had preserved, first in Spain, then in Ireland, and finally in

Scotland, the wisdom of Egypt, the literature and philosophy of Greece. Indeed, soon after their first settlement in Scotland, Ptolemy II, king of Egypt, the second founder of the great library of Alexandria, had sent an embassy to his cousin of Scotland, bringing, among other things, the works of Aristotle, which the polite natives hastened to read in the original Greek. . . .

These new revelations of their old history were, says a modern writer, 'a major cultural event' for Boece's contemporaries.[9] His book became a best-seller. While Major's work had fallen dead-born from the press, that of Boece was hailed as worthy of Livy. It had all the admired Livian virtues – and also the Livian prolixity. It was translated into Scots prose for the king, into Scots verse for the people. It was reprinted in Latin and translated into English. And the happy author was rewarded with a doctoral degree by his university, a tun of wine by his town, and a pension in cash by the king.

What were the sources whose gushing waters Boece now coloured and sweetened with his humanist rhetoric? They were, of course, Fordun and Fordun's continuator, Bower. But Boece also went beyond Fordun. Whereas Fordun had supplied occasional names for the series of forty-five imaginary kings between Fergus son of Ferchar and Fergus son of Erc, Boece went much further and took remarkable liberties. First, in the interest (we must assume) of plausibility, he reduced both their number and, by altering their relationship with each other, the number of generations which they spanned. Instead of forty-five kings covering thirty-three generations, he offered forty kings covering twenty-two generations.[10] Then he supplied elaborate and detailed biographies of these forty kings.

He described, almost in alternating series, a set of benign monarchs, admirable in their constructive purposes, and also a set of human monsters, vicious, violent and frightening. In the first category we have, for example, Josina, bred to the medical profession in Ireland, who persuaded the Scottish people of his time not to eat and drink too much – to the great benefit of the national health; and Dorvidilla, who issued the first salutary regulations on hunting with dogs, often repeated by subsequent rulers; and Donald, who in AD 203 introduced the Scots to the advantages of money, and likewise to the advantages of Christianity (ever since when, said Boece proudly, the Scots had remained rock-solid in the faith, without even a hint of heresy). On the other side were the villains. Such was Durstus, lustful and foul-mouthed, who ruled without his nobles' concurrence and cut down rich men to seize their property, but withal a cunning deceiver: so that, when the clan chieftains rose against him, he made them fair promises of good behaviour in the holy temple of Diana (for, as Boece helpfully explained, the Scots in those early days were still moon-worshippers), and then invited them to a grand banquet of reconciliation at his royal castle of Berigon – wherein he afterwards slaughtered them privily. Lugtacus was another tyrant who favoured vile creatures and ruled in similar abusive ways; but his private lusts were very specific and disgusting, focussed on the women of his own family – so that he repeatedly raped his aunts, his daughters, his sisters and their daughters. And then there was Ahirco: a wise young prince at first, a fine wrestler, but who also enjoyed literary company, especially that of historians. Unfortunately, after eight years in power, he went to the bad: becoming irascible and avaricious, taking up with disreputable company such as singers and dancers, and eventually turning so effeminate as to feel no shame in prancing about playing the flute. Cornered by some indignant gentlemen of Argyll, this coward committed suicide rather than face another kind of music.

Whence had Boece derived these details, which were not to be found in Fordun or his commentators, or in any other source known to us? He himself gave a perfectly clear answer. His source, he wrote, was 'Veremund, archdeacon of St Andrews, a Spaniard by birth, who compiled, in Latin, a history of Scotland from the beginnings of the race up to the time of Malcolm III, surnamed Canmore, to whom he dedicated the work'; and again, 'there was brought to me, by a messenger, a history of our people, by Veremund, formerly archdeacon of St Andrews, containing, though in an unpolished ancient style, abundance of detail from the beginning of the Scottish people up to the reign of Malcolm Canmore'. This manuscript, he said, had come, with others, from the island of Iona. For Iona, he explained, was the Record Office of ancient Scotland. And since he was never to be caught without a circumstantial story, Boece explained that Fergus son of Erc, in a period of exile before his invasion of Scotland, had joined Alaric the Goth in his expedition to Italy which culminated in the sack of

Rome in AD 410, and that, as his share of the booty, disdaining vulgar wealth (since the Scots were literate and philosophic men), he had chosen a chest of books, which he had deposited at Iona as the nucleus of a later collection. This collection, said Boece, though so important, had somehow escaped the notice of Edward I and his agents (as also, apparently, of the diligent Fordun and all his commentators and continuators), and had been reserved for himself to exploit in his present work of historical popularisation. After exploiting it, Boece (it was afterwards said in Aberdeen) destroyed these precious documents from Iona.[11] Though he presented his own copy of Fordun's chronicle to his university, he lightly cast on the bonfire those unique archives which had miraculously survived the depredations of so many centuries.

What are we to make of Veremund and his history? It cannot have been the lost 'History of the Scottish Kings' from the beginning up to the reign of Malcolm III which Fordun used, and whose title seems so exactly to describe it.[12] Is it, then, a complete ghost: a fantasy invoked by Boece to give spurious authority to his own inventions? This is suggested by the analogy of Geoffrey of Monmouth, whom Boece, in scope and method of fabrication, so closely resembles. Geoffrey, too, had fathered his stories on an archdeacon – Walter of Oxford; and the very language in which Boece describes the manuscript of Archdeacon Veremund recalls that in which Geoffrey had described the manuscript of Archdeacon Walter.[13] On the other hand, Boece is not the only writer to quote Veremund. Later in the same century, David Chambers, Lord Ormond, a Scottish judge, independently cited passages from Veremund which are not taken from Boece; and although the passages which he cited prove that their source is a forgery of the fifteenth or early sixteenth century (and is therefore later than Fordun), they suggest – unless Chambers was mistaken in his attribution – that such a document did exist; that it was a recent compilation; that it had not been destroyed after use by Boece; and that Chambers himself had seen it; as nobody else ever has.[14]

If there was such a manuscript source, and not merely the author's fantasy, behind Boece's *History*, we naturally ask, who wrote it, and for what purpose? The first scholar to examine the matter critically was Father Innes, in the early eighteenth century. He concluded that

Boece was the innocent victim of a deep political plot. Observing that many of Boece's early kings had been deposed and even killed by their subjects, he suggested that the document had been prepared by the political party among the Scottish nobility which had opposed, and finally killed, James III, in order to provide historical precedents and justification for their actions. Having concocted the document, these 'whig' magnates had then palmed it off, as a genuine historical source, on the unsuspecting Boece, in order that he should turn it into elegant Latin for popular consumption.

However, Innes' argument is not entirely convincing: for Boece's work, by itself, was never interpreted by its early readers as a 'whig' document; indeed, as we shall see, it would be used by royalist propagandists for another two centuries. Therefore it cannot have been, in itself, a radical document. After all, Shakespeare also portrayed the deposition of kings; but no one would see Shakespeare's historical tragedies as anti-royalist propaganda; and Innes admits that Boece himself held entirely correct political views. In these circumstances it seems over-subtle to ascribe such far-sighted intellectual machinations to the unruly noblemen of Scotland. It is more likely that Innes' view of Boece was coloured by later events: he saw the work of Boece not directly, but through the distorting medium of events which only began forty years after its publication. In the 1520s no such events could be forecast. The deposition and even murder of kings, though no doubt deplorable, had been a fact of life in Boece's own time: he had seen it in both England and Scotland; and he might well have imagined, in the distant past, similar tragedies, which seemed a permanently recurring part of history, without necessarily serving the interest of a political party, to which he himself was clearly opposed.

Besides, we must remember the nature and purpose of humanist history. Such history consisted, above all, of noble or deterrent examples. The historian was not expected to strain after pedantic accuracy of fact; but he was expected to show, on a high public stage, virtue rewarded and vice punished. Many of Boece's imaginary kings were virtuous. But as virtue unalloyed is somewhat dull, a sprinkling of vice was required to enliven the story; and vice, naturally, had to be punished. The deposition and death of wicked kings was thus necessary to the historian's art; and it served a moral purpose too: for it vindicated the virtue of the Scottish people.

For these reasons, Innes' argument seems implausible and unnecessary. That leaves us with two possible explanations. Either Boece was telling the truth when he stated that he was given a document – in which case the document (as is shown by Chambers' quotations) was a modern forgery, of which Boece was the innocent dupe – or his statement was a literary device, copied from Geoffrey of Monmouth: a fiction invented to supply an ostensible foundation for other fantasies, in the manner of Cervantes' Cide Hamete Benengeli or Sir Walter Scott's Jedediah Cleishbotham. Which of these two interpretations we adopt is a matter of choice, and depends on the credit that we give to Chambers. Since Chambers wrote in exile, it seems, on balance, preferable to suppose that he quoted from memory, and at second hand, from documents which he had never seen – like his contemporary John Leslie, bishop of Ross, who wrote in similar circumstances.[15] His evidence should probably, therefore, be discounted – leaving to Boece himself the credit for having invented the ghost of Veremund as an additional flourish of mythopoeic virtuosity.

Boece had set out to breathe life and colour into Fordun's dry chronicle. In that he succeeded. Thereby he deserves our gratitude: for without Boece we would never have had Shakespeare's tragedy of *Macbeth*.[16] Indeed, in describing the migration of Birnam Wood to Dunsinane, Boece, in a rare moment of scepticism, dismissed the episode prophetically as fit only to appear on the stage of the theatre: as it ultimately would.

Thus, within five years of its publication, the critical history of John Major was overtaken and stifled by a new, far fuller, far more popular version of the *History of Scotland*: a version which rescued the imaginary pre-historic kings of Scotland just as they seemed about to drown in the advancing tide of criticism. In the following decades, that tide would gradually dissolve and wash away the legendary past of other European countries. But not of Scotland. There, the whole troupe of primitive Scottish kings, so happily refloated and redecorated, would sail in their newly gilded ship, to the acompaniment of flutes and hautboys, like Cleopatra on the Nile, down the sacred river of tradition, while devout cheers arose from either bank: from Left and Right alike. For did they not prove that the Scots – the authentic Scots of Dalriada, the sole ancestors of modern Scotchmen – were an ancient and civilised people, Athens and Sparta combined, as famous for literature and philosophy as for valour in war; that they had brought the wisdom of Egypt and Greece to the far West; that they had been an aristocracy, a *Herrenvolk* in their country, living free of themselves, and subjecting the miserable Picts to their rule; that they had resisted and defeated the all-powerful Romans who had enslaved the miserable Britons south of the wall?

So glorious a past ought not to be lightly surrendered. Critical voices might be heard south of the Border, from the descendants of those miserable enslaved Britons; but they were not to be heeded. They might even be heard, fitfully, in pockets of Scotland. 'What our own Boece, following Veremundus, says about the origin of the Scots I regard as pure romance', wrote the learned judge Sir Thomas Craig, in 1605 – although even he somehow contrived to retain the conclusion, after he had discounted the evidence, concerning the superior antiquity of the Scottish people.[17] His doubts were echoed, a few decades later, by another equally learned Scot, Robert Gordon of Straloch, in Aberdeenshire itself, always a nonconformist shire (for a prophet must not expect too much honour in his own country).[18] But such voices, if raised, were quickly drowned by the chorus of orthodoxy. In 1578 John Leslie, bishop of Ross, the adviser, political agent and public champion of Mary Queen of Scots in her adversity, published in Rome a work on the origin, manners and history of the Scots. The history was taken from Boece, and included the exploits of the forty imaginary kings.[19] A century later, when James, duke of York, afterwards James II and VII, set up his court in Edinburgh, the forty kings were brought out of the shadows to glorify the royal line. The town council of Edinburgh welcomed the duke as a member of the royal family which had protected the city for two thousand years, and a Dutch artist was commissioned to paint the portraits of his royal ancestors. So the portraits of all those mythical kings can still be seen – forty almost identical faces, painted (it is said) from the same model – in Holyrood House. A few years later, that great oracle of the Scottish law, Sir George Mackenzie, was outraged by the historical doubts expressed by two learned English clergymen. With all his authority as the Great Panjandrum of polite learning in Scotland, he declared that the forty kings were an article of faith; and that if any of his countrymen attempted to question their authenticity, it would be his own duty as Lord Advocate to prosecute such a malefactor for high treason.[20] Twenty years later, at the time of the Union, the independence of Scotland was a point of such 'supreme delicacy and importance', we are told, that there was 'great hazard' in touching its questionable foundations;[21] and in the following generation, Father Innes would feel inhibited from publishing his criticism of the forty kings of Boece, not through fear of a charge of high treason (he took steps to prevent that by bolting abroad immediately after publication), but by 'an apprehension to be thought singular or presumptuous, and an aversion to be the first that should not only depart from, but contradict the common opinion of my countrymen'. His countrymen, he observed, clung to the myth of their extra seven centuries of history 'as if the honour of the nation did in great measure depend upon it'.[22] And they continued to cling to it even after he had published his great work of demolition. As late as the later 1770s Lord Hailes would bear rueful witness to the continuing power of Boece's 'fertile imagination', whose marvellous fictions had 'taken root in the minds of Scotsmen, and will never be eradicated': being constantly retold and re-copied. With the weary resignation of long experience, the learned judge said of his fellow Scots: 'although we have been long reformed from Popery, we are not yet reformed from Boece. . . . As fast as the cobwebs of fictitious history are brushed away, they will be replaced.'[23]

Bishop Leslie, James VII, Sir George Mackenzie, were all high-flying royalists. They defended the seven mythical centuries and the forty mythical kings in the cause of the Stuart monarchy. Perhaps if their party alone had sustained it, that myth would have fallen through the criticism of their opponents, the republicans or Scottish 'whigs', who, from the days of Mary Queen of Scots onwards, were the declared enemies of the house of Stuart. But by a singular chance the same myth was sustained no less vigorously, though for opposite reasons, by those opponents too. So, by equal and opposite pressure, the fabulous monarchs, whom either party might have pushed over, were artificially propped up. Indeed, the myth was even more vital to the republicans, the whigs, than to the royalists, the tories. The man who made it so vital was the first great agitator and propagandist of the whig cause, the man who was to the anti-Marian party what Bishop Leslie was to Mary: George Buchanan.

# 2

# George Buchanan

George Buchanan was, by universal consent, the greatest Latin writer, whether in prose or in verse, in sixteenth-century Europe. He was the undisputed literary hero of Scotland till the eighteenth-century Enlightenment. But very little of his life was spent in his native country. Once he had followed the well-trodden path from a Scottish university to the university of Paris, France was always his intellectual and generally his physical home. There he lived, mainly by teaching Latin, in a circle of humanist poets and scholars who all, vain though they were, recognised his pre-eminence. They hailed him – and it became his regular title, formally annexed to his name, even a substitute for his name – *princeps poetarum sui saeculi*, prince of the poets of his age. He was the greatest Latin poet, they said, since Virgil. His Latin prose style was no less perfect: unrivalled, it was claimed, since Tacitus. Only Erasmus could compete with him in that medium; and even Erasmus could only compete in that medium. If a perfect Latin style could confer immortality, as his contemporaries believed, the fame of Buchanan, it seemed, was secure.

Buchanan himself knew it. Though always poor, always dependent on patronage, he moved with perfect self-assurance in the highest society. His Scottish independence bordered often upon insolence. His appearance was 'rough-hewn, slovenly and rude': he wore, at least in old age, nothing finer than 'a rug-gown girt close about him'; but his patrician spirit and natural authority dissolved all initial reservations; and kings and queens listened to him with respect. The greatest of French poets, Pierre Ronsard, said of him that he had nothing of the pedagogue but the cap and gown. His Latin, too, was quite free of pedantry: it was the language of a statesman, a man of the world. Ronsard's friend and rival, Joachim du Bellay, wrote that Buchanan was the first to prove that a Scotchman was not necessarily a savage. The greatest of French historians, Jacques-Auguste de Thou, went further: he acknowledged him as an honorary Frenchman. To Montaigne, who was his pupil at the Collège de Guienne at Bordeaux, he was 'ce grand poète escossois'. The greatest classical scholar of the age, perhaps of any age, Joseph Scaliger, declared that in Latin poetry Buchanan left all Europe behind: in him, Scotland, the ultimate boundary of the Roman empire, became the last culmination of Roman eloquence.

Even those who hated Buchanan and his work – and his later political career made him many enemies – venerated him as a writer. King James VI of Scotland was his pupil, and resented, all his life, both the pedagogical methods and the political ideas of that overpowering tutor. Long after Buchanan's death, when James was monarch of three kingdoms, he would tremble at the mere approach of an innocent English courtier whose footfall recalled that of his old pedagogue. But even he found his resentment inseparable from admiration: admiration mixed with gratitude. When he was complimented on his genuine learning, he would reply that it was no wonder if he were a good scholar since he had had for his teacher the famous Buchanan. King James' views, on this as on other subjects, were shared by his able Scottish legal adviser, Sir Thomas Craig. Craig was a man of powerful mind and wide learning. He was a strong supporter of the king's policy of 'a more perfect union' with England. He opposed many of Buchanan's ideas, and wrote against him. But he too declared Buchanan unparalleled in the intellectual world. Whom, he asked, could the English put up against such a prodigy? 'He stands alone'.[1]

For two centuries after his death, Buchanan's literary fame remained undimmed. Politically, he might be extolled or denigrated: that depended on the politics of the judge; but in literature he was unchallenged. No man was less disposed to admire a Scotch whig than Dr Johnson. And yet even Johnson could suspend, for Buchanan, his own strongest prejudices. 'However unfavourable to Scotland', said Boswell, 'he uniformly gave liberal praise to George

Buchanan as a writer'; and when a Scotchman, seeking an easy triumph, exclaimed, 'Ah, Dr Johnson, what would you have said of Buchanan, had he been an Englishman?' 'Why, sir (replied Johnson, after a little pause), I should *not* have said of Buchanan, had he been an *Englishman*, what I will now say of him as a *Scotchman*, – that he was the only man of genius his country ever produced'.[2]

The external life of Buchanan, for his first sixty years, before he became a politician and a revolutionary agitator, can be described briefly. He was a Highlander by birth, 'born and bred in the mountains of Lennox', and almost certainly Gaelic-speaking.[3] He evidently knew the Highlands well, and he retained tribal loyalties. All his life he was a Lennox-man, devoted to the house of Lennox, hostile to its enemies, the house of Hamilton. 'It is well known', he would tell the monks of the Inquisition at Lisbon, 'how the family of Hamilton has always oppressed my family'.[4] (It is extremely unlikely that the hereditary feuds of Scottish clans were common knowledge in a Portuguese monastery.) Sometimes this tribalism is repellent, as in his triumphant poem on the judicial murder of Archbishop Hamilton. Sometimes it has a bizarre charm, as when he paraded it among the uncomprehending humanists of Europe.

All his life, also, Buchanan showed the pride, and the volatility, of the Celt. He was a pupil of that great Scottish scholar, whom we have already met as the first critical historian of Scotland, John Major. Having studied for a year, under Major, at the university of St Andrews, he followed him back to Paris in 1525–6. In Paris Buchanan discovered his own wonderful literary gift, and found a natural place for himself in a European humanist circle. From that moment he saw fit to despise his teacher, on whom, from the height of his new-found modernity, he would write a contemptuous epigram. The humanists were an arrogant breed, but they did not generally express open contempt of their teachers; and Major was no ordinary teacher.

Although he was loyal to his tribe, Buchanan does not seem for much of his life to have been strongly attached to his native country. At least, once he had discovered Paris, he showed a remarkable reluctance to return to the mountains of Lennox.[5] After nine years spent in France he returned to Scotland with a young nobleman whom he had been tutoring. So he found himself at court – but at

the half-French court of the young James V. When his engagement
to his pupil expired, he prepared to return to France; but he was
held back by an offer which no humanist could resist: the education
of a prince. The prince was the Lord James Stewart, a natural son of
James V whom an indulgent Pope had already made abbot of Kelso
and Melrose. Buchanan taught this well-endowed boy for two years.
Then an episode occurred which caused him to leave Scotland for
the third and, as seemed likely, the last time. He left in disgrace: a
disgrace which illustrates a permanent trait in his character.

At the court of James V in the 1530s, an outspoken, but somewhat
fitful, anti-clericalism was in fashion. The king's favourite companion
was Sir David Lindsay of the Mount, whose satires against the clergy
were appreciated by king and people alike. Observing this fact,
Buchanan (as he says himself) sought to please the king by writing a
series of Latin poems against the Franciscans. However – not for the
last time – he went too far. The poems were violent and obscene;[6] and
Buchanan had reckoned without the reigning royal mistress, who,
after the fashion of royal mistresses, was something of a *dévote*. They
were also ill-timed: they coincided with a sudden reaction against
'Lutheranism' at court. Buchanan was soon made to realise his error.
Instead of compliments on his wit and increase of royal favour, he
found himself arrested, along with other suspects, and thrown into
prison at St Andrews. However, he did not share the fate of the other
prisoners. While several of them were burned, he, perhaps through
royal connivance, managed to escape through his prison window
while his guards were asleep, and to bolt out of the country to
England. After a short stay in England, he returned to the continent.
For the next twenty-three years the continent was his home.

In those twenty-three years he led a roving life, a migratory cosmopolitan intellectual among other intellectuals, equally migratory,
equally cosmopolitan. They taught Latin in colleges or private
houses, compiled Latin grammars, wrote humanist manifestos, vied
with each other in the composition of Latin verses, flattered and
cultivated the great. Buchanan's first stop, after he had crossed the
Channel, was in Paris. Unfortunately, his arrival coincided with that
of a dangerous enemy. Cardinal Beaton, the clerical statesman of
Scotland who was afterwards to become the bugbear of Scottish

Protestants, arrived in Paris as special ambassador of the king of Scotland. Buchanan believed that he was not safe in the same city as Beaton, and looked for a safer refuge. Such a refuge was provided by a timely offer from a Portuguese friend in Paris, Andrea de Gouvea. Gouvea was a humanist teacher at the university of Paris, where his uncle, Diogo de Gouvea, was head of the Collège de Ste Barbe. Like Buchanan, Andrea de Gouvea was regarded as an honorary Frenchman. In 1534 he had been appointed head of the newly founded humanist Collège de Guienne in Bordeaux, and he now needed new teachers there; he wanted avant-garde humanists like himself; and he invited Buchanan, and some other friends, to come and teach Latin. Buchanan accepted at once. He spent three years in the congenial air of Bordeaux; it was there that he wrote his best poems; and it was there that he had as his pupil Montaigne.

After Bordeaux, Buchanan returned to Paris and taught at the strictly Catholic college of Cardinal Lemoine: an episode which he afterwards omitted to record in his brief autobiography, when that recollection would have proved inconvenient. But soon another invitation tempted him away again. His friend Gouvea had been summoned by the king of Portugal to preside over his new university of Coimbra; and once again Gouvea invited Buchanan and his little group of avant-garde colleagues from Bordeaux to join him. Unfortunately this experiment was less happy. The Portuguese Inquisition descended upon him; he was accused of various heretical practices; and he spent a year and a half immured in a monastery. It used to be supposed that Buchanan had brought this misfortune on himself by expressing his Protestant views; but such an interpretation was disproved when the documents of his examination were discovered and published. It then became clear that Buchanan was an incidental victim of an internal feud in the large and influential, but bitterly divided, Gouvea family. Buchanan's friend, Andrea de Gouvea, died suddenly after a year in his new post; but by that time denunciations had already been launched against him, and by extension his close associates; and Buchanan was caught up in the widening circles of investigation generated by the inquisitorial process. Eventually the inquisitors were satisfied; and Buchanan, having cleared himself of the charges, and professed himself a good

Catholic, was set free. By his own account, the monks had treated him well, and he was even invited to stay on in Portugal; but his friend Gouvea being dead, he preferred to leave. He sailed to England; but not finding the Protestant England of Edward VI to his taste, he returned to France and found employment as a tutor in the ultra-Catholic family of a distinguished and cultivated French general, Charles de Cossé, Maréchal de Brissac, who was also governor of Piedmont. Buchanan's pupil was the marshal's son, Timoléon de Cossé, named after one of Plutarch's heroes.

For five years Buchanan lived in the household of his new patron in France and in Piedmont. From that safe haven he poured out poems in honour of the Catholic rulers of France and, in particular, of the most Catholic of all, the leaders of reaction at a reactionary court, the great family of Guise. He celebrated the Duc de Guise's victory in recovering Calais from the English; he hailed the marriage of the young Mary Stuart, daughter of Mary of Guise, with the Dauphin of France; and when Mary Stuart sailed to Scotland to take up her crown, he, as the favoured poet of the Guise family, accepted an invitation to her court.[7] It was his first visit to Scotland since he had bolted through the prison window at St Andrews twenty-three years before. By the beginning of 1562 he was established at Holyrood House, with a pension of £250 Scots a year, reading Livy to the queen after dinner: Livy, the favourite historian of the conservative humanists, the model of Boece.

So, at the age of fifty-six, the greatest of humanist poets was back in his native land, and ready to begin the new career which was to give him a second title to fame, or infamy. At this period we may pause to ask some general questions. What, behind the shifting loyalties imposed by patronage, and the bewitching brilliance of his Latin style, was the true character of the man? What, if anything, were his consistent ideas?

The suggestion which used to be made that Buchanan was a Protestant hero, comparable with John Knox, is plainly untenable. At no time during his first fifty-six years did he appear as a Protestant; and although he stated, in the brief autobiography which he dictated just before his death, that in his student days in Paris he 'fell into the flames of the Lutheran sect', there is nothing in his writings to reflect this. At the end of 1552 his language remains that of an orthodox Roman Catholic;[8] indeed, the same inference can still be drawn from his language as late as 1558.[9] There is no trace of deep religious feeling in any of his writings; in fact, the whole cast of his mind was essentially secular. The charges which were brought against him by the Portuguese Inquisition implied anti-clericalism, but not heresy. The play of John the Baptist, which was objected against him, was indeed a powerful anti-clerical tract: its persecuting Pharisee, Malchus, has all the qualities ascribed by his enemies to Cardinal Beaton, from whose long arm Buchanan had fled to Bordeaux. It had clearly been denounced to the Inquisitors, by someone who had seen it performed there, as an anti-Catholic work. But Buchanan's defence, that it was an allegory of the persecution of Sir Thomas More – that Herod was Henry VIII, Herodias Anne Boleyn, and the Baptist More – would have been impossible if heresy had been involved. Even Buchanan's most famous devotional work – the translation of the Psalms into twenty-nine different Latin metres, which he composed during his imprisonment in Lisbon – was not so much a work of devotion as an academic exercise, an exhibition of humanist virtuosity. By his own account, Buchanan only began to study the controversies of religion in the late 1550s. He had been a student and a teacher when the writings of Luther, Erasmus and Calvin were distracting all Europe; and yet it was only when he was fifty that he began to take notice of these things.[10] A man who only begins to concern himself with religion in middle age cannot be said to be very spiritual.

Sir James Melville of Halhill, a younger contemporary of Buchanan, wrote of him that he was 'so facile that he was led with any company that he haunted for the time, which made him factious in his old days'.[11] It is a just observation, which Buchanan illustrated throughout his life. Indeed, he admitted as much himself: in excusing himself to the Portuguese inquisitors, he explained that he tended always to reflect the opinions of those around him, which was why (for instance) he had expressed 'Gallican', 'conciliar' opinions – that the Pope was subject to General Councils – when in Paris. In the same way, he had been anti-clerical at the court of James V, Erastian in the England of Henry VIII, radical in avant-garde Bordeaux, and would be ultra-Catholic in the household of the Maréchal de Brissac and in

the company of the Guises. Long afterwards, he would write a
famous satire against Mary Stuart's secretary of state, Maitland of
Lethington, whom he portrayed as a chameleon; but the real
chameleon was himself. His genius was essentially mimetic, not
original. Just as he could capture the style and cadence of the classical Latin writers, and imitate them to perfection, so throughout his
career he would borrow the sentiments of those with whom he
consorted and give them, by his rhetorical brilliance, a more cutting
edge, a brighter polish.

He would also, more often than not, go too far. Drunk with his
own virtuosity, accustomed to the competition of his humanist
peers, and to his own triumph in that competition, he would
indulge his rhetoric, exaggerate the views which he had borrowed,
and sometimes, in consequence, come to grief. This is what he had
done at the court of James V, in his aggressive youth, and it had
nearly cost him his life. He would do it again in his old age, at the
court of James V's daughter Mary Stuart, and it would make his
fortune as a revolutionary.

Such was the temperament of Buchanan. But what of his views?
Can we, behind these shifting attitudes, discover any consistent ideas?
It does, in fact, seem possible to do so. Like most of his cosmopolitan
humanist contemporaries, Buchanan was anti-clerical, but not anti-
Catholic. More than most of them, he was thoroughly secular in
spirit. In his ideas, like them, he was conservative. In no intellectual
direction did he show any originality whatever. In politics, the only
ideas which he admitted – the 'conciliar' ideas about the government
of the Church – were standard form in Paris. They went back to
Aquinas, and had been expressed by Buchanan's teacher, Major. His
most ambitious work, his didactic poem *de Sphaera*, was a defence of
medieval astronomy against the absurd novelties of Copernicus. In
Bordeaux, he wrote Latin plays for his students to perform, to wean
them away from their shocking new taste for plays in the vernacular.
As a humanist, Buchanan despised vernacular languages, and wished
to see them wither away as relics of barbarism: he looked forward to
a time when Latin would be restored as the universal language of
civilisation;[12] and in drama he looked back to Seneca, not forward to
Shakespeare. For the future, so far as Scotland was concerned, he

dissented, once again, from Major. He looked to the perpetuation of the 'old alliance' with France, not with England. For France was at the centre of his life: it was the intellectual capital of Scotland. In England he had little interest. He had passed through it after his escape from prison in St Andrews in 1539, and had submitted flattering poems to Henry VIII and Thomas Cromwell; and he had visited it again on his escape from prison in Lisbon. But he had found no temptation to stay there. He did not, like his teacher Major, love the English, or find music in the bells of Cambridge.

Such were the general views of Buchanan when he ended his long sojourn in France and set out to spend his declining years as an intellectual ornament of the French court in Holyrood House. On arrival in Edinburgh, he joined the Calvinist Church of Scotland. On the face of it, this may seem surprising. The Calvinist Church was indeed, by now, the established Church of Scotland; and, except for the royal chapel, there was no visible Catholic church left in the country: the old established Church had collapsed entirely. It could therefore be said that Buchanan, as usual, was conforming to his surroundings. But the queen was his patroness, and she was still a Catholic. Buchanan's action in openly joining the Calvinist Church, instead of continuing to entertain anti-clerical humanist views while professing the orthodoxy of the court, requires some explanation.

The explanation is to be found, partly at least, in the experience of that intellectual milieu to which, behind the temporary bonds of patronage, Buchanan was always committed: the humanists. In the 1540s the humanists of France had been, like himself, conforming Catholics. Those were still the years of the French Renaissance: of the reign of François I, the restorer of learning and the arts; and a critical, 'Erasmian' posture was still possible for those whose ultimate loyalty was, anyway, not to papal but to pagan Rome. But in the 1550s that had changed. As the Protestant threat became more serious – as it moved from intellectual and moral criticism towards social revolution – the ruling powers took fright, and the engines of repression were mounted against heresy. Humanist criticism of the Church was now brutally repressed, and the humanists had to choose between conformity and revolt: in effect, between that *sacrificio dell'intelletto* which was accepted as the price of survival by

Muretus,[13] and the preservation of the critical spirit under the new, and still apparently liberal leadership of Calvin. Almost all of Buchanan's humanist friends in France chose Calvinism. It was in the persecution of the 1550s that the Huguenot movement in France acquired its intellectual leadership, which in turn provided the leadership of the Calvinist International throughout the rest of the century and until the Thirty Years War. In those years, while Buchanan lived with a Catholic family, praising the leaders of the Catholic party, he must have felt himself gradually becoming isolated from his humanist friends. Naturally, he must have felt doubts, and asked questions. He himself says that it was then that he began to study the controversies of religion. Then came the invitation to Scotland, a Calvinist country. If he had felt uneasy as a Catholic in Catholic France, how could he be at ease as a Catholic in Calvinist Scotland? Only the bond of personal patronage would hold him back.

That bond was indeed necessary; but how strong was it? To us, looking back through the coloured glass of intervening history, Mary Stuart is a heroine (or a villain) of Counter-Reformation Catholicism. But in 1562 no one could yet see her in that light. She was a cultivated, pleasure-loving princess from the most sophisticated court in Europe. And the 1560s were not the 1550s. At the end of that repressive decade, the great wars of Europe had been wound up, and the rulers who had made them had died. With the new decade, a new era seemed to have begun: an era of peace, and perhaps coexistence. In France, the Catholic Queen Regent, Catherine de Médicis, a civilised *politique* who perpetuated the pagan traditions of Fontainebleau, had proclaimed religious toleration. In England, Queen Elizabeth, another sophisticated princess, had similar aims. Why should not Mary Queen of Scots do likewise? In 1562 it was widely believed that she would adopt the Anglican via media. That might have preserved the policy of coexistence. Alternatively, she might become a Calvinist herself, like some of the French princesses. As queen of a Calvinist country, it would be reasonable: just as reasonable as for the queen of Navarre. Mary's own uncle, the Cardinal of Lorraine, a prince of the house of Guise, advised her to do so. It seemed the obvious thing to do.

Besides, the court at Holyrood was itself divided. The strongest force there, the man on whom Mary most relied, was her half-brother, the Lord James, Earl of Moray. It was he who had come to France to persuade her to return to Scotland. He had also persuaded her to support the Protestant party, of which he was the leader; and he had himself crushed, on her behalf, a Catholic rising in the north. All the signs suggested that the Scottish court would become a Calvinist court in a Calvinist country, as other petty courts in the French *clientèle* would do: for Calvinism, though it never succeeded in capturing power in France itself, remained a French religion, the badge of French cultural domination; and the Calvinist rulers in the Palatinate, the Hague, Geneva would continue to move in the orbit first of Valois, then of Bourbon France.

Thus Buchanan, in becoming a Calvinist, was not necessarily defying his patron. He might even be jumping with the cat, or just ahead of it. And he was, of course, recommending himself to the dominant power at court, the Earl of Moray. Moray was himself a patron of literature, and he gladly extended his patronage to Buchanan. To have the most famous scholar in Europe as his mouthpiece would be a great asset. Thanks to the support of Moray, Buchanan soon became a member of the General Assembly of the Kirk; and other positions of influence or profit would follow. Meanwhile he wrote flattering Latin poems and profane masques for Mary. So long as Mary and her half-brother were in agreement, Buchanan could walk on the razor-edge of double loyalty and enjoy the best of both worlds. The difficulty would come if they should part.

In 1565 they had not yet parted; and Buchanan, being now at the height of his prosperity, decided that it was time to crown his long and successful career as a man of letters, and to ensure his future fame, by publishing his collected works. Hitherto, as far as we know, he had only written poetry. But of that poetry only a part had so far appeared in print. Many of his poems were dispersed in manuscript in the hands of his French friends. In order to collect them for orderly publication, it was necessary to pay a visit to Paris. Fortunately, in this year, he had a chance to make such a visit. The queen of Scots entrusted him with a secret diplomatic mission to the king of France. We do not know the nature of the mission; but it shows the confidential position which Buchanan, at some minor level perhaps, had acquired at court. While in France, he no doubt thought, he would be able to assemble his poems, and perhaps arrange for their publication by one of the great Paris printers. He would then return to Edinburgh, and spend his last years enjoying his well-established fame in a comfortable sinecure at the court. He was, after all, in his sixtieth year, and had earned an honourable retirement.

So, at least, he may have supposed. But when he arrived in Paris, he soon changed his mind. For there he found his humanist friends in great anxiety. The policy of coexistence had by now completely broken down, and the future looked very black. Threatened by an ideological civil war, the French humanists could hardly become excited about complimentary poems addressed to patrons who, by now, were sometimes their most hated enemies. So, with one accord, *velut conspiratione facta*, as if in league with each other, they begged Buchanan not to rest on his literary laurels or regard his career as closed; for although he was now an old man, there was still work to do. They reminded him that, in the past, he had promised to write a prose work, a history of Scotland: a continuation, perhaps, of the work of Boece. It may be that he had in fact already written some such history, or at least begun work on it; certainly some of his foreign friends believed that he had. But nothing had so far been made public. So now they urged him to resume the task. History was what was needed. Several of his closest friends had written, or were writing, histories. Diogo de Teive, who had been with him in Bordeaux and in Coimbra, had written on Portuguese exploits in India. Nicholas de Grouchy, who would be his last host on this last visit to France, had written on the constitution of the Roman Republic, proving that it was essentially a democracy. Why should Buchanan not now bring to completion his long promised and now so necessary work?

After a short stay, Buchanan returned by sea direct to Scotland. His position at court was now more satisfactory than ever. The Earl of Moray particularly cultivated him, obtaining a new pension for him, appointing him (for it was in his gift) to the Principalship of St Andrews University. Moray even had this secular-minded layman elected 'moderator' of the General Assembly of the Kirk. Buchanan responded with flattering verses. He also caused to be printed his obscene early poems against the Franciscans, and dedicated them to the austere Protestant hero. This was somewhat ironical, since Moray's mother was the royal mistress who had been so outraged by the same poems a quarter-century earlier. To the queen, Buchanan presented a more decorous work: his Latin version of the Psalms, begun when he was a prisoner of the Portuguese Inquisition. With the gift he offered her a dedicatory poem as perfect as any such poem in ancient literature. Then, to crown his felicity, he saw the queen married to the Earl of Darnley, heir to the Earl of Lennox, the head of his own Scottish tribe. When a son was born, the future James VI, Buchanan would write another celebratory ode, and would be pre-appointed the prince's tutor. Meanwhile he was, we must assume, reflecting on the history of Scotland, and realising his old plan, now revived, to continue or replace the work of Boece.

Alas, the felicity did not last long. Within a year of the royal marriage, a series of disasters began. In 1566 the queen was estranged from Darnley by the brutal murder, in her presence, of her Italian musician and secretary, David Riccio. In February 1567 Darnley himself was murdered, following the blowing-up by gunpowder of the house at Kirk o' Fields, to which his wife, with a sudden seeming return of affection, had taken him to recover from a serious illness. Soon afterwards the queen married Darnley's murderer. With these events, the policy of coexistence had broken down in Scotland as completely as in France; and Buchanan's loyalty to the queen broke down with it. Meanwhile Moray had already drawn away from Mary. The queen's marriage with Darnley, which had pleased Buchanan, had not pleased Moray: he saw in it the beginnings of a new and dangerous policy, and of his own eclipse. By the time of the murder at Kirk o' Fields, he was already the leader of opposition. Now he became the leader of rebellion: he resolved to overthrow Mary, and to secure for himself, if not (as some thought) the royal crown, at least the regency and effective government of Scotland.

Faced with the collapse of coexistence, and forced to choose which side he would support, Buchanan did not hesitate. All his loyalty to Mary had been dissolved by the murder of Darnley. From now on he was Moray's man: becoming the silver trumpet of revolution against his former patroness. When the Scottish nobles, 'the Lords of the Congregation', captured, imprisoned and deposed Mary, he became the most violent of agitators against her. The excitement of revolution inspired the old man with new life. He put his pen, and all his talents, at the disposal of the revolutionary lords. He supplied them with propaganda for foreign courts. He devised the insignia, the coinage, the public documents, of the new regime. When Mary, defeated in civil war, fled to England, and sought asylum at the court of Elizabeth, it was he who was sent thither, accompanying his patron Moray, to accuse her to the English ministers. And he accused her to some tune. He wrote the formal indictment of her, the terrible *Detection of Mary Stuart*, denouncing her as an adulteress and a murderer.[14] And he set out, by writing, to prove to all that she was rightly deposed and that the nobility of Scotland had the right to elect, in her stead, a new monarch, chosen from the ruling house: in effect, to replace her by her half-brother, his own patron, Moray, now Regent of Scotland.

Such was the background to Buchanan's activity as a revolutionary propagandist in the years from 1567 to 1572, the years of the Scottish revolution. It was also the background to his new activity as the historian of Scotland. History, his French friends had told him in 1565, was the science that was needed in these days of crisis. They would prove it themselves when their turn came. The ideas which they would advance, after the Massacre of St Bartholomew, to justify frontal war on the legitimacy of the house of Valois in France, had been generated in Huguenot circles under the pressure of events in the mid-century. They were ideas based on Aristotle and on history. From the same common stock Buchanan now drew his ideas. The French Huguenots would appeal to French history to show that the true, historic French constitution, brought into Gaul by the Franks, the Germanic invaders of the Dark Ages, was aristocratic, even republican: that the true, historic French monarchy was, at base, elective not hereditary, and depended on good behaviour. Buchanan would similarly appeal to Scottish history to show that the true, historic Scottish constitution was the same. And if the recorded history of the last thousand years did not support this theory – if, in fact, there was not a single historical instance of such formal deposition – what of that? Were there not forty earlier kings before that, one-third of whom (according to Boece) had been, in one way or another, deposed, tried or executed for their colourful crimes? Hitherto Buchanan had cited those phantom kings in tributary poems to Mary, as evidence of the glorious antiquity of her race. Now he would cite them as evidence of the ancient, whig constitution of Scotland.

The first appearance of the forty kings in this new capacity was at the very beginning of the Scottish revolution. In the summer of 1567, when Mary was a prisoner in Kinross castle, on an island in Lochleven, Queen Elizabeth sought to intervene on her behalf. Elizabeth had every reason to dislike and fear Mary, who was gaping after her crown; but she had no desire to encourage the rebellion of subjects or the deposition of monarchs. She therefore sent an ambassador to Scotland to persuade Moray and the confederate lords to consent to a compromise. She wished to see Mary restored to the throne, but on terms which would ensure a Protestant policy, in line with that of England. In other words, she wished to restore, and strengthen, the policy of coexistence. But in Moray's view the time for coexistence was over. Too much had happened in the past year, and he was determined not to compromise. If Mary were restored to power, he could see only the prospect of a gradual return to Catholic rule in alliance either with the French or the Spanish monarchy; power would be wielded by the Hamiltons; and Moray and his friends would be strung up. The only alternative, in his eyes, was a radical Protestant policy in alliance with the Crown of England – or, if Elizabeth were reluctant, with the Puritan party in England – and the Huguenots of France. He was therefore determined to make no concessions on the essential point of the restoration of Mary. Fortunately, in considering how to deal with the English ambassador, he had Buchanan at his elbow, and Buchanan had Boece at his fingertips.

So when the ambassador delivered his message, he received a summary reply. Whatever might be the rights of princes elsewhere, he was told, in Scotland it was different: on account of the peculiar Scottish constitution. 'It was said', the ambassador reported, 'the states of the realm and people assembled might in this case be competent judges; whereof they had in their own country sundry experiences in criminal offences committed by princes; and there was recited unto me sundry examples forth of their own histories, grounded (as they said) upon their own laws. But I believe', he added sceptically, 'it was but practices'.[15]

At the same time Buchanan wrote, for circulation in manuscript, his famous dialogue *de Jure Regni apud Scotos*: a dialogue which has been described (by Harold Laski) as 'possibly the most influential political essay of the sixteenth century'. In form, it is a discussion on the revolution in Scotland between Buchanan and Thomas Maitland, the younger brother of William Maitland of Lethington, Mary's secretary of state. (Afterwards Thomas Maitland wrote to Mary, protesting that his name had been taken in vain.) In substance, it is a 'whig' treatise, arguing that kings are subject to the choice and continuing approval of the people: or rather, of a council of nobles, who may correct and, if necessary, depose them. The argument is based on Aristotle, Aquinas, and the 'conciliar' writers of the Gallican Church; and, as far as the theory goes, would not have been rejected by Major. But a general theory of the accountability of kings was not, perhaps, the best way to win the support of foreign monarchs like Queen Elizabeth; and so Buchanan falls back on the particular constitution of Scotland. In Scotland, he says, the monarchy has always been fundamentally elective, like the chieftaincy of the Highland and island clans; and for evidence he turns to history. 'I could enumerate twelve or more kings', he says triumphantly, 'who were either condemned to perpetual imprisonment or only escaped the just punishment of their crimes by exile or a voluntary death'. The twelve or more kings are, of course, Boece's phantom kings: Culenus, Evenus, Ferchard, etc.; to whom, lest these should seem too ancient and irrelevant, he hastily adds James III – the only instance from modern times. James III had not been formally tried or deposed. He had been murdered in cold blood after being defeated in battle. But Buchanan covered himself, as the murderers had covered themselves at the time, by a convenient sophistry. The nobility in parliament, he could say, had afterwards formally condemned James III, and solemnly voted themselves immune from punishment on that account. They had thus retrospectively legalised his execution. It was thanks to this excellent constitution, Buchanan concludes, that Scotland has remained unconquered and free for two thousand years: the two thousand years since Fergus I (son of Ferchar).

At the same time Buchanan had begun work on his History of Scotland. How far he had carried it at the time of the revolution we cannot tell; for, like the Dialogue, it was not published till long afterwards; and, unlike the Dialogue, it was never circulated in manuscript. But it is probable that he was already engaged on the early part of the narrative – indeed that he was writing it simultaneously with the Dialogue, with which it has many phrases in common. The early part of the History, after all, was the necessary background to the Dialogue: it supplied the Dialogue's historical evidence, its necessary documentation. There, Buchanan described with unction the enormities of those wicked early kings: Thereus, Durstus, Evenus and the rest, who at that time must have come vividly to life for him, looming with real features out of the legendary mist. He was writing for a purpose, against time, under the pressure of great events, and with the exhilaration of a man deeply involved in those events. In revolutions, says Macaulay, men live fast. They must write fast too; for they may be overtaken.

It seems likely that Buchanan's aim, in these writings, was to secure the 'election' of his patron Moray as king of Scotland in place of the deposed Mary Stuart: for he did not argue for a republic; and his elective king was to be a member of the reigning family. Since Mary's son was disqualified as an infant, and the next legitimate heirs were the hated Hamiltons, it is difficult to see whom else he could have envisaged. Indeed, unless he envisaged Moray, his own theory could have been ruinous to him and his cause. The obvious objection was that Moray was illegitimate; and illegitimacy was normally held to be a fatal bar. But Buchanan knew how to deal with that difficulty. In his History he never mentioned or even implied Moray's illegitimacy: he invariably wrote of him as if he were the legitimate son of James V. And if that device should fail, he had another. By maintaining that Robert III, the second Stuart king, was also illegitimate, he indicated, by implication, that illegitimacy was no bar to succession: for if it were a bar, the whole Stuart dynasty since 1390 had been usurpers.[16]

For three years, from the murder of Darnley until the beginning of 1570, Buchanan, by virtue of Moray's patronage, was at the centre of revolutionary affairs. He could see himself as the guiding intellect of the revolutionary party. But then, in January 1570, Moray was murdered: shot from a window as he rode through Linlithgow. The assassin was James Hamilton of Bothwellhaugh, and he had been inspired and aided by the heads of the Hamilton family. The house from which he had fired the fatal shot belonged to James Hamilton, archbishop of St Andrews. With that shot, all Buchanan's hopes for the future collapsed. His Dialogue, already widely circulated in manuscript, his History, already partly written, had now lost their purpose. For some time he remained sunk in gloom. As the English agent, his close friend Thomas Randolph, reported, nearly two months later, he 'never rejoiced since the Regent's death'.[17] Half the purpose of his life – this second life as a sexagenarian political revolutionary – had gone.

Half? No, more than half; for it was the constructive half. Buchanan would still have to defend the revolution that had taken place: the deposition of Mary. So long as she lived, there was always the danger that she might come back, by a counter-revolution in Scotland, or by machiavellian diplomacy at the court of England: for who could predict the serpentine policy of Queen Elizabeth? Or, even worse, she might be replaced by the Hamiltons. That, indeed, would make a mockery of the revolution. In any such event, Buchanan himself would get short shrift. But what was now the positive alternative? All that Buchanan could hope for was that the revolution would be maintained; that the legitimate king, by living, would bar the way to the throne, and ultimately come to reign as the heir to Moray rather than to Mary. As the legitimate king was not yet four years old, that was a remote speculation: even his life was precarious; and even on the most favourable calculation, Buchanan himself would hardly reap any benefit: for he was already sixty-three.

Immediate danger, after Moray's death, was averted by the appointment of the Earl of Lennox to succeed him as Regent. Lennox was Darnley's father; he was committed to the revolution; and he was the chief of Buchanan's own tribe. Buchanan himself profited from Lennox's regency: he was a dependant of the Regent himself – letters should be addressed to him, he told a friend, care of the Countess of Lennox, currently in London.[18] He was made Director of Chancery and Lord Privy Seal, with a seat in the Scotch Parliament. But how long would Lennox last? He was fifty-four years old – fifteen years older than Moray – and had little support except from the revolutionary junto. The Hamiltons were in arms against him; the governor of Edinburgh castle, Kirkcaldy of Grange, transferred his loyalty to Mary; and the ablest politician in Scotland, the incalculable Maitland of Lethington, deserted the Regent to become the leader of the Marian party.

It was in these circumstances that Buchanan wrote his two – his only two – pamphlets in the vernacular Scottish tongue.[19] One was *Ane Admonition to the Trew Lordis* – a violent, indeed hysterical, attack on the whole Hamilton family who, said Buchanan, for over fifty years had stuck at nothing – not murder, not civil war – to grasp the Crown of Scotland. In particular, they had waged a perpetual vendetta against the family of Lennox. They had enforced the Regent's own exile in England. They had murdered the father; they had murdered his son. Now they were scheming to murder his grandson, the infant King James VI. They must be destroyed without mercy, root and branch: 'better it is to slay justly nor to be slane wrangfully'.[20] The other pamphlet was directed against Maitland of Lethington. It was the famous *Chamaeleon*: a subtler, wittier, more calculated attack; a brilliant satire, not a mere invective. Of both these pamphlets it has been well said that they differ from any other vernacular Scots prose of their time in their controlled structure. The sentences have form and point; and they have it because the old humanist, for most of his adult life, had thought, read, and spoken not in Scots but in Latin.[21]

The Hamiltons did not murder the young king; but the danger to the revolution from English intervention was very real. Having herself just survived an aristocratic conspiracy in the north of England, which drew nourishment from a faction in Scotland, Queen Elizabeth was anxious to bring the Scottish civil war to an end; and, once again, to end it by compromise: by restoring Mary on terms. The rebel lords in Scotland were determined not to readmit Mary on any terms; but they could not afford to alienate the English government, and they accepted an invitation to send commissioners to London and argue the case. In particular, they were to improve on the arguments which Moray had produced in 1568, and which had been set out in Buchanan's *Detection*. They were to produce positive proof that Mary had authorised the murder of Darnley, or some reason of state so compelling that Elizabeth could justify to the world what she had difficulty in justifying to herself: her support of rebellion against a sister queen. The three commissioners were duly appointed and sent to London. Their leader was the earl of Morton. They arrived in February 1571. Buchanan did not, this time, accompany them himself; but, as in 1568, he supplied their brief – or at least the central historical and theoretical portion of their brief.[22] It was in the form of a long document, a 'memorial', which Morton duly presented to the English commissioners appointed to deal with him and his colleagues.

Queen Elizabeth had asked for evidence of Mary's guilt, or other reasons for her deposition. Buchanan dismissed the question of guilt lightly – that, he said, had been adequately proved in his previous submission – i.e. the *Detection*. He rebutted the possible legal objection that Mary's abdication had been extracted from her under duress, quoting Roman law; then he turned with more relish to history. It was no new thing in Scotland, he insisted, for the people, represented by the nobility, to depose a wicked and unprofitable prince: 'for the nobilitie and people of Scotland, being a free people, in the beginning of their kingdom, choysit thair king, adjoyning to him ane counsall of the wisest; quhilk ancient custom the men of the Ilis and others, in chosing of thair chieftainis, yit still observis'. This had been so since time immemorial, and had been recognised by the kings themselves, except when they maintained themselves by tyranny, or flattery had sealed their eyes and indurated their hearts. Then, to prove his case, Buchanan trotted out his examples: Thereus, the eighth king of Scotland, Durstus the eleventh, and Evenus the thirteenth – not to speak of Ferlegus, Lugtachus, Mogallus, Conarus, Satrahel, Ahirco and other legendary rulers. All these accounts were taken, as Buchanan admitted, from the chronicles of Boece, to which 'the indifferent reader' is explicitly referred for even fuller details. In times which everyone would recognise as historical, a ritual reference was made to James III, whose doings 'were after his death disallowed by parliament'. Even Buchanan could not pretend that James III had been tried or formally deposed in his lifetime. At the close of the document, Buchanan quoted Calvin, Melanchthon, the canon lawyers of the conciliar movement, and Cicero.

The argument was in fact the argument of the Dialogue *de Jure Regni*. There was the same claim of a peculiar ancient 'whig' constitution; the same reference to the election of Hebridean chieftains; the same appeal to Boece's fabulous kings, with James III as an afterthought; the same appeal to classical writers. However, the document did not produce the desired effect. Queen Elizabeth, we are told, read it 'not without indignation' and tacitly condemned it 'as written in affront and wrong to kings'. But to the commissioners she simply replied that she was not satisfied with their reasons; and she urged them 'to take some speedy course for extinguishing the discords in Scotland'.[23]

The discords in Scotland were not extinguished. Next month Archbishop Hamilton was seized, tried hastily, and executed; an act which inspired Buchanan to write two poems of vindictive glee. Six months later, the Regent Lennox was captured at Stirling, and stabbed in the back while trying to escape. After his death, the Earl of Mar ruled for a year, and then died. The new Regent, the Earl of Morton, who succeeded him in 1572, began well. With English military aid, he captured Edinburgh castle from Mary's forces. The governor, Kirkcaldy, and his political adviser, the 'chamaeleon' Maitland, fell into his hands. Maitland died in prison; Kirkcaldy was hanged. Thereafter the revolution in Scotland was safe; its surviving profiteers settled down to enjoy the spoils; and the intrigues of Mary were directed not to the recovery of her Scottish throne but to the acquisition, by direct action – through foreign support and the assassination of Queen Elizabeth – of that of England.

In these circumstances there was no further need of Buchanan's propaganda. His Dialogue had served its turn in manuscript and could be forgotten. His History, which was to back up the Dialogue, had lost its immediate purpose, and was now becalmed. Scotland itself had now become a backwater. Five years earlier, its revolution had drawn the eyes of Europe; but now, as it settled down under a rapacious oligarchy, those eyes had been drawn elsewhere. For in April 1572 the Dutch Sea-Beggars, expelled from England, had seized

Brill, thus effectively beginning the revolution in Holland; in July the Prince of Orange had accepted the leadership of the revolt; and in August the Massacre of St Bartholomew not only renewed the wars of religion in France, but also sent Huguenot intellectuals to animate the revolt in the Netherlands. Now Holland, not Scotland, was the capital of European revolution; and Buchanan's old humanist friends were among its propagandists. The ideas which he had expressed in manuscript in 1567 were now published abroad by Théodore de Bèze, François Hotman, Hubert Languet, Philippe du Plessis Mornay. Buchanan had indeed got in first; but they had now overtaken him. *Franco-gallia, Le Réveille-Matin des Français*, and *Vindiciae contra Tyrannos* were now the manifestos of revolution: a revolution that would last longer, spread further, and strike deeper roots than 'the discords in Scotland'.

From all the evidence, it seems that in 1572 the steam went out of Buchanan's life. For five years he had lived on the crest of the wave. After a lifetime of dependence, he had become a political figure, the oracle of a revolutionary party, famous throughout Europe. He had tasted the intoxication of power, and had determined, or seemed to himself to determine, the fate of princes. But now all that was over. Moray was dead, Lennox was dead, Morton was unsympathetic; and Buchanan, a superannuated humanist, no longer consulted by the great, was relegated, in his old age, to the humble task of reading Plutarch and Livy, not with an amiable queen in the palace of Holyrood House, but with a small boy, whom he seems to have found thoroughly uncongenial, in Stirling castle. No wonder he was often irritable: abusing his charge as 'a true bird of the bloody nest to which he belonged'; and occasionally working off his frustrations by whipping the young prince.[24]

Moreover, in 1572, at precisely the moment of his political eclipse, Buchanan suffered an even graver blow to his pride. In that year, the literate public could read an attack – an altogether devastating attack – on the whole historical basis of Buchanan's political theory: the early chapters of Boece's *History*. The attack, which was posthumous, had been delivered by a Welsh antiquary, Humphrey Lhuyd.

# 3

# Buchanan's Nemesis

Humphrey Lhuyd was a man of some distinction. He was a medical man, a member of Parliament, and a friend, kinsman and client of the great. He was also celebrated as an antiquary, 'the most famous Antiquarius of all our country . . . after John Leland and John Bale'.[1] He was known abroad, too: in 1565 he contributed an essay on the Isle of Man to the atlas of the greatest living geographer, Abraham Ortelius of Antwerp. In this essay he declared himself a firm defender of the Welsh Brutus against the attacks of the unbelieving Italian, Polydore Vergil. So far, so good. When his essay was published in 1570, Lhuyd appeared as a conservative defender of ancient tradition. But meanwhile, he had moved on. In 1568 he had completed a map of Wales, also for Ortelius, and had posted it to Antwerp, accompanied, once again, by a learned commentary. Then he had died at the early age of forty-one. Ortelius did not publish the work till 1572. One of its earliest, and certainly most outraged, readers was Buchanan.

He had good reason to be outraged. For Lhuyd, while steadfastly averting his critical mind from Brutus, had concentrated it, with devastating effect, on Boece's *History*. With exact scholarship, made more maddening by bursts of ribald hilarity, he had exposed the manifold failings of Boece. He had blown out of existence all those extra seven hundred years of Scottish history, and had atomised, beyond any possibility of reintegration, all those forty kings whose vertiginous alternations of election, fornication and deposition had provided almost the entire historical basis of Buchanan's ancient whig constitution of Scotland. Not one of those kings, exclaimed Lhuyd gleefully, had ever existed. Boece's detailed account of their reigns, their victories, their laws, their virtues and vices, was a mere novel: a fable more fabulous than Lucian's *True History* or Ariosto's *Orlando* or that more popular work of chivalric fiction, *Amadis de Gaule.* No ancient author, said Lhuyd, had ever heard of the Scots. So far from being a nation of political philosophers who had perfected their constitution in the time of Aristotle and Alexander the Great, received an embassy from Ptolemy II, and defeated the armies of Rome, they first appeared in history in the closing years of the Roman Empire, when St Jerome described them as cannibals, dining off each others' breasts and buttocks and copulating like cattle in sylvan promiscuity. I do not mention this, Lhuyd hastily adds, in order to offend our northern neighbours, who are now a polished people, but only so that they may know what to think of their ridiculous historian. From now on, let them forget Boece and his forty kings and reconcile themselves to the fact that they, like the Germans and French and English – all famous nations – (but unlike the Welsh) were unknown before the time of the Romans.[2]

Alas, poor Buchanan! Imagine his predicament. Here he was, the greatest latinist of his time, the intellectual oracle of Europe, drunk with the flattery of the Republic of Letters, which had carried him into the world of politics and made him the friend and instructor of princes and statesmen, able to ride and guide the whirlwind of revolution. In the last six years, in the sour words of Father Innes, he had been 'suddenly transplanted from the mean situation of a grammarian, a poet or, at best, the head of a college' to be the president of a revolutionary assembly dictating to kings the terms of their rule 'under pain of trial and deposition'.[3] Now, at the height of his fame, and in his vain old age (he was now sixty-seven), he saw the political ideal which beckoned him upward vanishing into the remote future, and the intellectual system which sustained him pricked and deflated beneath him by an invisible pin extended from the grave of an impertinent Welsh antiquary.

What does a political philosopher do on such an occasion? Perhaps that is too difficult a question. Let us be content to describe what Buchanan did. He suspended work on his *History of Scotland,* which, it seems, was now almost complete. His dialogue *de Jure Regni apud Scotos* remained unprinted. It had done good service in manuscript, as propaganda in the heady days of revolution; but now that things were quieter he had laid aside his arms (he said) and was working for public peace.[4] Meanwhile he set out to destroy the credit of Lhuyd in the learned world, and worked off his frustrations by chastising, both physically and mentally, his unfortunate pupil, the child King James VI. In his own words, uttered to the scandalised Countess of Mar, who came to investigate the infant screams in the nursery of Stirling Castle, he was 'whipping the arse of the Lord's Anointed'.

Buchanan's attack on Lhuyd – pathological in its ferocity – was expressed in a new work which he now began, *de origine gentium Britannicarum*, on the origins of the British peoples – i.e., presumably, of the Welsh and the Scots. Of this work he seems to have completed only two chapters. These, as far as they go, are of great interest. In them, Buchanan, as a man of letters and a scholar, set out to study British origins through the Celtic languages – those same languages which he hoped to see disappear, but which remained useful meanwhile as a means of reconstructing the barbarous past.[5] But if he never completed the work, he did contrive to introduce into it the subject which, at that time, and for several years afterwards, was at the top of his mind: the enormities of the infamous Humphrey Lhuyd. Lhuyd, he wrote, was an absurd fellow who had dared to oppose the unanimous verdict of the learned world; he worshipped 'the rust of barbarism instead of latin civility'; he gave uncritical credit to any mouldy old piece of paper. His evidence was 'hodge-podge trash raked by him out of the dunghill', his ideas 'uncouth and slovenly affectations' compounded of 'boldness and stupidity', 'obstinacy' and 'scurrility'.[6] Meanwhile, in letters to his friends, he belaboured Lhuyd unmercifully. His friends hastened to appease the exasperated master. 'You are quite right', wrote Daniel Rogers, an old friend who, as a kinsman and collaborator of Ortelius, was particularly vulnerable, 'to chastise Humphrey Lhuyd, who poses as an antiquary and yet clings fast to futile and trivial old wives' tales, unsupported by any records of Antiquity'.[7] Here at least – for the reference must be to Brutus – Lhuyd's critics had a point.

Buchanan's sense of outrage at what Lhuyd had done can be seen and felt throughout these two chapters. Right from the beginning he spluttered indignantly, across four densely printed folio pages,[8] at Lhuyd's innocent suggestion that the natives of Britain, before the Romans came, might have pronounced the name of their country beginning with a P. How dared this upstart Welshman, thundered Buchanan, set his P-Celt fantasies, based on the ravings of old bards, scraps of worm-eaten paper, and analogies with the mouthings of contemporary common folk in his backwater of a province, against the high and majestic learning of the Romans and the Greeks, who had uniformly insisted on a B? Was this perhaps, even for a dyed-in-the-wool humanist, something of an over-reaction? Perhaps it was, Buchanan admitted. It was not in his nature, normally, to carp at and criticise people (he said); but really, Lhuyd deserved to be whipped for his scurrilous abuse of other writers. It would teach him better manners in the future. (Evidently Buchanan was unaware that Lhuyd had died before his book was published.) Which other writers? Well, Boece actually. Did Buchanan wish to defend Boece for transporting Queen Boudicca and her tribe of Iceni from East Anglia, and their allies the Trinobantes of Essex, wholesale into Scotland? Lhuyd had scoffed at this example, along with others, of Boece's unscrupulous and pretentious plan to create a history for the Scots where none had truly existed. This 'error' of Boece, along with others, Buchanan would pass over in silence. Yes, he said airily, Boece had made a few mistakes. But there was no need to shout about it. Every writer makes mistakes. Gravely he delivered himself of a platitude: only a perfect writer is free of all error![9]

As the ground slid from under him, Buchanan thought that he saw one place where he could still make a stand. Boece had placed the tribe of the Brigantes in Galloway. So, following him, had Buchanan in his briefing paper of 1571, mentioned in the previous chapter. Lhuyd declared that the Brigantes, with their Queen Cartimandua, should instead have been placed in Yorkshire, with their capital at Eboracum, which everybody (except apparently Boece) knew meant York. They were a British tribe, not one of those unheard-of Scots. Buchanan could no longer deny that the Brigantes had inhabited that large stretch of country subsequently called Yorkshire. But he was a dogged fighter, and he did not mean to give up on those Brigantes easily. By chance a piece of evidence came to light which seemed to offer Buchanan just what he needed, when he needed it. It was a slippery piece of evidence; but Buchanan grabbed it, and held on to it for all that it was worth – and more.

In 1577 the brilliant young classicist Joseph Scaliger published at Paris an edition of the Latin poetry of Tibullus: natural reading for Buchanan. In the course of his commentary on Tibullus, Scaliger brought into consideration what he thought was a complementary passage of Seneca, which he then daringly emended. The conventional reading of Seneca's passage referred to '*caeruleos scuta Brigantas*': that is, the Brigantes with their blue shields (*scuta*). Scaliger thought it more probable that the colour should refer to the Brigantes themselves, rather than their shields, from the well-known habit of British tribes painting their bodies with woad. What then did *scuta* refer to? Scaliger decided that this must be a misreading; and the real word must have been *scoto*, i.e. Scottish.[10] So, crowed Buchanan on reading this conjectural emendation, the Brigantes had been Scots after all, despite living in Yorkshire – and in the first century AD, contrary to what the loathsome Lhuyd had alleged. What a superb young scholar that Scaliger was!

Building on this discovery, Buchanan looked for other means of demonstrating the Scottishness of the Brigantes. No classical writer had mentioned any Brigantes in nearby Gaul, so they must have originated in Spain. No one ever arrived in Yorkshire directly from Spain; they always came via some stopping-off point. And the obvious stopping-off point was Ireland. Triumphantly, Buchanan then closed the circle and proved his theorem. Anyone coming out of Ireland in those days was a Scot! Besides, he said, with an airy wave of the hand, he had once read somewhere (it was in Fordun) that the early boundary between the southern and the northern parts of Britain lay along the river Humber. Any tribe living north of the Humber, as the Brigantes did, was therefore part of the Scottish nation.[11]

Did Buchanan really believe this flimsy stuff? Or was it, rather, a conjuring trick to distract the attention of his readers? For it is to be noticed that, in all his attacks on Lhuyd, Buchanan never mentioned Lhuyd's real crime: the curtailment of Scottish history by seven centuries and forty kings. That would only have given publicity to the evidence, which Buchanan must have recognised as decisive against himself. The nearest Buchanan came to naming Lhuyd's true offence is his charge that Lhuyd had ventured to correct certain (unspecified) statements by Hector Boece. Boece, Buchanan retorted, was a man 'not only well skilled in the liberal arts but also endued with singular humanity and courtesy'.[12] No doubt, we may reply; but what of his truthfulness and accuracy, which was what Lhuyd had challenged?

Lhuyd had put Buchanan in a thoroughly false position. Those seven centuries and forty kings of Scottish 'pre-history', lately exploded, occupied the whole of the first book of his History. Buchanan now saw that it was all based on just the sort of source material, the imaginings of irresponsible old bards, for the use of which he condemned Lhuyd. It was no more than rubbish – as, indeed, the English historian William Camden openly described it in his *Britannia*, published about a decade later.[13] Belatedly, Buchanan took up the proper position for a classically trained historian: there was no reliable evidence for the history of Britain earlier than the writings of the Romans and the Greeks. All of this evidence he would put together in a new chapter, marking the true beginnings of the history of Scotland. But what would he do about that pre-existent first book? He could not simply jettison it. For he had invested so much of his capital in that first book, both intellectually and politically. Without the history of those forty kings he had virtually no historical evidence to support his whig theory of the right of the nobles, representing the people of Scotland, to depose their rulers and elect new ones in their place. And without that intellectual justification, just what had he been doing in the practical politics of Scotland in recent years?

For several years after the shock caused to him by Lhuyd's posthumous publication, Buchanan seems to have been in a depressed state. Though pressed by his friends, he published nothing: neither his poems, nor his dialogue, nor his study of the origins of the British peoples. His History of Scotland was still unfinished. So far as we can tell, he could barely bring himself to write even a letter. The Scottish revolution had run out of steam, and Buchanan, it seemed, had run out of steam too. The epicentre of international revolution had now moved away from Scotland, to the Netherlands; and Buchanan, as its prophet, had been overtaken by the Huguenot émigrés – many of them his old humanist friends – whom the Massacre of St Bartholomew had driven thither from France. Perhaps if he had been left to himself, Buchanan would never have published the prose works which were to make him famous, or notorious, for the next two centuries and create the political myth of Scottish and English whigs. He was now old and rather disillusioned; his health was poor: he was suffering from gout; and his Scottish patrons were all dead. However, at the close of his life, a new impetus came from abroad which changed all that. It came indirectly from the Netherlands, directly from England.

In the later 1570s the Puritan party at the English court, headed by the Earl of Leicester and his nephew Sir Philip Sidney, were pressing Queen Elizabeth to intervene in the war in the Netherlands and, once again, as in Scotland, to support rebels against a legitimate sovereign. Once again, as in Scotland, they found the queen reluctant; and they needed to mobilise all the support that they could find: ideological as well as political. Among the activists who supported their cause were two English diplomatists who were old friends of Buchanan, Daniel Rogers and Thomas Randolph; and these two now pressed Buchanan into their cause. If the torch of revolution had been carried from Scotland to the Netherlands, why should not 'the bellows of revolution' (as James VI would afterwards call his old tutor)[14] be brought back into use to fan the flames? In particular, why should he not now complete and publish his theoretical and historical justification of revolt? Both Rogers and Randolph knew about his work. They had seen the manuscript of his dialogue and had been kept informed of the progress of his history. So, like his French friends fifteen years earlier, they pressed him, in the public interest, to resume his pen. They urged him to publish the dialogue and to complete the history.

Under this continuous pressure from England, Buchanan complied. In 1577 he allowed his old Senecan tragedy of John the Baptist – a brilliant anti-clerical poem – to be printed by a Huguenot printer in London. In 1579 he caused his dialogue *de Jure Regni* to be published in Scotland, with a somewhat hectoring dedication to his royal pupil, now twelve years old. Finally, after many a prod, and with many a groan, he finished his *History*. It had been, as a friend put it, 'a long sweat'.[15] Composing it, Buchanan wrote to Rogers, had been hard work even in his younger days; but now, 'while I meditate on mortality, between the fear of death and the shame of leaving it unfinished, how can it be other than slow and burdensome? I must not stop, and yet I have no pleasure in going on'.[16] However, the task was at last completed. The two chapters of *The Origins of the British Peoples*, containing his attack on Humphrey Lhuyd, were stitched on to it as an introduction, followed by a third and intermediate chapter, containing the classical accounts of the early history of Scotland. Then Buchanan simply renumbered his original first book, containing the seven centuries of 'pre-history', as the fourth book in the new structure; hoping, no doubt, that his inconsistency and fraud would go un-noticed. Finally, in 1582, the great work was published in Edinburgh. It, too, was dedicated to the young king. The king, at that time, was unable to express his feelings freely, for he had just been kidnapped, out hunting, by those noble gangsters who, according to Buchanan, had the constitutional right and duty to correct his faults by their virtues. A month later, Buchanan was dead; and the king, on recovering his liberty, prevailed on the Parliament to ban both the *History* and the Dialogue throughout Scotland.

Such was the origin of the two prose works which perpetuated Buchanan's fame and the new concept of the ancient whig constitution of Scotland. It has sometimes been suggested that Buchanan was an innocent subscriber to received ideas and that his 'errors', which include his wholesale adoption of Boece's early history, are still those of 'an independent thinker who believed in the sacredness and infinite importance of truth'.[17] Certainly even the greatest historians are led into error because their general convictions have acquired for them the character of a pre-cedent truth, with which individual facts must necessarily conform. But this defence cannot be offered for Buchanan. It is not merely that he shows himself capable of exact source criticism in other historical questions, but suspends it here. That, after all, could also be said of Lhuyd. What destroys such a defence is Buchanan's artful disingenuousness in his use of Boece. He knew well that the authority of Boece had been destroyed among the learned by Leland and, above all, by Lhuyd. Therefore he was careful not to use Boece as an authority for his later books, or in indifferent matters, but always preferred Fordun and other earlier writers. But for the early period, since Boece alone ascribed a power of deposition to the nobility, he invariably relied on Boece. On the other hand, while he scrupulously cited his later sources, he contrived never to cite Boece (or Boece's alleged authority Veremund) by name. At the same time he took care to make his borrowings from Boece more plausible by omitting the more extravagant stories of his predecessor. The conclusion is inescapable: Buchanan knew that Boece was historically worthless and could not be safely followed or openly cited; but since he depended on him for his essential thesis, he secretly used his work and made it more plausible by quiet adjustment in inessential matters.[18] The result was that the old fabrications were presented to the learned world in a more acceptable form. They now appeared not as the fabulous tales of the credulous and exploded Boece but as the critical conclusions of the great scholar Buchanan.

As such, they enjoyed a new life. It was in vain that James VI banned them in Scotland, as afterwards in England; in vain that he warned his son never to permit the circulation of those 'infamous libels'.[19] If they were banned in Britain, they would be published with impunity in Frankfurt and Geneva; and all through the seventeenth century they circulated and were read. Nor was the ban on them in Britain continuous. Indeed, their bibliographical history in Britain is a running commentary on the political history of the country. Suppressed (but circulating in manuscript) whenever the Stuart kings could command, they re-emerged into print whenever that authority was challenged, or in eclipse. In the effective reigns of James I and Charles I, they were naturally unprinted in Britain. An English translation of *de Jure Regni*, made in 1610, and a Scottish translation of the *History*, completed in 1634, remained in manuscript. But once civil war had broken out the works reappeared. In 1643, when the Scotch army entered England in support of the Parliament, the *History* was reprinted in Edinburgh, and every army chaplain, we are told, could produce it 'as readily as the Bible'; the officers read the work and their children learned Latin from it. In 1659, when the English Republicans feared the return of the Stuarts, English translations of both the dialogue and of the *History* were prepared for the press; but Charles II came back before they could appear, and the publication was stopped as 'very pernicious to monarchy and injurious to His Majesty's blessed progenitors'; and four years later manuscript copies circulating in Scotland were called in under penalty of proceedings for sedition and disaffection. In 1680, at the height of the whig challenge, a Scottish whig contrived secretly to publish a translation of the dialogue. In 1683, at the height of the Stuart reaction, the loyal university of Oxford publicly burnt the works of Buchanan, as of other dangerous writers; and in August 1688 the Scottish Privy Council again called in manuscript copies. It was not till the Glorious Revolution had driven James II out of his three kingdoms that those dreadful works would reappear from native presses. In 1689 the Dialogue, in 1690 the *History*, were published in English; and in 1700 an Edinburgh printer produced the first Scottish edition of the original text of the *History* since the first edition, published during the captivity of James VI, in 1582.[20]

Thus from the whig side, as from the tory side, the fabulous age of Scotland was sustained long after the fabulous early history of England and Wales had been jettisoned. Indeed, thanks to Buchanan on one side, and Sir George Mackenzie on the other, the battles of whigs and tories were carried back to the mythical Highland courts of Thereus and Durstus, Lugtacus, Ahirco and Satrahel. Only in the eighteenth century, with the Union of England and Scotland, the extinction of distinct Scottish politics, and the exclusion of the heirs of James II, did the issue lose its political relevance. Whiggism was now firmly established on a new, modern base. It had no need of such archaic precedents. It could even be said that Buchanan had triumphed: for had not the Grand Council of the Nobles, of England as of Scotland, deposed an unworthy king and chosen, from the royal family, a prince fitter to rule? Was not George I the eighteenth-century equivalent of Buchanan's patron, the Earl of Moray?

It was in this less heated atmosphere that a new character appeared and, in the Jacobite interest, but by pure scholarship, quietly destroyed the entire battleground on which the battle had been fought, and where Buchanan, it seemed, had won. This, therefore, is the point at which to introduce more fully a man who has already appeared casually in these pages: the first and greatest of Scottish antiquaries, Thomas Innes.

Thomas Innes was a member of an Aberdeenshire family that was remarkable for the staunchness of its loyalty to both the Stuart dynasty and the Roman Catholic religion.[21] His father, a gentleman of middling rank, had eight children – of whom five became priests. The two most important of those five were Lewis, the oldest, born in 1651, and Thomas, born in 1662. These two were sent to France for their education from the age of sixteen or seventeen: studying at the university of Paris, and living at the Scots College there. The two brothers rose to dominate the Scots College. Lewis became its Principal in 1682, and Thomas its prefect of studies in 1704, and ultimately Vice-Principal. Later they would be joined by a nephew, George Innes, who would succeed to all of those offices in turn. Lewis and Thomas were both keen antiquaries, as well as priests and Jacobites. After the revolution of 1688 they became custodians of the voluminous Jacobite papers deposited in the college, including the memoirs of the ex-King James II and VII himself. As they sorted carefully through the papers in the college archive, they also found the original document proving (contrary to Buchanan's account) that the Stuart line had descended legitimately from King Robert II of Scotland. They organised an impressive public ceremony of authentication in 1694, attended by the finest French historical scholars of the day, by various senior French legal officers, and by assorted Scottish and English peers from the Jacobite court at Saint-Germain-en-Laye nearby.[22] Lewis was also a politician. He became a close adviser, confidential secretary, and almoner to the Chevalier de St George: known to Jacobites as King James III and VIII, to whigs as 'the Old Pretender'. As Principal of the Scots College, and as a leading supporter of the claimant king, he consistently supported his younger brother, both morally and financially, in his interesting historical studies.

All the Innes family were deeply conservative, entrenched in Jacobitism, opposed to new-fangled ideas of any kind. They hated the Jesuits and resisted the 'modern', 'enlightened' ideas which, through them, were penetrating the Church of Rome. All three members of the Innes family in Paris were accused by the Roman Catholic establishment in France of 'Jansenism'. The Scots College, in general, was regarded as a hotbed of Jansenism, and the Innes family were regarded as the great patrons of that heresy, which they protected by conspiratorial secrecy. So alarming were the reports about the Scots College that the French clergy withdrew their financial support; and finally, in 1736, the nuncio in Paris was ordered to investigate. His report confirmed the worst suspicions. 'Your Eminence cannot imagine,' he wrote, 'what difficulty there is in obtaining any information respecting the college, whose administrators make a secret of everything ... Notwithstanding this excessive caution, we have learned sufficient from other sources to know that the college is in need of complete reform, and that the first measure of reform should be the removal of the three Inneses'. The worst of these three kinsmen, who, between them, were poisoning the Catholicism of Scotland, was, he said, Thomas Innes.[23]

Clearly we cannot regard Thomas Innes as a natural innovator. Indeed, so conservative was he that, on his visits to Scotland, he found himself in delightful harmony with his fellow antiquary, the reactionary Presbyterian Robert Wodrow, in joint detestation of the new ideas which threatened to liberalise the Kirk and would in fact point towards the Scottish Enlightenment. They were united in deploring the spread of critical thought in Holland and England concerning the doctrine of the Trinity, and in applauding the silencing of Professor Simson at Glasgow for similar heterodoxy.[24]

For Thomas Innes occasionally crept across from Paris into Scotland. In the early years, at least, this was extremely dangerous. His first recorded visit came between 1698 and 1701, the years following the Peace of Ryswick, when he was sent on the Scottish mission, based at Inveravon in Aberdeenshire. It must have been some time during this visit that an event occurred which caused the Anglican, but non-juring, Oxford antiquarian Thomas Hearne to stare in horror and admiration as he heard the story about two decades later. Innes, Hearne was told, had been going about in Scotland on his missionary business, carrying with him a fine collection of historical papers, collected and copied in his own hand, the fruit of ten years' work. Suddenly, the house in which he was staying was raided by the authorities, in hot pursuit of this dangerous hedge-priest. Innes saved himself by jumping out of a window. But he could not take his papers with him. They were seized and burnt. Innes had to begin his compilations all over again. It said a great deal about Innes' determination and temper, as Hearne recorded, that 'he bore this loss with great patience'.[25] Innes' second visit to Scotland – the visit on which he met Wodrow – was in 1724 to 1725, when he was concentrating on his research into the beginnings of Scottish history. He was in Scotland again in 1728, and in London in 1729 to oversee the printing of his work.

Innes had begun his studies of early Scottish history many years before;[26] but he had often felt inhibited by the fear of affronting the entrenched opinions of his countrymen. Indeed, he had had to struggle long and hard against the impress of his own Scottish patriotism in order to break through to a more impartial view. He had really wanted to believe in, and to support, the traditional story of Scotland's beginnings inherited from Fordun, and glossed by Boece and Buchanan. He had written half a book, fitting all his newly gathered information into the established nationalist scheme.[27] But then the scales fell from his eyes. He saw the fundamental falsity of that scheme. He realised that he had no honest choice but to dismantle the entire construction of received ideas, and build again on a completely new basis.

What was it, then, which enabled him eventually to separate himself from the 'half-learned prejudiced writers' of his time and country?[28] It had much to do with his being an outsider – though of a different kind from the Welshman Lhuyd. Virtually all of Innes' adult life was spent in exile: not only in clear opposition to the forms of state and church in power at home, but probably – at least in later years – without even much realistic hope of feeling again those entangling webs of emotion and interest to which Buchanan had succumbed on his return to Scotland. Moreover, he was an exile in France, at Paris. This was a great age in French culture generally, and a heroic age for men of erudition in particular. All French thinkers of that time, philosophers, clerics and historians alike, had to confront the powerful challenge of systematic scepticism. Malebranche, Bossuet, Bayle, to name just three of the most prominent French thinkers of that time, each represented very different responses to that challenge – and there were many more. Even with the very scanty information available concerning the life of Thomas Innes, we can connect him with a few of the greatest names in French historical scholarship. He was certainly associated with the Benedictines of the abbey of Saint-Germain des Prés; and he met and corresponded with their leaders, Jean Mabillon and Thierry Ruinart.[29] Their dedication to the discovery, accumulation, and sifting of ancient ecclesiastical documents, and their technical expertise in dating and evaluating such records, must have set the standards to which Innes himself worked. We can connect him also with Etienne Baluze, the prodigiously productive ecclesiastical historian who was at the head of the Colbertine Library between 1667 and 1700; who, along with Mabillon and Ruinart, authenticated the fourteenth-century Stuart document in the Scots College in 1694; and in whose rich repositories Innes found new materials for his work on the earliest age of Scotland.[30] In the background to Innes' book, occasionally appearing at its surface, lay his reading of the sixteen volumes of *Mémoires pour servir à l'histoire ecclésiastique des six premiers siècles*, which were published at Paris between 1693 and 1712, and which were the work of Tillemont – whose 'inimitable accuracy', as Gibbon would later say, 'almost assumes the character of Genius'.[31] We find him, in 1729, as he published his *Critical Essay*, referring to the twenty-volume *Histoire Ecclésiastique* (1691–1720) of the abbé Claude Fleury as the model of what he would most like to have been able to do for the history of Scotland.[32] In short, it was his lifelong exile in the France of Louis XIV that gave Thomas Innes that critical distance from Scotland which enabled him to break the mould of Fordun, Boece and Buchanan.

It seems likely that Innes' original agenda was more ecclesiastical than political. As the reference to Fleury's work shows, he wished to write a full modern ecclesiastical history of Scotland – down to the Reformation. He believed that he could show Scotland to have been Christianised from Rome more than from Ireland, contrary to the view favoured by Protestants. He also wished, of course, to demonstrate the vital historical rôle that had been played by bishops. But this ecclesiastical agenda was interfered with, at many points, by the established views on what had happened in Scotland's earliest centuries; and those established views were, in his opinion, politically motivated. So his ecclesiastical agenda had to be subsumed, for a time, in his political agenda. He would first have to demolish that misconceived scheme of early Scottish history in order to clear the way for his projected ecclesiastical history, which would be written later. Alas, by the time he had published his *Critical Essay*, the vigour of his health had been broken. He continued to work on the ecclesiastical history, slowly, and as his health permitted; but he could not finish it.[33]

Thomas Innes' researches in England and Scotland were financed by his brother, the Pretender's secretary, who recognised their value for 'the reputation of our country and *the support of monarchy*': i.e. the Jacobite cause.[34] Thus sustained, he visited various English repositories: his own footnotes show him burrowing among the archives in the Tower of London (to which he had been introduced by a Jacobite peer); in Cannons, Edgware, the great house of the Duke of Chandos; and in the famous library of Sir Robert Cotton in Downing Street. In Scotland we see him through the eyes of 'that sanctified scoundrel', that 'pretended whig saint and real Jacobite intriguer', Lord Grange, working constantly in the Advocates' Library in Edinburgh. The Presbyterians of the capital were at first suspicious of this busy Catholic researcher, but in the end he was allowed to pass: he was 'not engaged in politics', it was reported, being 'a monkish, bookish person who meddles with nothing but literature'.[35] We also catch sight of him here and there in the muniment rooms of old Jacobite houses – at Panmure, at Kelly, at Traquair, at Stobhall, at Drummond Castle. He obtained important help also from two Scottish scholars who, for one reason or another, were sympathetic to his project: from Professor John Ker of King's College, Aberdeen, a Jacobite sympathiser, and from Sir Robert Sibbald of Edinburgh, a one-time Catholic convert.[36] Then he returned to Paris to work up his materials into the bombshell which, as he believed, would shatter the orthodoxy of the Scotch whigs. In 1728 he was back in Scotland for a last round of research; then he went to ground in London to arrange the publication of his book.

This was no easy task, he found: publishers were not interested in Scotland, and he was not willing to publish by subscription – that would have given too much away, and deprived him of his secret plan of dedication. Fortunately, he found a kinsman in the publishing world, one William Innes, with whom he made an oral agreement. Thus secured, he prepared to return to Paris. But before leaving, he wrote to his Jacobite friend in Scotland, Henry Maule of Panmure, describing his work, its purpose and its conclusions. He had written 'with as much impartiality as one can write of one's own country', he said, 'but at the same time with all the regard for the true honour of it which truth could allow of'. He had been fair to all, he thought, – to Fordun, to Boece, 'whom I look upon as having written *bona fide*'; but he had 'another opinion of Buchanan', for which he had given his reasons. But all this, he added, must be kept a dead secret. He had told no Scotchman about it except the Maule family, 'nor do I desire so much as the content of my essay to be known till I be at the other side'.[37]

When he was safely on 'the other side', with the few free copies which were the only material return for his labour, Innes savoured his secret triumph. He inserted into the specially bound copy, which he had reserved for the purpose, a formal letter of dedication. It was addressed 'to the King'. The king was, of course, King James VIII of Scotland, III of England, alias the Old Pretender.

In his letter to 'the King', Innes spelled out the real purpose of his work. In the preface to his book, he explained, he had described 'the general motives of my undertaking, such as I thought proper to render public. But besides these, I had another motive that related to the rights of the Crown and Your Majesty's service'. These ulterior motives he could not openly announce 'without awakening the governing powers and manifestly hazarding the printer, the copies and the author be seized upon'. But now he could reveal all. In his researches into the antiquities of Scotland, he had observed with concern that 'the fabulous and seditious accounts of the ancient state of that kingdom left by our modern writers Boece and Buchanan', though palpable forgeries, are still accepted without question, 'and since the Revolution, these wretched libels of Buchanan are become as classic authors, put into children's hands in our Scottish schools'. So Innes has opened up the whole problem. 'Your Majesty will easily perceive that it was no easy matter, in these times, to publish in London a piece of this nature, which strikes at the root of the Revolution principles of Scotland'. Therefore he had concealed that purpose under the pretence of enquiring into the true date of the Scottish monarchy; but that purpose had, he hoped, been no less effectually achieved, 'and the dark contrivance of the forgery, and the source of the anti-monarchical principles of Scotland, no less fully laid open, than if I had openly declared my design . . .'.[38]

Scholars customarily overvalue the influence of historical truth as against historical myth. Thomas Innes, by exact scholarship, revalued the sources of ancient Scottish and Irish history, providing a base on which all later scholars would build. Incidentally he removed centuries of false history, and thereby destroyed the historical foundations of whig theories and the historical justification of the Hanoverian succession to the throne of Scotland. But did the political cause of Jacobitism gain anything from his work? Probably not. We may doubt whether the Chevalier de St George even read it. In fact very few people read it.[39] Even the greatest historian of the eighteenth century was not among them.[40] It was not reprinted for 150 years: 150 years during which there were at least eight editions of Buchanan's *History* in English. But the ablest of Scottish antiquaries in the century after Innes – a man equally out of tune with the establishment of his time – paid a notable tribute to him. John Pinkerton would say some hard things about Innes, as about everyone who had the misfortune to differ from him; but he recognised him as the only true historical scholar whom Scotland had yet produced: he was 'the industrious and acute Innes' who 'ought never to be named by a Scotish antiquary but with superlative praise'; and whose work 'forms a grand epoch in our antiquities, and was the first that led the way to rational criticism on them'.[41] With him, at last, the political myth of Scotland had been intellectually destroyed.

By Pinkerton's time, the destruction was accepted. It was acceptable, not because reason had at last prevailed over inveterate prejudice, but rather because Boece and Buchanan, by then, had ceased to matter. The Stuarts were now finished: after 1746 they were no longer a threat to the Hanoverian establishment. The whigs were finished too, it seemed: their work was done, their principles were accepted, and after 1760 they had disintegrated as a political party. It was the contest between these two forces which had sustained for so long the myth of the ancient Scottish kings and the ancient Scottish constitution. Now that contest itself had become meaningless.

But did this mean that Scotland was demythologised? Not at all. In a mythopoeic society, one myth surrenders only to another; and in the eighteenth century a Scotland that had abandoned its political mythology, because it was now free from politics, turned aside to seek an alternative myth in another department of life: in literature.

## Part II

# THE LITERARY MYTH

# 4

# The Search for a
# Celtic Homer

When a society renounces politics, it can find other ways of expressing its identity. After the Union of 1707, and more especially after the defeat of the last Jacobite rebellion in 1746, the Scots looked for such other ways. Some of them turned to economics. Recognising that the development of their country in the past two centuries had been arrested, and that their political activity had been (to say the least) unconstructive, they welcomed the end of political independence and devoted themselves to 'improvement'. While their landlords attended to their estates, planted trees and introduced new crops, and their merchants and manufacturers exploited the new markets opened by the Union, their thinkers escaped at last from the intellectual prison-house of the Kirk and explored the secular world. Some of them studied the mechanics of social change and discovered the science of political economy. Others turned from politics and history to literature. They looked to discover an old literature of Scotland, or to create a new.

In seeking to discover their own literature they were only following the fashion. The eighteenth century was a period in which Englishmen were making a cult of their own literature, declaring, grading, editing and commenting on their classics. This was the time when Shakespeare was raised up to be the national poet of England: when, as Gibbon would put it, 'idolatry' for that 'Gigantic Genius' was 'inculcated from our infancy as the first duty of an Englishman';[1] when the long series of critical editions of his works were published, when Pope and Johnson were happy to be his editors, and Garrick and Mrs Siddons restored him triumphantly to the stage. In 1741 the statue of Shakespeare was set up in Westminster Abbey; and in 1769 the cult would reach its climax in the great Shakespeare Jubilee, organised by Garrick, at Stratford-upon-Avon. Next to Shakespeare, Milton was exalted as the greatest of English poets. His republican past was forgotten or forgiven; he became a national classic, above party loyalty; and his most famous work was emended, like an ancient text, by the greatest of classical scholars, Richard Bentley. Anthologies of the beauties of English literature were collected and published; and it was as introductions to such a collection that Dr Johnson wrote his marvellous series of *Lives of the Poets*. In these circumstances, it was natural that Scots, seeking compensation for the end of their independent history and politics, should turn to discover and appreciate their native literature. Unfortunately, when they looked for it, they could not find it. There was none.

Some gallant attempts were made to remedy this unfortunate defect. In 1719 Lord President Forbes and Sir Gilbert Elliot presented to the public an ancient ballad entitled *Hardyknute*, of which the manuscript had been discovered (they had been told) in a vault in Dunfermline. This ballad was taken up by Allan Ramsay, the Edinburgh wig-maker, bookseller and poet, and reprinted a few years later in his *Evergreen*, an anthology of early Scottish poetry. Unluckily, suspicions were aroused, and it was afterwards established that the poem had been forged by its alleged discoverer, Lady Wardlaw, the wife of a baronet in Fife.[2] Even so, the Scots were reluctant to surrender even a fragment of their supposed ancient literature: half a century later, John Pinkerton would forge a second part of *Hardyknute*, and the bogus ballad would be the first poem ever learned by the young Walter Scott, 'and the last I shall ever forget'.[3] A generation later, a determined effort was made to produce a Scottish rival to Shakespeare. John Home, minister of Athelstanford in East Lothian, wrote a Shakespearean tragedy entitled *Agis*, which he took to London and sought to recommend to the arbiter of the London theatre, David Garrick. Garrick rejected it; whereupon the despondent poet went to Westminster Abbey and there recited a plaintive apostrophe in verse to the statue of Shakespeare. Garrick's judgment was no doubt correct. The author's kinsman and friend, David Hume the philosopher, admitted that he could never like the work: the author, he said, 'had corrupted his taste by the imitation of Shakespeare, whom he ought only to have admired'.[4] Undeterred, Home wrote another tragedy, *Douglas,* which in 1755 he also took to London and showed to Garrick, only to incur a second rejection. However, after being performed in Edinburgh – where the performance of a profane play written by a minister of the Kirk was a cause of great scandal, and drove the author to leave the ministry – Home succeeded in interesting a London producer; and the tragedy of *Douglas* was ultimately performed at Covent Garden.[5] It was a great success. At the first performance, we are told, an excited Scotsman rose in the theatre and cried out, in challenging tones, to the humiliated English, 'Whaur's your Wully Shakespeare noo?'[6] Unhappily the success did not last. After its brief initial triumph, *Douglas* was soon forgotten. It is not much performed today.

Where were the Scots to turn in search of a native literature which would humiliate their complacent English neighbours? What kind of poetry would, in the eighteenth century, have the desired effect of over-trumping Shakespeare and Milton? What qualities, in literature, appealed to the sensibility of that age? If we can answer these questions, we may begin to understand the extraordinary success of the great Scottish epic which ultimately achieved all these triumphs. It will be most convenient to begin with the most general question, the last.

In the eighteenth century two qualities in literature particularly appealed to the public taste: 'melancholy', or 'the pathetic', and 'the sublime'. The 'melancholy' of the eighteenth-century English was notorious abroad, and it found expression in a great range of literature, occasionally beautiful, more often maudlin and ridiculous. At the top of the scale we may put Goldsmith's 'Deserted Village' and Gray's 'Elegy in a Country Churchyard'; at the bottom, Young's 'Night Thoughts', Robert Blair's 'The Grave', Thomas Warton's 'Pleasures of Melancholy' and James Harvey's 'Meditations among the Tombs'. The second quality, 'the sublime', was more difficult to achieve. Though easily recognised once it had been realised, it was difficult to define. The most famous discussion of it was the Greek work of literary criticism commonly known as 'Longinus on the

Sublime'. In the eighteenth century this work acquired enormous popularity: at least fourteen editions of the text and at least eight translations were published in Britain alone – and it was equally popular abroad. In France it was translated by the oracle of modern taste, Boileau. In England it inspired the young Edmund Burke, whose *A Philosophical Enquiry into our Ideas of the Sublime and the Beautiful* was published in 1756.

Where was the 'sublime' to be found? In the eighteenth century as to Antiquity, to Burke as to Longinus, the great master of the sublime was always Homer. But could Homer ever be imitated? Was not the sublime, in Longinus' phrase, απηχημα της μεγαλοψυχίας, a reverberation of magnanimity, and therefore, by definition, inimitable by art? Was not Homer a unique genius? The greatest artist among modern British poets, Alexander Pope, had indeed translated the *Iliad*, and his achievement was acclaimed by all; but it was equally agreed by all that the translation lacked the spontaneous power and sublimity of the original: it was magnificent, but it was not Homer. At best it was Homer cramped into eighteenth-century formal court dress.

Fifteen years after the publication of Pope's translation, an important work on Homer was published in London. It was by a Scotchman. Half a century later, John Pinkerton would declare it to be one of the only two valuable works of scholarship yet produced in Scotland.[7] It was called *An Enquiry into the Life and Writings of Homer.* The author was Thomas Blackwell, professor of Greek at Marischal College, Aberdeen.

Blackwell's work, published in 1735, and reprinted next year, had a great effect on the eighteenth-century conception of Homer: indeed, transformed it. Hitherto, Homer had been seen as a divinely inspired poet, almost outside time and space, unique and unrepeatable. From this general opinion Blackwell dissented. While agreeing that Homer was the sublimest of poets, he insisted that he was not necessarily unique or unrepeatable. All literature, he believed, was socially conditioned; and the progress of literature was to be understood by studying it externally as well as internally, by relating it to its social context and the changes in that context. 'It is the different periods or steps, naturally succeeding in the progression of manners', he wrote, 'that can only account for the succession of wit and literature'. To this general rule even Homer was no exception; and the duty of the critic was not to be dazzled by his unique genius but to explain it by an examination of the social circumstances which had produced and conditioned it. He must ask 'by what fate or disposition of things it has happened that none have equalled him in epic poetry for 2,700 years, the time since he wrote, nor any that we know ever surpassed him before'. 'Since it is absolutely the conjuncture of manners and times that produces poets', Homer's uniqueness must lie in the uniqueness of that conjuncture – which Blackwell now set out to discover.

From Homer's poems, and from the writings of the ancients about him and them, Blackwell reconstructed both the life and the times of Homer. His reconstruction would not be entirely approved by modern Homeric scholars, but that is irrelevant to our purpose. According to Blackwell, the greatest poetry springs neither from a savage nor from a civilised society, but from a stage of society which lies somewhere between the two. Historically, the sublimest poetry seemed to be composed in 'the interval between the high liberty and enslavement of a state'; for whereas 'high liberty' – the anarchy of barbarism – was hostile to all literature, once society was 'enslaved' – that is, brought under effective control, polished and civilised – the spontaneity of genius was reduced within conventions and rules, and its free expression tamed and ritualised by systematic patronage. Civilisation, in other words, is incompatible with sublimity in literature: 'the same society cannot be thoroughly civilised and afford proper subjects for poetry'. This being so, it was useless to look for sublimity in modern poets. Sublime poetry could only arise in the kind of society which was now long past. Homer's good fortune, the cause of his apparently unique genius, was that he lived in precisely such a stage of society as Blackwell posited: the 'primitive' but not 'savage' society which obtained in the Greek cities between the Trojan war and the Persian invasions. 'Had he been born much sooner, he could have seen nothing but nakedness and barbarity; had he come much later, he had fallen either in times of peace, when a wide and settled policy prevailed over Greece, or in general wars, regularly carried on by civilised states, when private passions are buried in the common order and established discipline'.

Homer was lucky, then, in his time: in the social circumstances around him. He was also lucky in his own personal way of life. Living (as was presumed) in Chios, between Greece and Asia Minor, travelling in civilised Egypt, and hearing tales from the seafaring Phoenicians, he could draw upon a wide range of knowledge. This he owed to his function as a wandering bard. For the bards, as Homer himself has described them, were the product of a highly mobile society. They were a guild of men who preserved a tradition of knowledge. They were 'quoted as the fountains of history, the judges of politicks, and parents of philosophy'. They had an enviable personal independence, and yet they had free access to the great. They were familiar with high life and welcome at the petty courts of the Greek princes. Homer himself shows an intimate knowledge of such courts: he 'knows their rarities and plate and can hold forth the neatness and elegance of their *bijouterie*'. He is, in fact, by the accidental combination of personal genius and personal experience, the greatest of a whole tribe of bards. How fortunate for us that a man so gifted took up that particular profession with its opportunities! 'Homer's being born poor, and living a wandering indigent bard, was, in relation to his poetry, the greatest happiness that could befall him', for poetic genius, which had been bestowed on him by Nature, 'has its fits and seasons, which are provoked and indulged nowhere so happily as in the strolling unanxious life of an αοιδός or bard'.[8]

So Blackwell brought Homer down to earth, fixed him in time and space, gave him a character and a life, and thereby reduced him from an inimitable genius and a law unto himself, to the human product of a certain kind of society. Homer, said Blackwell, was not unique: he was only one of a tribe – the best of the tribe – and he owed the marvellous development of his poetic powers to a 'combination of lucky accidents': to 'his climate and country, his religion and language, the publick and private manners of his age, and his own profession and travels'. In short, 'his good fortune was far superior to his skills'; and a similar conjuncture of social circumstances and personal accidents could easily have produced, in another time or place, another tribe of bards, and among them another Homer.[9]

Was there another such society? Were there, anywhere else in the world, such indigent strolling bards with access to the petty courts of 'primitive' but not 'savage' princes? To a Scotchman in Aberdeen there must have been an obvious answer. In the Highlands of Scotland, as in Ireland, every chief had had, and some still had, a *senachie*, or bard, whose office, like that of the Greek *Homeridae*, was often hereditary. But such a parallel, in Blackwell's time, would be entertained only to be dismissed. Never had any scholar regarded the Irish or Scottish bards as 'the fountains of history', of political wisdom or of philosophy. 'If anyone appeals to the bards or senachies as custodians of ancient record', wrote Buchanan, 'they are utterly ridiculous'; for such bards are totally illiterate men, maintained by the chiefs to recite their genealogies: how can anyone put any trust in 'men whose whole life and fortune depends on flattery'?[10] On this subject at least, Buchanan's great adversary, Father Innes, shared his view. The 'ignorant venal bards', he wrote, were absurd creatures of no credit whatever, insolent and mendacious 'parasites that lived by the flattering of great or rich men'.[11] And Innes' contemporary, Martin Martin, a native of Skye who knew the bards better than any (for he had travelled over the whole of the western Highlands and islands as factor of the Macleod), was even more contemptuous. The *senachies*, he wrote, had a very singular way of study: 'they shut their doors and windows for a day's time, and lie on their backs, with a stone upon their belly and plaids about their heads; and, their eyes being covered, they pump their brains for rhetorical encomium or panegyric'.[12] This was hardly the method of the Greek bards, as presented by Blackwell, travelling, observing and learning among the courts and cities of the eastern Mediterranean.

Shortly after Martin's observations, and while Blackwell was working on his book, an English officer stationed in Inverness, one Captain Burt, whom we shall have reason to cite again, was making use of his opportunities to study Highland life. He, too, personally encountered and described these Highland *senachies*. The bard, he wrote, was the genealogist of the chief's family who 'celebrates in Irish verse the original of the tribe, the famous warlike actions of the successive heads, and sings his own lyricks as an opiate to the chief, when indisposed for sleep'. Burt gives a particular account of an occasion when he had dined alone with a Highland chief and his kinsmen. Two bards were 'set at a good distance at the lower end of a long table, with a parcel of Highlanders of no extraordinary appear-ance, over a cup of ale'. They were not treated with any civility, or invited to the chief's table, or offered a glass of wine. One of them, however, being ordered by the chief, sang 'one of his own lyricks' about 'some clan battle', until the chief, 'who piques himself upon his school learning', stopped him, 'and cried out to me, "there's nothing like that in Virgil or Homer". I bowed, and told him I believed so.'[13]

Thus the general view held of the Highland bards at the time when Blackwell was writing his book was that they were worthless parasites; and Blackwell, in describing Homer as 'a strolling bard', was careful to forestall any comparison with them. The Greek bards, he wrote, practised a dignified profession: there was no need for Homer's admirers 'to vindicate him from it, as a mean and contemptible calling'. It was not to be compared with any modern equivalent, 'for I should be unwilling to admit the Irish or Highland *Rŭners* to a share of the honour, tho' their business, which is to entertain a company with the recital of some adventure, resembles a part of the other'.[14]

However, if the modern bards, from Buchanan's time onward, were regarded (except by their own chiefs) with uniform contempt, there were some men who believed, or chose to imagine, that their prede-cessors, in the remote past, had been of a higher quality. Early in the seventeenth century, John Johnston, an Aberdonian scholar and humanist who had studied and taught abroad until he was fetched back to Scotland by his friend Andrew Melville to be professor at St Andrews, celebrated the worthies of Scotland. As a disciple and imitator of Buchanan, he naturally included the mythical kings; and he also provided them with mythical poets. The ancient Caledonians, he wrote, 'had their Homers and Virgils, whom they called bards'; but he did not go further, or show any knowledge of their language or supposed works.[15] As a humanist and Latin poet, he was probably merely enlarging on a phrase of the Roman poet Lucan whose reference to the Celtic bards, as the immortalisers of dead heroes, was to become a commonplace in the eighteenth century.[16]

More specific was the statement of the famous deist, John Toland, a contemporary of Innes and Martin. Toland was an Irishman; he knew the Irish language; and although he combined fantasy with his learning, and credulity with his scepticism, he had undoubtedly studied Celtic antiquities. In a series of letters to his friend Lord Molesworth, intended as material for a History of the Druids, Toland touched on the Celtic bards who, he said, 'are not yet quite extinct, there being [some] of them in Wales, in the Highlands of Scotland, and in Ireland'. He himself, of course, was particularly familiar with the Irish. These bards, he wrote, were essentially parasites 'whose licentious panegyrics or satires have not a little contributed to breed confusion in the Irish history'. They lived free of cost, since 'out of fear of their railing, or love of their flattery, nobody durst deny them anything'; but in time they became 'such a grievance that several attempts were made to rid the nation of them; and, which is something comical (what at least our present poets would not extraordinarily like), the orders for banishing them were always to the Highlands of Scotland'. Thus the Scottish bards, according to Toland, were refreshed by the repeated deposit of the human rubbish of Ireland. However, if Toland, like everyone else, despised the modern bards, he too was more generous to the ancient bards whom the Romans had found in the Celtic lands. Some of these bards, he wrote, were 'mere quibblers' but others were 'truly ingenious . . . and among the bombast of the British and Irish bards there want not infinite instances of the true sublime'.[17]

Whether Toland had any evidence for such a judgment is not clear, nor does he seem to have applied it to the Scottish Highlands; but from him, as from Johnston, an enthusiastic reader might infer that the ancient Celts, in Caledonia as in Britain, Ireland and Gaul, had poets superior to their degenerate successors. An enthusiastic reader of Blackwell might even go further: he might suppose that, in Scotland as in Greece, the 'primitive' stage of civilisation could have produced its Homer.

Few would have dared to suggest this at the time. In 1735 the Highlanders of Scotland were still regarded with contempt – a contempt occasionally sharpened by fear. But ten years later an event occurred which was ultimately to change all that. The 'Young Chevalier', 'Bonnie Prince Charlie', landed in the western Highlands; the clans – or many of them – rose to support him and to supply him with an army; the forces of government in Scotland collapsed before him; he entered Edinburgh in triumph, held his court in Holyrood House, and led his victorious army into England. When he reached Derby, there was panic in London; the Bank of England, to hold up the press of clients seeking to withdraw their money, was reduced to paying out in sixpences; and, in the words of David Hume, the most perfect system of government in the world trembled before a few thousand wild Highlanders, 'the bravest, but still the most worthless', of its subjects.[18] However, this most formidable of all Highland revolts was also the last. A year later the adventure was over; the prince's army had retreated into Scotland, and its last relics had been slaughtered at Culloden. Thereafter, the Highlanders would never again be a threat to the settled life of Lowland Scotland and England. The 'Forty-Five' had been the last fling of an archaic society, already on the verge of dissolution; and under the impact of severe repressive laws, it would quickly and finally dissolve.

With the defeat of the rebellion of 1745, and the imminent dissolution of Highland society, the attitude of Englishmen and Lowland Scotchmen towards the Highlanders rapidly changed. These Celtic barbarians who so recently had been denounced and feared as vagabonds, thieves, blackmailers and rebels, but who were now found to be helpless and impotent, gradually acquired the romantic charm of an endangered species. Their loyalty to their chiefs, which had hitherto been regarded as contemptible servility, now became admirable and touching constancy. Who could fail to be moved by their fidelity to the defeated Chevalier, hunted like a partridge in the mountains with a huge price on his head? Their chiefs themselves, recently so dangerous by reason of their incorrigible treachery, now became romantic warrior-princes; and their 'venal', 'mercenary', 'lying', 'parasitic' *senachies* became the last poets of a noble but doomed cause.

Nor was this change of attitude merely local or national. Politically the experience of Britain was peculiar, but intellectually it fell into place in a European movement from which it drew new strength and to which it gave a particular application. For the same years in which British attitudes towards the Highlanders were changing saw, in Europe, the beginnings of a new general fashion: the cult of 'primitive' society and the attribution to it of purer morals, simpler virtues, more 'natural' poetry than could be found in the artificial civilisation of the West. It was the age of Rousseau, of Herder, and of the German poets of *Sturm und Drang*. In this new climate of opinion, the cult of sublimity and melancholy, hitherto satisfied with overgrown graveyards, ruined abbeys and deserted villages, found a new and more lively embodiment in primitive peoples crushed by the march of progress, and expressing their last prophetic message in high, tragic strains.

To this new mood of the later eighteenth century, even Homer, sublime though he was, was not quite equal. Homer, after all, represented the victors, not the vanquished, in the heroic struggle. The Greeks sacked Troy. Homer was also altogether too robust, too extrovert, too crude for eighteenth-century sensibility. He lacked – except on rare occasions when he placed himself in Trojan shoes – the ideal strain of melancholy: as Voltaire wrote, he never drew tears from his readers.[19] Nor were his heroes altogether noble savages, such as were required by the new doctrine. Sometimes they were just savages. Achilles, exclaimed Voltaire, was little better than a cannibal, or a redskin brandishing his tomahawk.[20] Critics began to complain not only of the barbarism of Homer's heroes – their human sacrifices, their greed for plunder, their exultation over the dying or dead, their savage spirit of revenge – but also of their lack of social propriety and their defective table manners. They dined without spoons or forks, tablecloths or napkins. In the *Odyssey*, Nausicaa, a king's daughter, went down to the river to do the family washing, sitting 'on a waggon of greasy clothes'. Worst of all, neither the poet nor his heroes seemed conscious of these social gaffes: they were 'not sensible of the lowness of their manners'. A truly sublime epic poem, it was now thought, should not be disfigured by such barbarism, such brutality and grossness. Its heroes would combine primitive simplicity with modern decorum: they would be both magnanimous and refined, able to shame the sophisticated eighteenth century not only by their more splendid language but also by the superior purity of their manners and morals. By this ideal standard even Homer was judged wanting. There was room for another 'primitive' poet, greater than him.

Was it conceivable that such a poet had existed, or, if he had, that his work could now be recovered? To anyone who asked that question in the later 1750s, the answer was clear. In 1755 there had been discovered, in the German monastery of Hohenems, a surviving manuscript of the *Nibelungenlied*, the tragic poem of the barbarian heroes of Germany. It was published two years later at Zurich by J.J. Bodmer. The poem, it is true, is not very elevated: the Nibelungs were far more gross and barbarous than the heroes of Homer; but the discovery showed what was possible. Who could tell what treasures of ancient literature might lurk in forgotten corners? The ancient Germans might be a rough lot, but perhaps other races – the mild Celts, for instance, whom these rough Germanic invaders had pushed into the outer fringes of Europe – would be found to be less objectionable on that count: to be at once heroic and refined.

Yes, the Celts. Obviously the Celts. For where in Europe was there a more constantly defeated people? Whether in Wales, or in Ireland, or in Scotland, they were always being pushed back, always uttering melancholy poetic cries. And of course they had 'bards', who, at least in the distant past, had been credited with sublime poetry. By 1755, the year of the discovery of the *Nibelungenlied*, the Celts were already being groomed for their part. In that year Thomas Gray, the most learned of English poets, who showed a special interest in Celtic poetry, wrote his poem 'The Bard', which was published, two years later, by his friend Horace Walpole. In it, the Welsh bard, the last of his race, utters his prophecies of doom against the Anglo-Norman conqueror of his people, King Edward I:

> On a rock, whose haughty brow
> Frowns o'er old Conway's foaming flood,
> Robed in the sable garb of woe,
> With haggard eyes the Poet stood;
> (Loose his beard and hoary hair
> Stream'd like a meteor, to the troubled air)
> And with a Master's hand and Prophet's fire
> Struck the deep sorrows of his lyre.
> 'Hark, how each giant oak, and desert cave
> Sighs to the torrent's aweful voice beneath!
> . . .[21]

Such, in 1755, was the stylised portrait, almost the stereotype, of the Celtic bard in the twilight of the heroes of his race. All that remained to be discovered was his Scottish incarnation, and the song that he sang.

Two years after Walpole's publication of Gray's poem, a young Scotch Highlander made himself known to Walpole and Gray, offering, in effect, to discover the epic poem of Celtic Scotland. A year after that, out of the recesses of the Highlands and islands, he produced it. It had all the qualities which the age required. It was epic, melancholy and sublime. It was primitive and yet pure: pure in morals, pure in sentiment. It dated from the heroic age of the ancient Caledonians who, at the beginning of the third century AD, had gloriously resisted the legions of the Roman Emperor Septimius Severus; and yet it was suffused with tragedy: for that heroic generation had entered its twilight. The poet himself, like Homer, was blind; but unlike Homer, he was not a mere wandering bard: he was a king's son, a royal but now lonely figure who had seen all his peers, and his own son, perish in the wars and himself had survived only to lament their fate in majestic poetry. As a poet he had the attributes, and was surrounded by the apparatus, which Gray had given to his Bard: the white hair, the flowing robe, the lyre, the jutting rock, the foaming torrent. His name was Ossian. The young Highlander who had discovered and translated his work, and who had thus given to Scotland the great literature which it had so far totally lacked, and which it now so desperately needed, was James Macpherson.

James Macpherson was born in 1736 at Ruthven, in the parish of Kingussie, Inverness-shire, in the valley of the river Spey. This was Macpherson country. A few miles up the valley was Cluny castle, the seat of the chief of the clan. James Macpherson's father, a poor farmer, was closely but perhaps illegitimately related to the chief, and James was always deeply involved with his kinsmen. In 1745 the chief, Ewan Macpherson of Cluny, after much hesitation and tergiversation (for he was an officer in the Hanoverian army), had brought his clan to join the rebels; and next year, James, at the age of ten, had seen the broken remnants of the Highland army fleeing through his valley, pursued by the Hanoverian forces. After the rout, the chief lived in hiding nearby for nine years, protected and supplied by the devotion of his clan, before escaping to France; the Spey valley is full of houses, or caves, which have legends of his narrow escapes. His story was that of the Young Chevalier himself – only prolonged for nine years. During those years James Macpherson witnessed the Lowlanders' revenge: the attempt to destroy the substance and forbid the outward form of distinctive Highland life. In such circumstances, the survivors of the clan clung tightly together; and in the absence of the chief, the lead must have been given by the neighbouring Macpherson laird at Strathmashie castle, a few miles up the valley from Cluny. Indeed we are told, on what looks like sufficient authority, that the laird of Strathmashie took young James into his own household; and that James lived with the laird's family at Strathmashie during many years of his boyhood and youth.[22] This opened up to him opportunities for development and advancement that were otherwise inconceivable. In particular, it brought James early into close and prolonged contact with the laird's son, Lachlan, known as 'young Strathmashie' or 'Strathy', who was thirteen years older than him, a strongly defined and leading character in his own right, and who would prove a firm friend and guide to James for many crucial years ahead. At the age of sixteen James was sent to Aberdeen University – first to King's College, then to Marischal College. There he studied Latin and Greek, becoming, we are told, 'an exceedingly good classical scholar'.[23] The Principal of Marischal College and the Professor of Greek, at that time, were one and the same person, Thomas Blackwell, the author of the *Enquiry into the Life and Writings of Homer*. Blackwell had now held his chair for thirty years, and had ruled his college for six. He was recognised as by far the greatest scholar in the place; and by his influence and exertions, we are told, had raised 'a poor neglected college to high repute'.[24] His work on Homer must have been familiar to Macpherson.

After leaving the university, Macpherson took a post as a schoolmaster in his native village of Ruthven. It was one of very few schools in a wide area,[25] and there was little hope of promotion to a less provincial post. It was probably at this time that he became interested in Gaelic poetry.[26] He was not the first to show such interest. Gaelic ballads were already being collected; and Macpherson certainly read the translation of a Gaelic ballad and the accompanying essay which one such collector, Jerome Stone, had published in the *Scots Magazine* in 1756. Stone there wrote that he had collected in the Highlands poems 'which for sublimity of language, nervousness of expression, and high spirited metaphors are hardly to be equalled among the chief productions of the most cultivated nations. Others of them breathe such tenderness and simplicity, as must be greatly affecting to every mind that is in the least tinctured with the softer passions of pity and humanity'; or, more briefly, which combined sublimity with pathos.[27] Macpherson must certainly have been encouraged also, in that remote and unlettered valley, by the example and conversation of his boyhood friend and model, Lachlan Macpherson of Strathmashie, living not far from the Ruthven schoolhouse, who was now making a name for himself in that province as a wit, a scholar, and a poet. 'Young Strathmashie' was fluent in Gaelic, with 'a happy facility for writing it in Roman characters'; and he was learned in Gaelic subjects, Irish as well as Scottish. He wrote poems in Gaelic under his Gaelic title of Fear Shrath-Mhathaisidh.[28] James Macpherson could not yet compete on equal terms with his kinsman and friend: for although he spoke Gaelic fluently enough, he did not, it seems, speak it very correctly; and his acquaintance with the Gaelic literary tradition was that of an amateur rather than a scholar. But he, too, studied poetry and wrote poems of a fashionable melancholy kind with a kind of Jacobite, Celtic tinge, though in English. One of his early poems was entitled 'On Death'; another was 'a sort of heroic poem in several cantos' entitled 'The Hunter'.[29] Some other poems he published in the *Scots Magazine*. A longer poem entitled 'The Highlander' he published separately in 1758. These poems excited, at the time, no interest.

By 1759 Macpherson had given up school-teaching and taken a post as private tutor in the house of a local family, the Grahams of Balgowan. His pupil was Thomas Graham, who would afterwards distinguish himself as a soldier and be created Lord Lynedoch. To this connection Macpherson owed much. It was probably through his predecessor as tutor, the Rev. George Fraser, minister of Redgorton in Badenoch, that he obtained his first and historically most important

Gaelic manuscript, the famous Book of the Dean of Lismore, to which we shall return. For the manuscript had been in the minister's family for a century; it was currently in the hands of the Rev. Thomas Fraser of Boleskin, the uncle of George Fraser; and it certainly passed, at about this time, into the hands of Macpherson. This book contained, in a collection of various writings inscribed by different persons in the Fortingall area of Perthshire during the first half of the sixteenth century, poems ascribed to 'Oisin'.[30] Through the Grahams of Balgowan, Macpherson also discovered his first patron in the public world. For in the summer of 1759 he accompanied the Graham family on a visit to the little Border spa of Moffat. On the way the party stayed at Logierait in Perthshire; and there Macpherson met the son of the local minister, Adam Ferguson.

In 1759 Adam Ferguson was thirty-six years old and already well known in Edinburgh, where he would afterwards be famous as a historian and philosopher. His immediate interest, for Macpherson, lay in the fact that he was a Highlander and Gaelic-speaking: indeed, he had preached a sermon in Gaelic to the Highland soldiers who had fought for the government against the Young Chevalier in 1745. He was also familiar with Gaelic popular poetry, and had inspired his friend John Home, the author of *Douglas*, with his interest. Home's interest had soon turned to enthusiasm. Now, at Logierait, hearing that Macpherson shared their interest, and was accompanying the Grahams to Moffat, Ferguson gave him a letter to John Home, whom he knew to be there on his regular summer visit. The consequences of this introduction were so enormous that James Macpherson could write, fifteen years later, that Ferguson was 'the man who drew me from obscurity. His politeness and friendship to me . . . are debts and claims on me that oblivion itself can scarcely obliterate'.[31]

At Moffat, Macpherson duly met John Home. Since the great controversy over *Douglas*, John Home had resigned from the ministry, in which he had suffered such persecution, and had found a safer and more promising post as private secretary to Lord Bute, who was the governor and friend of the Prince of Wales, afterwards King George III. But Home retained his connection with Edinburgh, and was a distinguished member of that group of literary men known as the Edinburgh literati. These were the men who had supported him in his battle with the obscurantists of the Kirk, and who now dominated the intellectual life of the Scottish capital. Their leader was the philosopher David Hume. Other prominent members of the group were Hugh Blair, an Edinburgh minister, Alexander Carlyle, minister of Inveresk, Henry Home, Lord Kames, a judge and scholar, and the historian William Robertson, soon to be principal of the university. Thus, by becoming known to Ferguson, and through him to Home, Macpherson had placed his foot in the enchanted circle of the Scottish literary elite, who were also in close touch with the arbiters of taste and makers of policy in London. As the means of his entry had been through Gaelic literature, he naturally discussed that subject with Home at Moffat.

In the course of this discussion Macpherson, who had literary ambitions and must have seen Home as a potential patron, revealed that he had in his possession certain Gaelic poems which he had collected from oral recitation in the Highlands. He recited some of these poems in Gaelic, which Home did not understand. Home pressed him to translate them. After some resistance, Macpherson consented and produced an English prose version of a poem on the death of Oscar, the son of Ossian. Afterwards he produced several more translations. Home was 'highly delighted' with the translations and soon afterwards, being joined by Alexander Carlyle, showed them to him. Carlyle, by his own account, 'was perfectly astonished at the poetical genius displayed in them'. The two men agreed that they had made 'a precious discovery, and that as soon as possible it should be published to the world'.[32] They returned to Edinburgh in high spirits and informed their fellow-literati of their great find.

Their fellow-literati shared their excitement. Even the sceptical David Hume, who at first was 'inclined to be a little incredulous', was won over by John Home's circumstantial account, and became, for a time, a warm advocate of the newly discovered Gaelic poety. But the man who now took the lead in the whole affair was Hugh Blair. Blair lectured on English composition at the university, and had already established himself as the oracle on all matters of literature. The next year he would be appointed professor, and afterwards regius professor, of rhetoric and belles-lettres. The success of his lectures would be enormous. Thirty years later an admiring acolyte would hail him as the man who had reformed the national taste, diffusing 'a skill in elegant composition, and taste to relish it, throughout all Scotland'.[33]

When Blair heard of Home's discovery he sought out Macpherson and persuaded him to come to Edinburgh. Macpherson duly came; and, on arrival, found the whole literary establishment already converted to his cause, and insistent that his poems be published. Blair himself undertook to organise the publication, to defray the costs, and to write a preface. But since Scottish support alone was not enough to ensure success, Blair sought to engage English interest. Advance copies of two of the poems were therefore sent, through Sir David Dalrymple, afterwards Lord Hailes, a learned antiquary known and respected in England, to the English arbiter of taste, Horace Walpole, and, through him, to his friend Thomas Gray.

Both Walpole and Gray read the poems with enthusiasm. Gray was 'so charmed with the two specimens of Erse poetry' that he wanted to see more – and particularly, in order to form some idea of the language and the rhythm, copies of the original Gaelic. Who were the authors, he asked? Of what date were the poems? Were there any more such to be found? Of course, one had to be careful about accepting them as genuine – he remembered Lady Wardlaw's *Hardyknute* – but really he did not care: even if the poems were modern forgeries, 'I would undertake a journey into the Highlands only for the pleasure of seeing' the author. Gray's comments were passed on to Macpherson, who was much encouraged by them. He now wrote to Gray direct, enclosing more poems. Gray found Macpherson's letters thoroughly unsatisfactory. They were, he reported, badly written and badly reasoned: betraying, as he imagined, evident signs of an intention to deceive, without being clever enough to carry it off successfully. But the effect on Gray of Macpherson's letters was paradoxical; for they convinced him that the poems must be authentic. At least, he thought, the writer of these letters could not himself have been the author of those poems. This was an argument which would be used again and again in the subsequent controversy. How could that raw Highland booby be anything but the mere conduit for poems so pathetic and sublime? Nevertheless, having advanced the argument, Gray soon found himself doubting again. He could never quite decide whether

Macpherson was the inspired author or the lucky discoverer of the poems. 'In short', he wrote to Walpole, 'this man is the very Demon of Poetry, or he has lighted on a treasure hid for ages.'[34]

Meanwhile the poems, with Blair's preface, were published at Edinburgh in 1760, under the title *Fragments of Ancient Poetry, collected in the Highlands of Scotland, and translated from the Galic or Erse Language*. There were sixteen poems altogether. In his preface Blair took it upon himself to guarantee their authenticity and antiquity. The poems, he said, were 'coeval with the very infancy of Christianity in Scotland'. He then went on to say that 'although the poems now published appear as detached pieces in this collection, there is ground to believe that most of them were originally episodes of a greater work which related to the wars of Fingal'. 'There is no doubt', he went on, that these poems, of which the translation was 'extremely literal', 'are to be ascribed to the Bards' – that is, not the degenerate modern *senachies* but the primitive bards mentioned by Roman writers – and 'there is reason to hope that one work of considerable length, and which deserves to be styled a heroic poem, might be recovered and translated, if encouragement were given to such an undertaking'.[35] Thus Blair clearly declared his belief in the Gaelic Homer and angled for patrons to come forward and finance the discovery of his works.

How could Blair be so confident and so explicit? What grounds could he have to believe? How could he dismiss in advance any possible doubt? How could he, who admitted that he was 'entirely ignorant of the Gaelic language', vouch for the literal accuracy of the translation? No originals had yet been seen by anyone. Blair's statements, by his own admission, were based on 'conversations I had held with Mr Macpherson'.[36] But why did Blair swallow, and support by his authority, all the assertions of a young man of twenty-three? The answer must be that those assertions coincided so perfectly with his own preconceptions that he could not resist them. They were factual confirmation of what he was already determined to believe. Perhaps they even originated with him. Perhaps – we cannot exclude the possibility – Blair was the driving force in the dialogue, suggesting, eliciting and systematising the contributions of the naive Macpherson.

In his famous work, *On Scotland and the Scotch Intellect* – a work which has proved easier to dismiss than to refute – H.T. Buckle argued that the Scottish intellect, even in its most enlightened period, was not inductive, like the English, but deductive: that it reasoned not empirically but a priori.[37] No better confirmation of this theory could be given (though Buckle himself did not notice it) than the arguments consistently used on behalf of Macpherson by Hugh Blair. In fact it is now known that of the sixteen 'fragments' produced by Macpherson and authenticated by Blair, fourteen had no basis at all in authentic Gaelic tradition, other than the names of the persons involved, which had been borrowed for this occasion from genuine ballads. Those fourteen 'fragments' were not translations but original compositions by Macpherson. Among them was 'The Death of Oscar', the first work by which Macpherson had won the interest of John Home: a short romantic melodrama, presented in primitivist pastiche.[38]

Blair and Macpherson evidently hoped for patronage from England. Copies of the new book were sent into England, and Blair's angling preface was sometimes reinforced by particular letters. Thus the copy sent to the poet William Shenstone was accompanied by a letter stating that 'if these specimens were well received by the public, and if suitable encouragement were given to the ingenious translator, he would oblige the world with the translation of the epic poem mentioned in the preface, which consists of upwards of nine thousand lines; but the dependent situation of a tutor cannot afford him leisure to undertake so great a work'.[39] The substance of this letter was almost certainly supplied by Macpherson himself, who would on other occasions anonymously puff his own work.[40] It is interesting to note that he was writing as if the discovery of the epic poem were already guaranteed, and he knew exactly its length. In conversation with the Edinburgh literati, he was even more explicit. There was, he told them, 'a country surgeon somewhere in Lochaber' who had the whole epic by heart, and from whom he could doubtless obtain it; 'but as he is somewhat old, and is the only person living who has it entire', there was no time to lose . . ..[41]

The appeal to England was unsuccessful. When Gray and Walpole read the published *Fragments* their doubts returned, and Gray wrote to Scotland to express them and to ask for expert guidance. His letter was passed to David Hume. Hume wrote back strongly supporting the authenticity of the poems. He explained the circumstances in which Macpherson had produced them at Moffat, and which had convinced John Home. Then he gave the historical background as already announced by Macpherson and Blair. 'In the family of every Highland chieftain', he explained, 'there was anciently retained a bard, whose office was the same with that of the Greek rhapsodists; and the general subject of the poems which they recited was the wars of Fingal; an epoch no less celebrated among them than the wars of Troy among the Greek poets . . .'. Moreover, now that the poems were published, all the Highland gentlemen in Edinburgh, and even 'Adam Smith, the celebrated professor in Glasgow', declared that they had heard these poems in identical form in different parts of the Highlands. Their authenticity was thus beyond doubt.[42] Adam Smith was indeed much taken by Macpherson's *Fragments*, as he had been by Lady Wardlaw's *Hardyknute*, which he still assumed to be genuine; but as he did not know Gaelic, his authority is somewhat weakened: presumably it was second-hand, from 'the Highland gentlemen'.[43]

Walpole and Gray remained sceptical, or rather in a state of suspended judgment. Reason suggested that the poems were modern forgeries, said Gray, and yet he would like to believe that they were genuine and ancient, if only because he had never known a modern Scotchman 'that could read, much less write, poetry; and such poetry too!' Walpole was a little firmer in his scepticism. The result was that neither of them was prepared publicly to underwrite the poems, or took the hint about a subscription to enable Macpherson to discover the epic poem still lurking in the Highlands. That was left to the Edinburgh literati.

The Edinburgh literati rose to the challenge. By now their literary blood was up and the honour of Scotland was at stake. Now, after fifteen centuries, they found themselves accidentally on the scent, indeed close on the brush, of the still elusive Scottish Homer. And yet, unless they were very quick, they might lose him after all, and lose him finally. Everything seemed to depend on that aged country surgeon in Lochaber: what a disaster it would be if he should die

before he had passed on his knowledge! So, once again, Blair took the
lead. He canvassed opinion in Edinburgh to discover the most promising scheme for raising money to send Macpherson to the Highlands
for the purpose of 'recovering our epic'.[44] Then he organised a dinner
of 'many of the first persons of rank and taste in Edinburgh'.
Macpherson was invited to come and state his case; and it was
agreed, then and there, to raise a subscription so that Macpherson
could 'disengage himself from all other employment and set out
without delay' to the Highlands to procure 'more of these wild
flowers'.[45]

Thus already, in the summer of 1760, before he had presented any
evidence, Macpherson knew exactly what he was going to find. It was
a Gaelic epic of over nine thousand lines, concerning the wars of
Fingal, whom he described as a Scottish hero of the third century AD;
and although it could perhaps be reconstructed from different
sources, there was one (and only one) man, known to him, who had
the whole poem by heart. In these circumstances it is rather
surprising that Macpherson, on being freed from his tutorial post
and subsidised to go and collect the poem, did not go at once to
Lochaber and take it down from the aged country surgeon there.
Instead, he headed for the Hebrides. Perhaps that old country
surgeon had suddenly died. Perhaps he had never been born.

However that may be, Macpherson clearly knew where to go. He
could rely – all through his life he could rely – on his kindred; for all
Macphersons hung together, regarding themselves (somewhat ques-
tionably) as a clan. First of all, there was his cousin, Lachlan
Macpherson, 'young Strathmashie', whom we have already met.
Strathmashie was an essential companion to James Macpherson, at
least on the first part of his western tour. He acted as his interpreter
where necessary, took down oral recitations, and transcribed and
translated manuscripts for him. He was also, no doubt, socially
useful, for he knew the lairds and chieftains of the Highlands. He
would play an important, though mysterious, part in the story.

In Strathmashie's company, Macpherson travelled to the island of
Skye, staying with local lairds or ministers on the way, hearing recita-
tions and seeking manuscripts. In Skye, at Portree, he obtained from
Alexander Macpherson, a local blacksmith, a manuscript volume of

poems. He spent a night at Skinnader with Captain Alexander Morrison, a man of some education and literary tastes, fluent in Gaelic.[46] Morrison was interested in Macpherson's purpose and would remain a valuable accomplice in later years. But Macpherson's most useful host in the island was another Macpherson. This was the Rev. John Macpherson, minister of Sleat.

The Rev. John Macpherson was not, it seems, a kinsman – or at best he was a very remote kinsman – of our hero. He came of a long line of clergymen settled and beneficed in Skye. He himself had been brought up at Duirinish, on the mainland opposite the coast of Skye, and before being called to Sleat had been minister in the Hebridean island of Barra, in the presbytery of Uist. He was Gaelic-speaking, and had some pretensions to antiquarian scholarship. He knew everyone in Skye, and in the islands. Through him Macpherson was assured of welcome and interest throughout the Hebrides.

Moreover, at the minister's house, James Macpherson was lucky enough to discover yet another Macpherson, coming originally indeed from his own native valley. This was Ewan Macpherson, who had been born in Kingussie, and was currently a schoolmaster in Knoydart. Ewan Macpherson was steeped in Gaelic culture. His family had moved, a year after his birth, from Kingussie in Badenoch to Glenorchy in Argyll. In Glenorchy, up to the age of fourteen, he had listened to Ossianic recitations countless times, and with an enthusiasm which nothing in later life could match (as he declared in his seventies) from a member of the MacNicol family who was both bard and *senachie*. After a few years elsewhere, he had returned to Badenoch; and he had lived for a couple of years with his older brother, then minister at Laggan. In 1751 he had been appointed SPCK schoolmaster at Loch Carron in Ross, where he had remained until moving to Knoydart five years later.[47] Thus Ewan Macpherson, by reason of his poetical interests and his wide acquaintance with the Gaelic-speaking heartland, was a man who could be very useful to James Macpherson. Above all, he could read the old Gaelic script. James Macpherson swept Ewan into his wake and employed him to hear recitations and transcribe documents while he himself remained at ease among lairds and clergy. The unfortunate schoolmaster had not bargained for this; he had probably hoped to spend the summer in other pursuits. But James Macpherson overbore him: he was an overbearing man, something even of a bully. At Sleat, James Macpherson may also have met the minister's son John, who was afterwards to play a vital part in his life; but at this time he was a boy of just fifteen.

No doubt it was at the suggestion of the minister of Sleat that James Macpherson undertook the next stage of his journey, to the Hebrides. The minister knew the Hebrides well, and the ruling family there, the Macdonalds of Clanranald, whose ancestors, the Macdonald Lords of the Isles, had once been the greatest power in Gaelic Scotland. He also knew their hereditary bards, the MacMhuirich family: thirty years ago he had heard the MacMhuirich of the time, an old man, reciting, from a Gaelic manuscript, tales of Cuchullin, Fingal, Ossian, Gaul, Diarmid and others, to a crowded Highland audience.[48] It was well known that Clanranald, alone of the Hebridean chiefs, possessed ancient Gaelic manuscripts,[49] so it was natural for James Macpherson to be directed to him. Equally naturally, he once again conscripted the protesting schoolmaster, whose services were now doubly necessary since Strathmashie, it seems, had to leave the party in Skye. Ewan Macpherson wriggled hard, and at Dunvegan attempted to break away; but the whole establishment of the castle was turned upon him and he was 'in a manner compulsorily obliged' to go on. The party thus moved on from the Macleods and the Macleans of Skye to the Macdonalds of the isles: first to Sir James Macdonald, the proprietor of North Uist, whose bard, John McCodrum, enraged Macpherson by mocking his incorrect Gaelic, then to Benbecula and South Uist, Clanranald's capital. They stayed one or two nights with Clanranald senior at Ormiclate in South Uist and a week at Benbecula with his son Clanranald the younger. They also stayed with Angus MacNeill, the minister of Howmore, South Uist, who was a convenient neighbour of the reigning bard, Neil MacMhuirich.

The MacMhuirich family, like so many Hebridean families – like the Macbeths or Bethunes, who were hereditary physicians to the same chief – had come originally from Ireland.[50] The first bard, Muredach O'Daly, had come over to serve the Lords of the Isles in the thirteenth century; and his successors regularly went back to Ireland for their bardic training. As the reward of their service they had a grant of land and a high position at the Hebridean court. In 1411 one of them, Lachlan MacMhuirich, had composed a famous 'incitement' to the battle of Harlaw in which the Lords of the Isles challenged the crown of Scotland. After the forfeiture of the Lordship of the Isles, the MacMhuirich dynasty continued to serve the Macdonald chieftains, who remained powerful in the west and in Ireland. They composed panegyrics and dirges and celebrated the wars of Montrose – or at least the part played in them by the Macdonalds.[51] They also compiled, as the tools of their trade, manuscript volumes in which they recorded their repertoire. Some of these documents were kept in Clanranald's archives; others were in the custody of the MacMhuirich family. No doubt it was from one of these books that the Rev. John Macpherson had heard the old bard reciting Ossianic poetry thirty years earlier.

At the time of James Macpherson's visit, the family was represented by Neil MacMhuirich, eighteenth in succession from the founder Muredach. He would also be the last; for after his death the chief would decide that he could no longer afford the luxury of a bard, and the office would be abolished. The MacMhuirich family would thereupon lose their land – which was now a farm at Stailgarry in South Uist – and, with it, their inspiration.[52] But that would be in the future. In 1760 Neil MacMhuirich was still active as Hebridean laureate, and James Macpherson, while staying with the minister of South Uist, became friendly with him and learned about his manuscripts. Appeal was made to Clanranald, and on the authority of the chief several manuscripts were handed over to Macpherson. One such manuscript was highly valued by the family, and Macpherson was required to give a written bond for its return. 'Clanranald senior' also gave him an order to a clansman in Edinburgh to lend him another manuscript; but there is some doubt whether Macpherson ever collected this book. Macpherson carried off Clanranald's manuscripts in triumph. They were to become his trump card, his secret weapon. Clanranald would never see them again.[53]

But secretly, it seems, James Macpherson already had one trump card up his sleeve before he even set off on his visit to the western isles. During that journey he confided to his captive helper, Ewan

Macpherson, that although he was, of course, keen to make all enquiries, 'he had previously received a manuscript from a clergyman in Perthshire, which contained, he believed, all of those poems that were likely to be found'.[54] James did not show this manuscript to Ewan; and perhaps he had prudently left it at home. But from that description, it must surely have been the Book of the Dean of Lismore.

After two months of fieldwork, Macpherson returned with his spoil to his native glen, and there went to ground with his cousin Strathmashie and Strathmashie's most intimate local friend, the Rev. Andrew Gallie, then missionary in Badenoch. Gallie too was a Gaelic-speaker. Together, the two Macphersons worked on the manuscripts and notes which they had collected; and Gallie was sometimes called in to decipher a word or interpret a phrase. Strathmashie clearly played an important part in the whole process, in Ruthven as in the islands, in textual reconstruction as in discovery and collection. He was a good Gaelic scholar and 'an excellent Gaelic poet'; whereas James Macpherson, according to Captain Morrison, 'was no great poet, nor thoroughly conversant with Gaelic literature'.[55] Strathmashie seems to have written out several drafts or copies of the original material collected, or of what was being constructed out of that original material; and he distributed some of those copies to friends. One such document he sent to another cousin, Sir John Macpherson of Lauriston, who in due course would produce it as independent evidence in support of James Macpherson's texts. Another would be given to Gallie, who would similarly serve it up as independent corroboration. In fact, neither of these documents possessed any independent authority; they were simply copies of what was available, or being made, at Ruthven.

By November 1760 Macpherson was ready to leave Ruthven with his transcriptions. He was well satisfied with his haul. He had, he wrote, 'gained all worth notice' in the islands; and although he spoke of visiting Western Argyll and Mull, he probably did not go there at that time.[56] It was now winter, and he may have preferred corre-spondence with known collectors of Gaelic poetry. We know that he obtained thirteen poems by correspondence from the Rev. James Maclagan, minister of Amulrie, some other poems from the

Fletchers of Glenforsa on Mull, and planned, but failed, to visit Glenorchy in Argyll, in order to tap the recitations of the MacNicol family.[57] By mid-January he was back in Edinburgh, and could write that in his brief foray he had been 'lucky enough to lay my hands on a pretty complete poem, and truly epic, concerning Fingal'. The poem, he added, was demonstrably old, superior to anything known in the Gaelic language, and 'not inferior to the more polite performances of other nations in that way'.[58] In other words, he had brought back exactly what he had promised to find.

The Edinburgh literati, of course, were delighted. Was not this just what they had prophesied, on a priori grounds? Here at last was the Gaelic Homer. Now all that was needed was to prepare an English translation of the new-found epic for the press. Once again Blair took charge. He found lodgings for Macpherson immediately below his own house, and there the work was completed. Some papers 'which appeared to them to be old manuscripts' – for they were 'much stained with smoke and daubed with Scots snuff' – were shown to Adam Ferguson and some other Gaelic-speakers; and they recognised Macpherson's translation of those passages as exact.[59] At dinner, Macpherson would read his translations to the admiring Blair.[60] With remarkable speed, he produced a continuous English version of the whole epic.

When the English text was in its final form, Macpherson set off to London to find a publisher. He carried with him a letter of introduction from David Hume to Hume's own publisher, William Strahan. Macpherson, Hume wrote, had already had some success with his *Fragments*; now he 'has also translated a larger work, a narrative poem of great antiquity, which lay in obscurity and would probably have been buried in oblivion if he had not retrieved it'; and he added that the bearer was 'very worthy of your friendship, being a sensible modest young fellow, a very good scholar, and of unexceptionable morals'.[61] Hume may afterwards have regretted this letter, for he was to find that Macpherson was neither sensible nor modest, and that exception could be taken both to his scholarship and to his morals. However, Hume's patronage was not in fact necessary, for Macpherson had already secured far more powerful support. When his book was published, it carried an eloquent expression of gratitude for the generosity of 'a certain noble person' too grand for him to name. This, as a later reference would show, was the Earl of Bute, now Prime Minister of Britain. Bute's patronage had no doubt been obtained for Macpherson by Bute's secretary, John Home.

While in London, arranging the publication of his epic, Macpherson showed his manuscript to Horace Walpole who, once again, was enchanted by this Gaelic poetry: his doubts as to its genuineness, he wrote – doubts fitfully engendered by the lyrical *Fragments* – were now 'all vanished'.[62] Walpole now agreed with Gray – indeed outran Gray in enthusiasm. He accepted the new discovery in toto. *Fingal*, by the mere fact of its discovery, had proved the authenticity of the *Fragments*.

*Fingal*, an epic poem in six books, composed by Ossian the son of Fingal, was published at the beginning of December 1761 (though the title page carried the date 1762). In a somewhat confused 'advertisement' which preceded the preface, Macpherson stated that 'some men of genius whom he has the honour to number among his friends' had advised him to invite subscriptions for the publication of the original Gaelic text as a better way of proving its authenticity than by depositing manuscript copies in a public library. However, no subscribers having appeared, 'he takes it for the judgment of the public' that neither course was necessary. Even so, it was his intention one day to publish the originals as soon as they could be transcribed for the press. If not, copies would be deposited in a public library 'to prevent so ancient a monument of genius from being lost'. In the Preface, Macpherson described the origin and success of his researches and the discovery of the epic, which he now laid before the reader 'as I have found it'. 'How far it comes up to the rules of the *Epopaea*' he left the critics to decide; but he expressed his own view that *Fingal* was 'truly epic', being 'beautiful in simplicity and grand in the sublime'. In other words, it complied with the a priori rules of Professor Blair. After the preface came a 'dissertation on the antiquity of the poems of Ossian, son of Fingal'; then the text of the epic, followed by sixteen short poems, one of which, *Temora*, was described as being a fragment of another epic, still awaiting discovery. All the poems were translated not into verse, but – at the suggestion of John Home, we are told – into rhythmical biblical prose.

The poem of *Fingal* is today totally unreadable. Its story is of inexpressible tedium; its characters are as bloodless as the ghosts who provide its supernatural machinery; and they reiterate only the most high-minded sentiments and vapid rhetoric. The context is an unchanging background of bleak crags, twisted oak trees, purple heather, raging storms and misty islands. But to the taste of the later eighteenth century, which had grown weary of Augustan formality, it provided, in instant form, everything that was most desired. It was sublime; it was melancholy; it presented the noblest of noble savages; and its rhythmical prose was a relief from the mechanical regularity of heroic couplets. Pope had put the Greek Homer into a literary straitjacket; but the Celtic Homer was free. He was also superior to the real Homer in every respect in which the real Homer was now being criticised.

We have seen that the critics had begun to object to the crudities of the Greek poet and his heroes. How vastly superior were the early Scottish Highlanders and their poet! Here were no human sacrifices, no petty thieving, no princesses washing knickers in the river. Indeed there was nothing common, or even concrete, at all. All was high-minded humanity, sensibility, chivalry. As Sheridan put it to Boswell, Ossian surpassed 'all the poets in the world . . . he excelled Homer in the Sublime and Virgil in the Pathetic'; his morality was so elevated that Mr and Mrs Sheridan 'have fixed it as the standard of feeling, made it a thermometer by which they could judge the warmth of everybody's heart'. Finally, these poems marked 'a great discovery' in another respect. They were an important contribution to anthropology. Till they had been published 'we could not imagine that such sentiments of delicacy as well as generosity could have existed in the breasts of rude uncultivated people'.[63] Now it was clear that they could: Ossian proved that the Noble Savage was not a myth but reality.

If such was the reaction in London, it is easy to imagine the spirit of triumph which reigned in Edinburgh. The literati were united in complacency at having brought to light this treasure of ancient Scottish literature. Once again, the leader of the chorus was Blair. In

1762 Blair and Macpherson both visited London and dined out in glory. Returning to Edinburgh, Blair – now Regius Professor and more oracular than ever – delivered a series of lectures on literature which seem an almost preconceived answer to the invitation in Macpherson's preface. Macpherson had invited critics to determine how far *Fingal* came up to 'the rules of the *Epopaea*', and to this a priori question Blair, as the voice of Criticism, now gave an a priori answer. *Fingal*, he declared, complied with those abstract rules, and complied with them so fully that 'although there were no external proof' of its authenticity, we could still assume, and assume 'for certain', from its structure, language and ideas, from its 'grandeur of sentiment, style and imagery', that it is 'a genuine venerable monument of very remote antiquity'. In other words, its authenticity was proved by its conformity with the theories of Blair.

Blair's lectures were not ostensibly on Ossian; but whatever his immediate topic, always Ossian is brought in, and always it is Ossian who comes out best. There is 'rudeness and indelicacy' in Homer and Shakespeare which is avoided by Ossian. 'The works of Ossian abound with beautiful and correct metaphors', with 'tender images', and with 'the most beautiful instances' of that most epic of literary devices, the invocation or apostrophe. But above all, the distinguishing marks of Ossian's poetry are its sublimity and its pathos. Here he is superior to Homer. Homer may be 'a more cheerful and sprightly poet than Ossian', but he lacks pathos and the high epic strain of melancholy. 'Ossian's ghosts', in particular, 'are drawn with much stronger and livelier colours than those of Homer'. Homer indeed has always 'been greatly admired for sublimity', but even so he cannot reach the heights attained by Ossian, whose works 'abound with examples of the Sublime'. Indeed, his whole subject demands it: 'amidst the rude scenes of Nature and of society such as Ossian describes – amidst rocks and torrents and whirlwinds and battles dwells the Sublime, and naturally associates itself with that grave and solemn spirit which distinguishes the author of *Fingal* . . . Never were images of more aweful Sublimity employed to heighten the terror of battle'.[64]

Unhappily, even while Blair was expounding to his crowded classes the undoubted authenticity, antiquity, sublimity, pathos, etc., of the newly found Celtic Homer, the more critical literary men and scholars of London were beginning to entertain grave doubts. The first hint of the controversy to come is contained in a private letter from Horace Walpole. Walpole, whose doubts about the ancient Celtic poetry had vanished when he first read *Fingal* in manuscript, changed his mind when he reread it in print. 'Fingal is come out', he wrote to his friend George Montagu, soon after its publication, and added, 'I will trust you with a secret, but you must not disclose it; I should be ruined with my Scotch friends. In short, I cannot believe it genuine.'[65]

# James Macpherson
# and *Fingal*

Horace Walpole was not alone in his doubts. In the year following the publication of the newly discovered epic, while it was being hailed as a literary, historical and moral revelation throughout Europe, the men of letters in London found increasing and, in the end, overwhelming reasons for scepticism.

First, there was the style: the style of Ossian was not that of a 'primitive' poet: it fitted a little too happily into the taste of the moment. It also contained some passages suspiciously similar to passages from Milton and the Bible, among others;[1] and although these similarities would afterwards be explained away by Macpherson as being independent observations of 'Nature, the great original', this explanation was not judged sufficient by the literary critics, who found the parallels rather too close.

Secondly, there were historical objections. Macpherson's Fingal was represented as king of 'Morven' in Caledonia in the third century AD, and Ossian, his son, sang his exploits in the 'Erse' language in the same century. But what were the Scots, and their 'Erse' or Irish language, doing in Caledonia so early? Historically, they only arrived there in the sixth century AD. Before that, the country belonged only to the Picts. All this had been scientifically established by Innes in 1729; and although Innes himself had not expected to be read by Englishmen, it might be assumed that Scotchmen who undertook to judge the question were familiar with his work.

Then there were internal objections. These were both general and particular. In general, why were the poems so lacking in concrete detail? They seemed never to touch the ground: no one could deduce, from their thin, high-falutin' rhetoric, the economy, the state of civilisation, the morals, even the religious beliefs of the Caledonians – except that their morals were exquisitely refined and their religion happily free, like that of the eighteenth century, from vulgar superstition: the upper air was peopled only by the spirits and ghosts dear to the early romantic writers. How different, in this respect, were the poems of the Ionian Homer, so full of vivid detail and domestic incidents! By avoiding such detail, Ossian did of course escape the charge of vulgarity levelled at Homer by the polite critics of the later eighteenth century, but only to incur the suspicion of forgery. For the critics could not fail to notice that when Ossian did descend to particulars, he was frequently guilty of demonstrable anachronisms: late medieval ideas of knight-errantry, halls, towers, palaces in third-century Scotland. Could that be, the critics asked, why he so seldom risked such a descent? This was the view of Walpole, who referred to the poems's 'sterility of ideas, the insipid sameness that reigns throughout, and the timidity with which it anxiously avoids every image that might affix it to any specific age, country or religion'. This timidity did not, he thought, bespeak 'a savage bard': 'few barbarous authors write with the fear of criticism before their eyes'; and he added that if one removed from *Fingal* its essential furniture – 'the moon, a storm, the troubled ocean, a blasted heath, a single tree, a waterfall, and a ghost' – there was nothing left to anchor it in time or space.[2]

Finally, there was the problem of Ossian's language. If the poems of Ossian had been preserved in their original form, in ancient manuscripts, they must necessarily have been written in an archaic language which must be very different from that still spoken in the Highlands: as different (at least) as Anglo-Saxon from modern English, or Gothic from modern German. On the other hand, if they had been transmitted orally, and gradually modernised in the process, could they really be regarded as ancient poems at all? And anyway, could they really have been so transmitted? Was there any other instance of a long epic poem carried by oral tradition through fifteen centuries? On the face of it, there seemed no way out of this dilemma that did not require assent to absurdity.

Once these suspicions were entertained and expressed, it was reasonable to ask Macpherson, and his champion Blair, for further and better particulars than those stated so dogmatically in their prefaces and dissertations. It was not enough to say that the antiquity of the poems was self-evident, or to justify them by discovering in them what were dogmatically declared to be the essential characteristics of epic poetry. Inevitably scholars would demand to see the Gaelic text, to examine the manuscripts, to cross-examine the living sources from whom Macpherson had collected both his oral and his written evidence.

While such varying doubts circulated in the literary air of London, converging and coagulating at convivial dinner parties in salons, clubs and taverns, and expressed, sometimes, in hilarious anti-Scottish satires from Grub-Street,[3] the first open challenge came from overseas, from the rival Celtic society of Ireland. For while the wits of London were acute critics of literature, they were not Celtic scholars. None of them knew anything about Celtic society, or the Gaelic language. Few, if any, of them had experience of the living Celtic world. On such subjects, detailed and conclusive evidence could only be produced by Scottish or Irish scholars; and since the Scots seemed united in uncritical support of Ossian, the burden of scholarly criticism fell, of necessity, on the Irish. But before coming to the Irish intervention in the debate, it will be convenient, in order to put the matter in perspective, to anticipate the scholarship of the next 150 years, and give some account of the true history, as far as it has been established – and it would not be established till a century after Macpherson's death – of the genuine Ossianic poems of the Celtic world.

The genuine Ossianic poems belong to a cycle of Irish Gaelic poems originally composed in Leinster in the later Middle Ages. They are not the oldest such cycle: they cannot be traced back beyond the English conquest of Ireland in the twelfth century, although they occasionally draw on material from the earlier 'heroic' poems of an Ulster cycle. They consist of stories of Fionn MacCumhaill, a mythical hero, represented as the captain of the Féine, or mercenary bands serving Cormac, king of Ireland in the third century AD. These warriors were a *corps d'élite* with their own rules and rites; they had served Cormac's father, and grandfather; but under Fionn, a mighty hunter, poet and prophet, they became intolerable to the Irish; and King Cairbre, the son of Cormac, had destroyed them in the battle of Gama in 283 AD. 'Oschin' features incidentally in these poems. At first he is simply the last survivor of the heroes of the Féine; later, as their seer and poet, he takes the central position. Throughout the seventeenth and eighteenth centuries these 'Ossianic' poems continued to be recited or sung in Celtic Ireland, and some of them were recorded in Irish manuscripts. The substance of some of them was even used as evidence by the two seventeenth-century Irish historians of Ireland, Geoffrey Keating and Roderic O'Flaherty.

Essentially, therefore, the poems were Irish in origin, Irish in substance, and Irish in preservation. However, as we have seen, Celtic Ireland, its population, its language, and its traditions, had overflowed into the Highlands of Scotland; and since the Highland bards often learned their art in Ireland, and drew on an Irish repertoire – and indeed, according to Toland, were often themselves the refuse of Ireland – Ossianic poems were naturally carried to the Highlands to be recited or sung there too. They were probably first imported in the later Middle Ages, when the Macdonald Lordship of the Isles reunited the western Highlands and Ulster, previously severed by the intervening Scandinavian kingdom of Man and the Isles. Thus they were known to John Barbour, the fourteenth-century Aberdonian poet of the *Bruce*. They were mentioned – only to be dismissed as idle tales – by that other Aberdonian man of letters, Hector Boece. With one important exception, however, they were not recorded in early manuscripts; for the Highlanders were, and always had been, less literate than their kinsmen in Ireland. The exception is the so-called 'Dean of Lismore's book' which, as we have seen, had come into Macpherson's hands, most probably before his visit to the Hebrides, perhaps even before he went to Moffat: a manuscript collection of Gaelic poems and other writings made early in the sixteenth century by the family and social circle of a learned Gaelic-speaking priest who was vicar of Fortingall in Perthshire and also, under another hat, dean of Lismore in Argyllshire. Many of the poems in this collection – which amounts to about 2,500 lines of verse in all – are Ossianic ballads, and some of them are ascribed to 'Oisin' himself; but even here, the characters and the scenes are always Irish.[4] Apart from this collection – the largest extant manuscript collection, whose survival we may owe to Macpherson – the Ossianic poems, like the other Gaelic poems, were transmitted, in the Highlands and islands of Scotland, very largely by oral tradition, and thus often modified, no doubt, in the process of transmission.

But they were transmitted within a closed society, and in a closed language. Celtic culture was generally distinct from that of eastern, Lowland Scotland; and in the sixteenth century Celtic society contracted, turned in on itself. The literate world – that is, almost exclusively, the English-speaking Scots – despised it. The only purpose for which a literate man might learn Gaelic, in the two centuries between the 'Dean of Lismore's book' and the rebellion of 1745, was not to explore that culture, to share its literature, but to destroy it, to convert the Highlanders away from their idle life of vagabondage and blackmail, thievery and balladry, to the truths of Presbyterian Christianity. In 1567, the year of the Scottish Revolution, John Carswell, Protestant Bishop of the Isles, published a Gaelic version of John Knox's Book of Common Order. His purpose, he explained, was to wean the Gaelic-speakers from their own profane literature and vain, hurtful 'lying, worldly stories' about Irish heroes such as 'Finn mac Cumhal with his warriors'.[5] The Gaelic works published in the seventeenth century were all instruments of evangelism; and when Gaelic vocabularies were published, the purpose was the same. The first significant attempt at a Gaelic dictionary was published in 1741, and its express purpose was not, of course, to introduce English-speakers to Gaelic literature, but to teach the Highlanders English and so reform their deplorable characters and idle way of life.[6]

One English-speaking layman who did penetrate the Gaelic world for secular purposes was Martin Martin, whom we have already met. He was factor to the Macleod, and he travelled in the western islands in order to collect rents and dues, and exercise authority for his chief. His account of Hebridean society would become very popular in the eighteenth century. In it he remarks that the natives of Skye (of whom he was one) had many stories of Fin Mac Coul, 'with which', however, 'he will not trouble the reader'.[7] It never occurred to him, in the 1690s, that such ballads could be of interest to educated men. Another was William Buchanan, who published an essay on the family of Buchanan in 1723. He too was Gaelic-speaking, and he gives an account of the Feans or militia of Fin, and speaks of 'rude rhymes' on the actions of Fin Mac Coul, their general, which circulated in Ireland and among the Scotch Highlanders.[8] His writings were contemporary with those of Toland and Blackwell, so contemptuous of the Highland bards.

But by now we are in the early eighteenth century and already the closed Highland society is beginning to disintegrate. After 1746 it collapsed. The petty courts of the Highland chiefs dissolved; the tribal bards were discontinued; and the antiquaries moved in to collect the poems which were now ceasing to be recited or sung. The process had already begun before Macpherson inserted himself into it: clergymen like James Maclagan had begun to collect such poems; a few of them had been published; and we have seen that John Home had developed an interest in them. So the time was ripe for a more systematic collection and publication. But what the first Scottish collectors did not sufficiently realise (although Toland of course had stated it) was that Celtic Scotland was the outer fringe of Celtic Ireland; that the Gaelic ballads of Scotland, in general, were of Irish origin; and that the Ossianic ballads, in particular, were all originally Irish. Once again we see the results of the systematic falsification of early Scottish history, the insistence that the early Scots were a distinct nation, independent of Ireland. Macpherson himself had never been to Ireland; and although the scene of the poems, even in the form which he gave them, was throughout Irish, he claimed them as the literature of ancient Scotland.

That was his first falsification. But there was also a second. Macpherson claimed that he had found the whole epic in the Highlands and islands of Scotland. He never specified his sources, but he insisted that *Fingal*, as published by him, was a faithful and literal translation of a continuous poem of which the ballads then known, or afterwards to be discovered, were 'spurious pieces', corrupt and degenerate fragments, 'disgustful to true taste'.[9] He did indeed use genuine ballads, and by now – thanks to the research of late nineteenth-century and twentieth-century scholars – we know, as his contemporaries could not, precisely which ballads he used. But he used them as occasional raw materials for a spurious modern epic poem, and then declared that the genuine ancient poems were spurious and only the spurious modern poem was genuine. And this fraud he protected by refusing to discuss the evidence. In this way – as his intimate friend, the local minister Andrew Gallie, would afterwards state – he claimed the credit that is due to one 'who restores a work of merit to its original purity'.[10]

So much can be said for certain. But there still remain two interrelated mysteries. The first concerns the manufacture of this long continuous poem, described as an epic. The second is the psychology of Macpherson himself. However, it will be best to leave these two problems for the moment, and to return to the narrative of events: to the doubts which were raised about the authenticity of *Fingal*, and to the first explicit challenge. This challenge was made, not indeed by, but on behalf of the true proprietors of Ossian: the Irish.

The first champion of the Irish was Ferdinando Warner, a learned English clergyman who, in 1756/7, had published a two-volume work of ecclesiastical history. His researches on this subject had led him into Irish history, and he had conceived the idea of a complete history of Ireland, which he hoped to finance by a grant from the Irish Parliament. For this purpose he visited Dublin in 1761, and there studied the manuscript sources for early Irish history, which of course included much legendary matter. On his return to England, he found that *Fingal* had been published and was in every hand. He read it, and was astonished. Here were the legendary Irish heroes with whom he had become familiar, from widely separated centuries, mixed up together and placed in a Scottish context. In order to clear the way for his own Irish history, Warner decided to dispose of this fashionable nonsense. He therefore wrote a scholarly pamphlet refuting Macpherson's work and censuring him for having distorted the whole of early Irish history by his usurpation. He further rebuked Macpherson for his hectoring style and for his ignorant prejudices against 'the innocent antiquities of the poor Irish'.[11]

The impartial English clergyman was seconded by a number of Irishmen. In the same years, 1761/2, Edmund Burke happened to be

back in his native country, and on his return to London he told David
Hume 'that on the first publication of Macpherson's book, all the
Irish cried out, "we know all these poems, we always heard them from
our infancy"'. But he added that, when questioned, none of them
could quote 'the original of any one paragraph of the pretended
translation'.[12] In other words, they recognised the old names and the
occasional stories which lay behind the supposed epic, but not the
form into which it had been cast. Later, the Scotch Highlanders who
asserted the genuineness of *Fingal* would do the same.

Macpherson made one attempt to still these early doubts – or at
least to provide himself with an argument for later use against them.
In 1762 (according to his own later statement) he announced, in a
printed advertisement, that his original manuscripts were deposited
in the shop of his publisher, Mr Becket, in the Strand, and could be
inspected there by the curious. According to his own account,
nobody sought to inspect them, and he withdrew them. There is no
reason to doubt that Macpherson did make this offer, and he
certainly could have deposited the manuscripts which we know that
he possessed.[13] But it seems that he was not anxious for any of his
manuscripts to be inspected by anyone expert enough to judge them.
The announcement was somewhat inconspicuous; and there were of
course very few persons, if any, in London, who could have read them
critically. Only among Irish scholars could such critics be found; and
there was no question of inviting their comments.

Some of the ablest of these Irish scholars lived abroad on the continent of Europe – as the best Scottish scholars had done before 1707
– and they first learned of the newly discovered poems through
foreign publications. For Ossian had very quickly become known in
France. Three distinguished Frenchmen – the future statesman
Turgot, the founder of the *Encyclopaedia* Denis Diderot, and the most
successful translator of English literature, Jean-Baptiste Suard – had
published translations of the *Fragments* and of some of the poems
accompanying *Fingal*. These translations had aroused interest, but
also some doubts; and these doubts were made public in June 1763
when Terence Brady, an Irish physician in Brussels, published a letter
in the *Journal des Sçavans* claiming the poems for Ireland. Next year
an anonymous writer, who was probably an Irish priest living in

France, published a long series of articles showing that both the Scots and their Celtic poetry were originally Irish, and that Macpherson had falsified the early history of Scotland in order to credit the Scots with a romance which he himself had composed out of later Irish material.[14]

These Irish voices may have reinforced the scepticism of the literary men of London, but they had no effect at all on the settled faith of their colleagues in Edinburgh, who were now completely spellbound by the dogmatic rhetoric of their *Coryphaeus*, Professor Blair. Early in 1763 Blair published the substance of his lectures as a *Critical Dissertation on the Poems of Ossian*. The work was an uncritical panegyric. Then he came south to London to bask in his fame as the discoverer of the Celtic Homer. At first all went well. Wherever two or three Scotchmen were gathered together, the talk was of the great Scottish poet and his prophet Blair. However, one day Blair suffered a rude shock. It came when he was introduced to Dr Johnson, and the subject of Ossian was mischievously raised by one of those present. On this subject, Johnson's views were already known. From the beginning, he had strenuously denied the authenticity of the poems and, says Boswell, 'what was still more provoking to their admirers, maintained that they had no merit'. In an attempt to defend his own position, Blair rashly asked Johnson 'whether he thought any man of a modern age could have written such poems'. 'Yes, sir,' replied Johnson (who was unaware that Blair had written his *Dissertation*), 'many men, many women, and many children'.[15]

How well Johnson emerges from every literary controversy! Other critics doubted the authenticity of *Fingal* on historical or scholarly grounds, but they did not deny its merit. Walpole, Gray, Hume, all expressed admiration of the poetry even if they questioned its origin. All these men were imprisoned in the taste of their time. Only Johnson stood firmly outside and above it. He saw, from the start, that the poem not only lacked scholarly authority: it was also, as literature, worthless. 'The poem of Fingal', he said on another occasion, 'was a mere unconnected rhapsody, a tiresome repetition of the same images'; and to Sir Joshua Reynolds he remarked, 'Sir, a man could write such stuff for ever, if he would abandon his mind to it.'[16]

By the autumn of 1763, David Hume, on a visit to London, found scepticism, in literary circles, almost universal, and he decided that the problem must be faced: otherwise not only the Scots, already unpopular owing to the rule of Bute, but their most enlightened representatives, the literati of Edinburgh, might find themselves ridiculous. So he wrote firmly to Blair. After polite praise of Blair's *Dissertation,* he gently opened the matter. *Fingal,* he wrote, was now generally considered by competent judges in London to be a forgery and, unless its authenticity could be established, it was doomed to fall into contempt and oblivion, from which its beauties, such as they were, could not save it. This being so, it was essential that Blair, as its principal champion, take steps to establish its true origin. This general English scepticism, said Hume, was increased by 'the absurd pride and caprice of Macpherson himself, who scorns, as he pretends, to satisfy anybody that doubts his veracity'; but it was justified by certain real difficulties which had converted Hume himself. In particular 'the refined manners' ascribed to the ancient Caledonians were implausible, 'notwithstanding all the art with which you have endeavoured to throw a varnish on that circumstance'. And the preservation of so long a poem by oral tradition alone over a course of fourteen centuries was so extraordinary as to require 'the strongest reasons to make us believe it'. Hume therefore urged Blair, 'in the name of all the men of letters of this and, I may say, of all other centuries, to establish this capital point, and to give us proof that these poems are, I do not say so ancient as the age of Severus, but that they were not forged within these five years by James Macpherson'. 'These proofs', he insisted, 'must not be arguments but testimonies. People's ears are fortified against the former; the latter may yet find their way, before the poems are consigned to total oblivion.' In particular, Hume urged Blair to establish the truth of Macpherson's claim to have found part of *Fingal* in an ancient manuscript which he had obtained from Clanranald. 'Get that fact ascertained by more than one person of credit; let those persons be acquainted with the Gaelic; let them compare the original and the translation; and let them testify the fidelity of the latter.' He also urged Blair to write to the Highland clergy and gentry for evidence not merely that Ossianic ballads were recited but that these ballads were indeed demonstrably the originals of Macpherson's translation.[17]

Thus challenged, Blair consented; and Hume wrote to express his satisfaction. 'You need expect no assistance from Macpherson', he wrote, 'who flew into a passion when I told him of the letter I had wrote to you. But you must not mind so strange and heteroclite a mortal, than whom I have scarce ever known a man more perverse and unamiable'. In any case, Macpherson was now slipping out of the picture. Having established himself by means of Ossian, he was now seeking prosperity through a public career. He was preparing to go to America, as secretary to the new British governor of Florida; 'and I would advise him', added Hume, 'to travel among the Chickisaws or Cherokees, in order to tame him and civilise him'.[18]

Blair certainly got no assistance from Macpherson, who told him haughtily that he would make no concessions to 'public distrust of his veracity';[19] but Blair duly sent a questionnaire to the clergy and gentry who had assisted Macpherson during his expedition into the Highlands and islands. The gist of their replies was similar. Yes, they said, Ossianic ballads were undoubtedly sung and recited in the Highlands, and they remembered, or thought that they remembered (as the Irish had done), that they had heard all this before. Yes, Macpherson had certainly obtained some manuscripts from Clanranald – the only manuscripts known to exist in 'these islands' – and had been in touch with Clanranald's bard, MacMhuirich. But beyond that it was impossible to go. Only Macpherson himself knew exactly what material he had obtained; and if he refused to co-operate there was little hope of satisfaction. So far, so good. Blair had received factual answers to factual questions. But mixed with this dry testimony, there was also a note of national triumph. The Highlanders, having suddenly discovered that the vain, idle, lying ballads of their worthless mercenary *senachies* were now recognised as a great national epic, were not going to underprice them. So, instead of apologising for these rude rhymes, they extolled them to the skies. These poems, they now said, were works of the highest genius. No translation could do justice to the beauty of the original Gaelic poetry, whose sublimity could but feebly shine through the dull medium of Macpherson's prose. 'The glory arising to our country and ancestors from these noble monuments of genius', wrote the Rev. John Macpherson, James Macpherson's host at Sleat, must inevitably arouse the envy of the English who, having nothing to compare with them, would naturally pretend that they were spurious; but such malicious objections should be ignored: 'Ossian was the Homer of the ancient Highlanders' and the genuineness of his namesake's translation 'seems to be abundantly probable'. Another clergyman mildly reproved Blair for his 'good natured indulgence' to the 'unreasonable prejudices' of the English in raising the matter at all; such absurd cavils really did not deserve notice. Another (following Macpherson) dismissed any discrepancy between the familiar ballads and the new epic by rejecting the former as 'Irish imitations of the works of Ossian'; and there was general agreement to defend what the Rev. John Macpherson described as 'a cause in which Dr Blair, Mr Macpherson and, let me add, I myself, are so deeply interested, especially as it is a national one'.[20]

Among these vague and general replies, there was, however, one that was perfectly concrete. It came from James Macpherson's friend and travelling companion, Lachlan Macpherson, the laird of Strathmashie. Strathmashie described how he had assisted Macpherson in collecting the poems, and had 'taken down from oral tradition, and transcribed from old manuscripts, by far the greatest part of those pieces he has published'. Some of the manuscripts which he had seen in Macpherson's hands were of great antiquity: one, in particular, was written as far back as 1410. Since the publication, he added, 'I have carefully compared the translation with the copies of the originals in my hands, and find it amazingly literal, even in such a degree as to preserve, in some measure, the cadence of the Gaelic versification.' Since later scholarship has identified almost all the authentic manuscripts actually used by Macpherson, and has collected a vast mass of Ossianic poetry from oral recitation, in all of which there is barely a single line that is exactly reproduced in Macpherson's Ossian, this concrete statement seems, at first sight, a palpable lie. However, let us not leap to conclusions: we shall return, in due course, to this important document. Like the other Highlanders, Strathmashie ended by thanking Dr Blair for the pains he had taken 'to illustrate the beauties and establish the reputation of the poems of Ossian, which do so much honour to the ancient genius of our country'.[21]

Unfortunately, in his enquiry, Blair seems not to have followed Hume's most precise instruction: to check the history and content of the manuscript which Macpherson had received from Clanranald. Had this been done, much future confusion might have been avoided. But perhaps Blair, by now, sought reassurance rather than truth. Certainly he was easily reassured. The replies of Macpherson's friends were, he declared, 'strong and irrefragable evidence' of the authenticity of the poems.[22] Hume was less easily satisfied. As he afterwards put it in conversation with Boswell, he would not now believe that *Fingal* was an ancient poem 'though fifty bare-arsed Highlanders' should swear to it.[23] From now on, this former believer was convinced that Macpherson had himself forged the poems.

Meanwhile, Macpherson, before leaving for Florida, sought to improve his fame and income by publishing another volume of Gaelic poetry. This consisted of another epic poem, *Temora*, in eight books – the 'second epic' of which he had previously published a fragment – and five short poems. The new volume was dedicated, in a flamboyant style, to Bute, who had paid the whole cost of publication. This time Macpherson did not claim to have carried out any further study in the field: the Gaelic text, he said, had come to him through the post to London.[24] Nor has modern research discovered any Gaelic ballads which correspond, even loosely, with any part of the new work beyond the first book.[25] Only the passage already published with *Fingal* has any authentic base. It seems that success had made Macpherson careless: Gaelic epics were now easy money to him and he no longer took trouble over them. Even the Edinburgh literati were momentarily shaken by *Temora*. But not for long. They soon recovered their nerve, and were not amused when David Hume teased them for their touching but absurd loyalty to the Celtic Homer.[26]

In 1765, while Macpherson was still in America (though he had deserted the governor of Florida after a quarrel), his supporters in Scotland struck two further blows on his behalf against the 'malevolence' and 'unreasonable prejudice' of his English and Irish critics. The first of these blows was struck by Blair. Confirmed in his views by the answers to his questionnaire, Blair now wrote an 'Appendix' to his *Dissertation*, and this 'Appendix' was printed in a new edition of the works of Ossian containing *Fingal, Temora* and the shorter poems. In it Blair explained that when he wrote his *Dissertation* he had no reason to suppose that anyone would doubt the genuineness or the antiquity of the poems, for 'in Scotland their authenticity was never called in question'. Blair himself could vouch for Macpherson, who was incapable of deceit. However, 'in England, it seems, an opinion has prevailed with some that an imposture has been carried on', and therefore he had consulted a number of Highland gentry and clergy who all swore that the works were genuine – although, he added, this was surely unnecessary 'where the consenting silence of a whole country was, to every unprejudiced person, the strongest proof'.[27]

'. . . The consenting silence of a whole country . . . the strongest proof'. The mind boggles at such a statement and its implications: a charter for unreasoning bigotry, national prejudice, or collusive guilt. But what is most astonishing is not the statement itself, but the identity of the man who made it. For it shows that it was not merely the 'bare-arsed Highlanders' who, as Sir Walter Scott would put it, 'had adopted the poems of Ossian as an article of national faith' more unquestionable than Scripture.[28] Had that been the case, the result would have been very different. By themselves, the Highlanders, as throughout history, would have been ineffective: after the first wild charge, they would have scattered and disappeared. But Blair gave to the disorganised, unconvincing Highlanders, in this intellectual matter, that necessary foreign leadership which the Young Chevalier had given them, in politics, a generation earlier. Regius Professor in what was then the most distinguished university in Britain, he brought with him the whole academic establishment of Edinburgh. Just as, two centuries before, it was Buchanan the cosmopolitan, modern, humanist scholar, the friend of Continental Reformers, the tutor of his own king, the representative, to foreigners, of the Scottish Renaissance, who had used his authority to validate the already exploded political mythology of the ancient constitution of Scotland, so now it was the Edinburgh literati, the makers of the new 'improved', 'enlightened' Scotland of the eighteenth century who, by their solid support and propaganda, made effective the myth of the ancient Scottish literature.

Blair was delighted with his own Appendix. Since it had been so successful among the believers in Scotland, he expected equal success among the unbelievers of England. He even boasted that, by it, he had converted 'that barbarian Sam. Johnson'.[29] In this he was mistaken; but he did at least score one temporary success. This was with Thomas Percy, who, in the autumn of 1765, having just published his *Reliques of Ancient English Poetry*, paid a visit to Edinburgh. Percy had originally been excited by Ossian, but by now he had come to share the general English scepticism. Blair therefore seized the opportunity of his visit to recover him for the faith. He introduced him to Adam Ferguson; and Ferguson (according to Percy) called in one of his own students as an expert witness. The student was, like Ferguson, a Gaelic speaker; and he sang to Percy a Gaelic ballad which, as translated by him, bore a convincing resemblance to a passage in *Fingal*. Percy was convinced by this demonstration; and in the second edition of his *Reliques*, published two years later, he declared his conversion. Unfortunately the conversion did not last long: Percy afterwards changed his mind again, and was persuaded that, in Edinburgh, he had been the victim of an imposture. Sixteen years later, having been forced into public controversy on the subject, he recalled the episode and was mortified to find that Blair and Ferguson both obstinately refused to remember it. The student who had been the essential actor in it was Ferguson's favourite pupil, a young man who lived in his house, whom he treated as his son, and with whom he would remain on the closest terms for the rest of his life. His name was John Macpherson, and he was the son of the Rev. John Macpherson, minister of Sleat.[30] He was also a man who would play a significant part in the later story.

The minister of Sleat also entered the battle himself. In 1763 to 1765 he took up his pen and wrote *Critical Dissertations on the Origin and Antiquities of the Caledonians*. The main purpose of this work seems to be to provide an appropriate historical background to the epic poems of Ossian and to explain away certain inconvenient objections. According to the minister, Scotland was the original centre of Celtic civilisation in Britain; it was from Scotland that Ireland had been peopled; and it was Scotland which, in its otherwise undocumented heroic age, in the third century AD, had produced the poems of Ossian. Unfortunately, explained the minister, in the seventh and eighth centuries, Scotland fell behind in civilisation, and so 'the *senachies* and *fileas* of Ireland', exploiting the temporary weakness of the Scots, unscrupulously filched their literature, falsified their history, and 'assumed to themselves the dignity of being the mother-nation'. Hence the present Anglo-Irish conspiracy to deny to the Scots their national antiquities.

Having thus put the Irish in their place, the minister also took the opportunity to deal with other objections which had been raised against the authenticity of *Fingal*. Why, it had been asked, was there no reference to religion in Ossian? Because, came the authoritative reply, the bards 'sung merely mortal subjects', religion being reserved to 'the more dignified race of *Faids*'. For this reason even Ossian, 'though one of the first men of the state', could not – 'such were the prejudices of those times' – breach that monopoly. That Ossian was Caledonian, not Irish, was proved by the 'decisive' argument of the language in which he wrote his poem. That such a poem could have been transmitted orally over fifteen centuries was proved by the fact that it had been so transmitted. In other words, the genuineness of the poem was assumed and used to destroy all objections to the genuineness of the poem. Finally, the silence of James Macpherson himself was adequately explained. If the learned editor of Ossian has not deigned to answer these and other objections, explained the minister, that is because such trivial arguments are beneath him: 'when objections worthy of his notice are raised, he will certainly pay them all due regard'. Meanwhile, if 'some drawcansir', some blustering braggart, should arise to repeat the claims of Ireland, let him beware! The author has a knock-out answer in the form of a collection of manuscript notes, which, however, he is holding in reserve. 'These notes', he adds in a footnote, 'are now in the possession of Mr Macpherson of Strathmashie in the county of Inverness: a very ingenious and learned gentleman who has made the antiquities of Ireland his particular study'.[31]

In all this, a close parallel can be observed with James Macpherson's 'Dissertation' prefixed to *Fingal*: indeed, the very language is often the same, and it is tempting to suspect shamelessly deliberate collusion between the two authors, each of whom flattered the other. Certainly their work was complementary. The minister's aim was to rewrite the history of Scotland in order to accommodate in it the heroic age of Ossian, and to destroy the impertinent claims of the Irish both to historical priority and to the bard. Having done this, he would then use Ossian's epic as a source for Scottish history, and Scottish history as a confirmation of Ossian's epic. This plan was perhaps concerted between the minister and James Macpherson when they were together in Skye: for James Macpherson, we are told, had been announcing the forthcoming publication of the minister's book, in 'a strain of high commendation' 'some years before its appearance',[32] and the minister had evidently sent material to James Macpherson which was afterwards needed for his own book.[33]

The minister of Sleat died in 1765, before he could publish his *Critical Dissertations*; but it was sent to the press after his death by his son, John Macpherson: the same young man who, two years earlier, had been produced to convert Thomas Percy. Thus once again, the Macpherson clan rallied around their most famous member, in defence of the epic in which they were all now deeply interested. Particularly interesting is the note about Strathmashie, who appears once again as the *intellectus agens* of the tribe in its literary activity. Unfortunately, by the time the minister's book was published, it was too late to appeal for confirmation to Strathmashie. He had died, after a long illness, in August 1767. But we shall return to him later.

Objections worthy of James Macpherson's notice would never be made. On his return from America in 1766, he was greeted by a formidable critique from another Irish scholar, Charles O'Conor of Belangare, known already as a considerable antiquary from his *Dissertations on the History of Ireland* published thirteen years earlier. O'Conor now reissued those *Dissertations* in an improved edition with substantial alterations. His new preface proclaimed the level at which he was working. He thanked Samuel Johnson for encouragement, Edmund Burke for inspiration, Ferdinando Warner for scholarly guidance, and Thomas Leland, librarian of Trinity College Dublin, for his efforts to bring more of the original sources of Irish history and literature into the public domain. At the end of the book O'Conor added a sixty-page appendix, exposing Macpherson's Ossianic pretensions. O'Conor was amused by the audacity of

Macpherson's 'blast from the epic trump', which was obviously the product of a lively imagination; he was less amused by the petulance and aggression towards other writers displayed, especially, in the dissertation defending the almost indefensible *Temora* of 1763. As poetry, O'Conor allowed Macpherson's 'modern romance' some real merit; 'historical merit it has none'. *The Poems of Ossian* were packed with chronological absurdities, indeed 'conscious untruths'; and they revealed a lamentable ignorance of the geography of Ireland, which was their alleged setting. The whole story was founded on 'nightmare assumptions and ricketty etymologies'. What were modern scholars to make of a man who asserted, contrary to all the surviving documentary evidence, that the Gaels were the pre-historic people of northern Britain – their name indicating that they had originated in Gaul; that the Romans had called that part of the island Caledonia through slightly mispronouncing the first sound of their name; that the Picts and the Scots had been the same people, sharing the same language – Bede, who had said something quite different, being dismissed as a 'pious and credulous writer'; and that all of this could be proved by the oral tradition of a society which had allegedly remained 'pure and unmixed' in the Highlands and islands of Scotland throughout almost two millennia? So incredulous was O'Conor at the scale of the forgery that at one point he felt inspired to imitation. He invented a comic dialogue between the bold, confident Macpherson and the anxious, protesting Ossian: in which Macpherson urged Ossian on to make it all up, blithely assuring him that no one would notice! After all was said and done, said O'Conor, Macpherson's 'epics' would just have been 'an innocent fraud' and no one would have minded, if only the author had not tried to make everyone take them seriously as antiques.[34]

This was a weighty and well-aimed challenge. Macpherson, however, ignored it. He only condescended, in a book published five years later, to sneer in a footnote at O'Conor as a recent purveyor of 'some wild, incoherent tales concerning the ancient Irish', and to dismiss O'Conor's etymological objections as mere 'subterfuges'.[35] Nor would he ever again deign to discuss the Ossianic controversy in print. He left the defence of his work entirely to others: to Blair in Edinburgh; to the gentry and the ministers of the Highlands, to whom its authenticity was now a matter of faith; and, in London, to a group of immigrant Highlanders whom he could now afford to patronise and command. For by now Macpherson was a man of means and power. *Fingal* had made him. It had brought him to the notice of the prime minister and had been the ladder by which he had climbed to the public stage, where we shall shortly follow him. Now he was established at a far higher level, and he could afford to kick it down.

In the remaining thirty-one years of his life James Macpherson would touch in public only indirectly on the old subject. In 1771 he published an *Introduction to the History of Great Britain and Ireland*, which can be seen as a companion work to that of the minister of Sleat – of which, indeed, it is an extension. Its purpose was, once again – as an English antiquary would write – to check the advance of critical history in Scotland, to discredit the Irish origin of the Scots, and to make Scotland 'the mother-nation' of Ireland.[36] This meant a repudiation of the work of Innes. Macpherson condescended to allow some merit to 'the ingenious father Innes' for his demolition of earlier legends; but Innes, he wrote, being ignorant of Gaelic, 'fell into unavoidable mistakes'. Fortunately he had been corrected by 'a learned clergyman in one of the Scottish isles', whom it would be insufficient praise to describe as the greatest of Scottish antiquaries, and who had lately reduced 'into form and precision the antiquities which Innes had left in confusion and disorder'. This learned clergyman was named in a footnote. Needless to say, he was 'Dr John Macpherson, minister of Sleat in the Isle of Skye'. In all this new work, James Macpherson was careful not to use Ossian as a historical source. As he explained, there was no need to use him, for Macpherson's own historical reconstruction was an identical account. The 'perfect agreement' between Ossian and the 'system we have established' is, said Macpherson, the agreement of independent sources, each proving the other right.[37] A contemporary critic had some reason to write that Macpherson's portentous *Introduction* 'was published on purpose to support the imposture of Fingal'.[38]

Two years later, with the encouragement of his constant patron Adam Ferguson, Macpherson published a translation of Homer's *Iliad* into the same biblical prose which had made the fortune of

Ossian. No doubt the purpose was, at least in part, to show the similarities of the two ancient epics. Unfortunately the device which had been so successful with the Celtic Homer failed with his Greek predecessor. The translation was received with almost universal derision. The most that can be said of it is that it proved his point that Homer, at least in Macpherson's translation, was a worse poet than Ossian. After that fiasco, Macpherson gave up both poetry and Scottish history. From now on, he had other, and bigger, fish to fry. These fish were not the salmon of his native lochs and streams but the rich exotic fish of the Indian Ocean, to which we must now turn; for it provides the essential context of the second stage in the history of Ossian.

For in 1766, the year of his return from America, Macpherson began a new life. Outwardly it was unconnected with his previous career as the discoverer of Ossian; but in fact, at a deeper, more secret level, it was a continuation of that career; and at the end the two strands of his life, never entirely separated, would come together again in an uncomfortable manner. The essential partner in this second life, who was as vital to its success as Blair had been before, was our young friend John Macpherson, now twenty-one years old and fresh from Edinburgh University. James Macpherson was already indebted to him and to his father for their support over Ossian; and from now on they were (as James himself would put it) 'united in the strictest friendship'. It was an alliance of interest, which would make the fortune not only of the two principals, but also – for a time – of a whole clan of hungry Macphersons.

Like James Macpherson, John Macpherson was tall, strong and handsome. Like him, he had been (before going to Edinburgh) at King's College, Aberdeen. Like him, he was a poet and an accomplished classical scholar. But in other respects these two allies were very different. Whereas James was morose and unpleasing in society, graceless in movement and behaviour, proud and reserved in speech,[39] John was gay and affable, lively and convivial, a natural courtier and diplomat. Nathaniel Wraxall, the MP and political commentator, who knew John Macpherson well in later life, would wax lyrical in praise of this brilliant social and diplomatic virtuoso.

Though ambition was 'the master spring of all his actions', says Wraxall, he was infinitely patient, of unruffled temper and philosophic mind; his hospitality was liberal; he was an agile dancer who 'could perform a *strathspey* at seventy almost like a youth of eighteen'; and he would delight the company by singing French and Italian songs or Highland ballads.[40] We have already encountered him as a student in Edinburgh, singing a Gaelic ballad for Thomas Percy during the latter's visit to the house of Adam Ferguson. John Macpherson owed as much to Adam Ferguson as did James Macpherson. For just as Ferguson had introduced James to John Home, and thus made possible the marvellous success of Ossian, so he appointed his pupil John Macpherson to teach the two younger sons of the Earl of Warwick, who had been sent to Edinburgh to be under his care: a connection which proved very valuable afterwards.

Wraxall was a personal friend and admirer of John Macpherson, and mentioned only his virtues. Those who observed him more critically regarded him as devious and self-seeking. But all agreed that he was a man of infinite address, eloquent in speech, and a great flatterer. 'Your name', Warren Hastings would write to his wife on one occasion 'gently glided from the tongue of the Highland snake'; and he referred at another time to that tongue which 'drops honey upon this as upon every occasion' – but honey, it is clear, which was mixed with poison.[41] Another contemporary commentator, unsure how to read John Macpherson's real intentions beneath his genial flattery of everyone, described his slow and soothing words as falling from his tongue 'like the drops from the laudanum bottle, and with the same effect'.[42]

Such was the man who, from 1766 onwards, replaced Blair as the essential ally in James Macpherson's career. The first result of their collaboration was the publication in 1768 of the Rev. John Macpherson's Caledonian History, so vital to the vindication of the authenticity of Ossian. But then the two blood-brethren moved on to what would prove to be a very different and even more lucrative field of investment. This was the new empire which Clive had won for Britain in India.

The young John Macpherson had already discovered India.[43] In March 1767 he had obtained a passage, nominally as purser, on an

East Indiaman commanded by his uncle. The ship was bound for China, but Macpherson dropped off at Madras. There he found his way to the Nawab of Arcot, a prince of vast wealth but deeply in debt to the East India Company, and at loggerheads both with it and with another local prince, the Raja of Tanjore. Macpherson, who was particularly adept at ingratiating himself with princes, soon won the Nawab's confidence. According to his admirer Wraxall, he impressed the Nawab by 'the elevation of his sentiments, his apparent superiority to money, and the conciliation of his manners'. A less partial observer says that it was by showing the Nawab 'some electrical experiments and the phenomena of the magic lanthorn, sights very extraordinary to Asiaticks'.[44] At all events the Nawab gave him money and jewels and entrusted him with a letter to be delivered personally to the Earl of Chatham, then prime minister. Macpherson thereupon left his uncle's ship, which sailed on to China without him, and returned to England to throw himself into the backstairs politics of Westminster. On arrival, he found that Chatham was no longer prime minister; but with the help of the father of his two pupils, 'my patron and friend the Earl of Warwick', he was received and trusted by the new prime minister, the Duke of Grafton. Meanwhile James Macpherson, already established in the corridors of power by the favour of Lord Bute, and known as a man of letters through *Fingal*, was eager to help and be helped by his young friend.

During 1768 and 1769 the two Macphersons served the Duke of Grafton's government as hack-writers against its most formidable enemies, 'Junius' and John Wilkes. They wrote, under varying names, a series of pamphlets, poems and satires. In their own view, they were marvellously successful. 'I cannot but be a little vain', John Macpherson wrote to his cousin the Rev. Martin Macpherson, minister of Golspie in Sutherland. 'Could you imagine that during all the political fire and action in this seat of mighty Empire, two Macphersons have been the only pillars of government? ... Under about forty different signatures, Fingal and your friend have fought and routed the seditious warriors in our political writings here.' The government recognised its debt. James Macpherson was rewarded with a pension of £300 a year (he already had a pension of £500 a year for life out of the revenues of Florida) and John with the post of

Writer in the East India Company at Madras. In 1770 John returned to Madras and, once again, set out to cultivate his local patron, the Nawab of Arcot.

From now on the two Macphersons were deeply involved in East Indian affairs. John in India pushed his own fortunes and those of a group of Highlanders, mostly kinsmen, whom James, in London, found means to send out. James in turn protected his rear, invested his money, wrote pamphlets in his interest, and cultivated successive governments. Soon John was a member of the Nawab's Durbar and aimed to replace the governor of Madras: 'I would give you £10,000 sterling', he wrote to James, 'if you would bring this matter round'. A regular supply of diamonds now passed from the Nawab to government officials in England. In 1775 James was appointed agent of the Nawab in London with a salary of 15,000 pagodas a year plus expenses. In India, John struck up an alliance with the governor of Bengal, Warren Hastings: but without commitment, for James in London warned him that Hastings was unlikely to survive the political intrigues at home: 'you look after yourself. Do not tie yourself to Hastings. When he comes home he will fall into obscurity like his predecessors: the wretch is altogether without significance'. This passage, like all the more delicate passages in the correspondence of the two Macphersons, was written in Gaelic, which they used as a secret code between themselves. Little did Hastings know, when he forwarded the letters of James to John, what dynamite lay among 'the arcana in a Celtic strongbox of which you have the key'.[45]

In 1776 John Macpherson overplayed his hand and was summarily dismissed by the governor of Madras. His past was raked up. He was accused of treachery, of nightly visits to the Nawab to undermine the Company; and compromising documents were exhibited against him. But he was not dismayed. He returned to England with secret instructions from the Nawab, bought a seat in Parliament, and set out to repair his fortunes by supporting Lord North. In this he was successful; and in 1780 he judged that it was safe to return to India. But first it was necessary to protect his rear. For this purpose James Macpherson had also cultivated Lord North: he was described by John Macpherson as 'Lord

North's best and most confidential literary friend'.[46] Already an experienced journalist, James was, by 1775, running a London evening newspaper in conjunction with another Scotsman, Robert Macfarlane.[47] Shortly thereafter, he had begun to draw from the Treasury an annual salary of £600 or £800 to manage the newspapers of the capital in the government's interest: using threats or inducements to control the flow of news.[48] He too now bought a seat in Parliament. It was the Cornish rotten borough of Camelford and cost him £4,000. James now described himself openly as 'Minister Plenipotentary of His Highness the Nabob of the Carnatic to the Court of St James'. With his rear thus secured, John Macpherson returned to India in the winter of 1781/2. He had been appointed by Lord North, in defiance of opposition, a member of the Council in Calcutta. From that powerful position he could now intrigue to replace, not the governor of Madras, but the governor-general of India, Warren Hastings.

Throughout these years, the two Macphersons, as true Highlanders, had been organising and maintaining a regular Macpherson mafia. James organised the London end. There he held court among a group of Highlanders who ran errands for him, fought his backstairs battles, and lived on his bounty. They would act as his janissaries in the battles of Grub Street. Meanwhile, impoverished kinsmen from the valleys of Badenoch flocked out to India with peremptory recommendations from him. Among these adventurers were two sons of the late laird of Strathmashie, two illegitimate sons, a nephew and two cousins of James Macpherson himself, and the brother of the Rev. Andrew Gallie, the third party in those gatherings at Ruthven from which the text of *Fingal* had emerged. Once in India, John Macpherson saw to it that they did not starve; and in London, James Macpherson looked after their financial and political interests, and was paid liberally for his protection. Huge presents of money – sometimes as much as £10,000 and £11,250 'to consider as your own property for ever' – were regularly sent to him by those whom he described as his 'eastern friends'; and it was they who paid his election expenses: for it was most important, they agreed, that he be in Parliament 'to continue your long and unwearied endeavours to serve your friends'. In return, James Macpherson watched the political barometer at home, advised them on tactics, and sought to guarantee them against the consequences of sudden changes in the volatile climate of Westminster.

One such change – a veritable revolution – occurred soon after John Macpherson's return to India with the fall of Lord North in 1782. At first, even James Macpherson was shaken. He sent the news to John by a special overland express: 'the whole power of the state has fallen into the hands of our political enemies ... the removal of you all will be the least of their vengeance'.[49] But the great gift of James Macpherson was his sangfroid. As Warren Hastings himself wrote, 'he is the only man in England who possesses a cool and prescient mind. All the rest, great and small, wise as well as foolish, despond on every sudden reverse of fortune and presume on a ray of prosperity'.[50] Very soon James Macpherson was to show this gift, and reassure his 'eastern friends'. His own power, he was now sure, was above the reach of such accidents. 'New men,' he wrote to one of his cousins, 'it is positively said, will be sent to govern you, to put an end to *venality* and *corruption*'. But there was no cause for fear: he had given firm instructions to 'my friends in power there' – that is, to John Macpherson – 'urging the necessity of placing you all in such situations as will enable you to serve your friends as well as yourselves. I have not the least doubt but immediate attention will be paid to my request. ... Should you once get into situations, I shall always have sufficient influence here to preserve to you those situations'. His friends were naturally delighted and coughed up liberally: recent changes, they wrote tactfully, 'must have fallen heavily upon your sporran'. The translator acknowledged these gifts gracefully: 'I am highly pleased that the conduct of my dear friend Mr John Macpherson has so well answered your as well as my expectations. I knew him always to be a most noble fellow and that his friendship for me would be sensibly felt by my relations. I trust that, though the complexion of the times is gloomy, he will still have a long time in India to serve himself and his friends'.

Mr John Macpherson did not fail either himself or his friends. The revolution of 1782/3 left them all unscathed; and now they set out to capture the highest prize of all: the governor-generalship of India.

That meant, first of all, the removal of the current governor-general, Warren Hastings. James Macpherson, in London, was confident that it could be achieved. He was already in the habit of giving orders to Hastings – including lists of 'friends' to be promoted, such as Allan and John Macpherson, 'who are among my nearest relations' and whose success (he wrote) was one of his chief reasons for taking up Indian affairs.[51] Now, he moved closer in to the kill. In February 1783 he wrote to John that 'if you were against him, you might possibly be in the Chair in India'. 'Hastings is jealous', he wrote three months later, 'because it was I who saved India'; and a little later, 'I know that you wish the big governor to hand the business over to you. He should do that if he had any honour'. 'The whole world here knows that he would fall if my hand did not support him'. Early in 1784, when yet another revolution had taken place at Westminster, James Macpherson's sangfroid did not desert him. 'Pitt will keep you in your place', he wrote to John, 'and I will set you on a good footing with anyone who goes out'. Finally, at the right moment, he struck. In 1785 John Macpherson and his allies on the Supreme Council brought Hastings down; and who should succeed him but John Macpherson, now Sir John Macpherson, baronet? At this event there was jubilation among the friends, and a comfortable replenishment of James Macpherson's sporran.

In some of his friendly letters to Hastings, John Macpherson had reproached him for not building up a party through patronage, for not seeking to improve his fortune; and he dwelt on the folly of coming home *poor*.[52] Macpherson had no intention of making the same mistakes. His own rule in India, according to his more virtuous successor, Lord Cornwallis, was 'a system of the dirtiest jobbing' and 'peculation', sustained by 'duplicity' and by 'subtle and perse-vering intrigue'.[53] Unfortunately for Macpherson, it did not last long. After only twenty months he was recalled – much to his surprise and dissatisfaction. His 'friends' were very dissatisfied too: they main-tained that he had a right to a tenure of five years. At least he should be given the reversion of the governorship after Lord Cornwallis, and should resume his place on the Supreme Council . . .. But they pressed in vain. The government was determined that Macpherson should not stay in India in any capacity. So he returned to England

and was re-elected to his old seat in Parliament. Unfortunately, here too his tenure was brief. He was promptly unseated for bribery. After that he had fewer friends.

In the general debacle of the Macpherson mafia there were many casualties; but one man at least survived intact. In 1783, at the height of its success, James Macpherson went into partnership with an old and particular friend, Sir Samuel Hannay, a Scotch merchant in London. The purpose of the partnership was to invest the substantial sums which the 'eastern friends' were now accumulating in India, and James Macpherson duly urged them to take advantage of this opportunity, dwelling on the independent fortune, perfect honesty, and concentrated industry of his new partner. Unluckily, Sir Samuel did not quite live up to the prospectus; and in 1788 Macpherson decided, in view (as he said) of his other engagements and avocations, to slip out of the association. So he passed on his share of the business to one of his 'eastern friends' who, from poverty, had risen to affluence in India. This was his cousin, Colonel Allan Macpherson, who, after the fall of Sir John, was returning from India to set up as a laird in Scotland. It was time, he felt, to move from the hazards of Indian politics to the safe dignity of a well-endowed estate in his home country.

Colonel Allan Macpherson had already invested some of his gains in the estate of Blairgowrie, Perthshire, which he had bought from James Macpherson's former pupil, Thomas Graham of Balgowan; and he was now planning, with James Macpherson's aid, to add to it the even more desirable estate of Raitts in Kingussie. This was an old Mackintosh property, whose last owner had fled, pursued by criminal charges, to America; and Allan Macpherson had long eyed it from India, preferring it (as he wrote) 'to every spot in that country'. He had substantial funds in London and the partnership with Sir Samuel Hannay would ensure that they were profitably invested. Unluckily, this last venture proved ill-timed. For only two years later Sir Samuel died, and it was revealed that he was £150,000 in debt, and his firm bankrupt. The colonel was suddenly ruined; and although he contrived to cling to his estate of Blairgowrie, now deeply mortgaged, he had to surrender all his other acquisitions. The purchaser was his cousin James who, as the original agent in the transfer, knew their value, and who, by his timely escape from the bankrupt firm, was happily solvent.

The crash of the firm of Hannay and Macpherson in these circumstances was very embarrassing to James Macpherson. Harsh things were said about him – that he had saved himself by throwing his friends into the gap; 'that his character is blasted for ever and his credit in the City totally ruined'. Perhaps this was unfair: his nephew, who was ruined too, thought it unfair. But James evidently decided, at this time, to leave London and retire to the fine estate which this accident had brought into his hands. In Badenoch at least he would be someone: a Macpherson who had returned from the fray with glory and spoil.

In his youth, how he had longed to escape from that valley! Then, of course, he had been poor. But now he could return to it in style, and enjoy it; for he was rich. He was also popular. For now Duncan Macpherson of Cluny, chief of clan Chattan, heir to the proscribed fugitive of 1746, was back in the valley, welcomed by his kinsmen as Charles II had been welcomed by his subjects in 1660; and James Macpherson was the General Monck of that restoration: for he had used his influence with government to achieve it. He had acted as Cluny's agent in the long process, not only to ensure that the chief was restored, but also that the rival claims of the Mackintoshes to headship of the clan were defeated. Naturally, he had been paid a price. With that, and the estates of Raitts, Phoness and Etterick, and Inverhaven, now surrendered by the suddenly impoverished Colonel Allan Macpherson, and Banchor, bought from another branch of the Macphersons, he had a substantial landed property. All that he needed to complete it was a substantial house. So while his chief was building his enchanting modern 'castle' of Cluny, a few miles up the river, the translator of Ossian hired the most fashionable architect of the age, Robert Adam, to build him a solid but prosaic Georgian mansion which he named, unimaginatively, Belleville.[54] There he lived as a laird, a local worthy who had brought fame to that distant valley: 'a fine specimen', as the historian of Inverness-shire describes him, 'of the generous, chivalrous Highlander'.[55] There, in 1796, he died. But he was not buried there. By his will he left £500 to build a monument to himself on his estate; but he directed that his body should be taken to London and buried, among the poets of England, in Westminster Abbey.

And indeed why not? For it was as the poet of Ossian, not as the laird of Belleville, that he would earn immortality; and in spite of his obstinate silence, he must have known it. During those last thirty years, while Macpherson had been prospering in backstairs politics, his creature Ossian had been making his spectacular conquest of Europe. Nothing that his critics could do or say could arrest that triumphal progress. The almost universal scepticism of English scholars, the indignation of the Irish, the ridicule of the aged Voltaire – the last, unavailing enemy of the new romanticism[56] – all were swept aside. The 'works' of Ossian were translated into almost every European language. In Italy their translator, the learned abbé Cesarotti, who regarded Ossian as 'the greatest poetical genius of all time', would form a circle of Ossianic adepts: young disciples whom he would call Oscar and Malvina, reserving for himself the name of Ossian.[57] In Germany they would be seized upon by Herder, translated by Klopstock, cited as the equal of Shakespeare by the young Goethe. 'The Scotchman Ossian is greater than the Ionian Homer', declared J.H. Voss, the German translator of Homer. In Switzerland, Madame de Staël would declare that there were two streams of poetry in Europe: one in the south, flowing from Homer, the other in the north, whose source was Ossian. In France the fortunes of the poems would be even more spectacular, for they would be the favourite reading of Napoleon, who would read them on his return from Egypt and on his last journey to St Helena. Napoleon's Marshal Bernadotte would carry them to Sweden and, in homage to Ossian, give the name of his son Oscar to successive kings of Sweden. Meanwhile Ossian would have invaded and conquered the pictorial arts. Angelica Kaufmann, the Danish painter Abilgaard, the French disciples of David – Gerard, Girodet, Ingres – would portray Ossianic themes; and the dream of Ossian, Ossian calling up the ghosts with his lyre, Ossian welcoming the ghosts of the French heroes who fell in his wars, would decorate the apartments of Napoleon in Paris and Rome.

Naturally this triumph was celebrated in Scotland too. In 1771 the Edinburgh painter Alexander Runciman, returning from Rome, was summoned by his patron, Sir John Clerk of Penicuik, to decorate Ossian's Hall in the great house newly built for him by Robert Adam. Twelve great scenes from *Fingal* soon covered the walls, and Ossian himself looked down from the ceiling, singing to his lyre. A few years later, in 1781, the inhabitants of Kingussie, Macpherson's birthplace, planned to set up, 'in the most centrical situation in London', a veritable temple of Ossian, to the glory of their local hero, his high priest. It was to be called 'Ossian's Gallery', and was to house a great exhibition of paintings illustrating the works of Ossian and 'executed by the greatest masters in London' – a show to rival the recent Shakespeare Jubilee in Stratford-upon-Avon. Such a gallery, said its promoters, would not only 'add new lustre to the justly celebrated Poems of Ossian' – for 'the Poems of Ossian will afford ample scope for the pencil in all that is grand, sublime and striking in painting' – but would also be highly profitable to the promoters: yielding, they calculated, £1,851 per annum on an investment of £6,400, a return of 30 per cent. In spite of these inducements, Ossian's Gallery was not built[58] – perhaps the inhabitants of Kingussie were insufficient as a pressure group – but in 1783 a modest temple was consecrated to him in Perthshire. The Duke of Atholl converted a rustic 'hermitage', built by his father, into 'Ossian's Hall'. There, on the banks of the river Braan near Dunkeld, the visitor, on entering, saw a room, unfurnished except for seats facing a large painting of Ossian, wild-haired and white-robed, leaning on his harp under an oak tree bent by the storm, while his widowed daughter-in-law, the melancholy Malvina, listened to the sublime strains. Then suddenly, at the touch of a button, the picture would disappear, revealing a real waterfall tumbling from several hundred feet above. Unlike Ossian's Hall at Penicuik, the temple on the river Braan still survives; but the Ossianic painting and its machinery, which would inspire Wordsworth, has gone. Later nineteenth-century dukes of Atholl, it seems, no longer worshipped at that shrine.

Also in 1783, but in London, the painter James Barry exhibited at the Society of Arts, Manufactures and Commerce in the Adelphi a huge picture of 'Elysium', in which were assembled the notable of all ages: 'Charles I in his Vandyke dress, Homer in rags, Leo X in his purple, the Black Prince in armour, and Ossian in flesh and blood; for even that nonentity he has sent to heaven,' said Horace Walpole, 'although, indeed, after obliging him previously to go and be born in Ireland' – for Barry, being himself Irish, was not to be taken in by Scotch impertinence, and had deliberately refashioned the image of Ossian as one of his own countrymen.[59]

If visual propaganda, refusal to argue, and 'the consenting silence of a whole nation' could triumph over evidence, Ossian's place in the history and literature of Scotland was secure. Unfortunately his foreign base, though wide, was weak: he rested on a fashion in taste which must change; and the critics, though they had been silenced in France and had not yet appeared in Scotland, were still active in England: so active that even Macpherson was forced, on one occasion, to take notice of them. That one occasion occurred in 1775.

By that time the public controversy about Ossian had died down, and it seemed that there was a tacit agreement not to revive it. The English did not believe in Ossian; but why deprive the Scots – who were less objectionable now that Bute had disappeared from the political scene – of their tribal mascot? In April 1774, when Mason was editing the letters of Gray for publication, Walpole urged him to print nothing that might revive that controversy, and thereby arouse 'a nest of hornets – nay of hyenas'. He advised Mason quietly to 'reserve the objectionable letters, and your own notes, to a future edition'.[60] Mason accordingly cancelled, before printing, most of the passages which might offend the vain and irritable Macpherson, who was now living regularly in London and could so easily make trouble. His tact was unnecessary. For the controversy was about to be revived in language far more forcible than the tremulous indecisions of Gray. Dr Johnson was on the move.

# 6

# The Controversy
# over Ossian

Johnson's views on the authenticity of Ossian were already formed
when he set out, in the autumn of 1773, on his personal tour of the
Hebrides. He suspected, on the evidence of style and content, that the
work was not genuine; he considered that, in the face of this evidence,
Macpherson had a duty to submit to the scrutiny of scholars the
ancient manuscripts which he claimed to have used; and he interpreted Macpherson's refusal even to discuss the matter as confirmation of his own suspicions. In fact, Johnson believed that Macpherson
could have no manuscripts – or at least no ancient manuscripts – for
he believed that 'the Erse language was never written till very lately
for the purpose of religion'; but he was willing to be convinced by
evidence. 'There are, I believe, no Erse manuscripts', he wrote. 'If there
are manuscripts, let them be shown.' Till they were shown, the most
that he would concede was that Macpherson had picked up names
and episodes from oral tradition. But, like Hume, he refused to
believe that oral tradition could have preserved an epic poem nine
thousand lines long over fifteen centuries.[1]

Johnson was wrong on one point. It was not true that there were
no ancient Gaelic manuscripts in Scotland. Most of Macpherson's
manuscripts were indeed modern compilations; but the Book of
the Dean of Lismore and the Little Book of Clanranald show that
the language had been written, for secular purposes, in the sixteenth
and seventeenth centuries. However, these were exceptional; and
Johnson's opinion, though too forcefully expressed, was not basically
unjust. Nor was Johnson prejudiced against Celtic studies. He had an

interest in the Gaelic world, – what else could have impelled him, at the age of sixty-four, to undertake that heroic expedition? – he was eager to study Celtic society, and, like Boswell, he wished to preserve the Gaelic language.[2] He was, after all, a lexicographer. He would afterwards show his interest by his patronage of the Gaelic scholar William Shaw.

With these presuppositions, Johnson set off to the Hebrides and there made persistent enquiries about Ossianic poetry. He followed Macpherson's footsteps to Skye and there pressed an unfortunate minister who had too readily reassured Blair. In general, his enquiries confirmed his presuppositions. He satisfied himself that there were indeed Ossianic ballads, which he had never denied; but he equally satisfied himself that there was no basis for Macpherson's epic poem, and that the Highlanders who so readily swore that they had heard the poem, or parts of it, really only recalled names and episodes from such ballads, not continuous literature. 'Well, sir,' he replied to a minister who recited Gaelic passages which resembled Macpherson's version, 'this is just what I have always maintained. He has found names and stories and phrases, nay passages in old songs, and with them he has blended his own compositions, and so made what he gives to the world as the translation of an ancient poem.'[3]

When he returned to London, Johnson wrote his *Journey to the Western Islands*. In it he expressed his conclusions on the subject of Ossian and the value of the evidence which had satisfied Blair. He believed, he wrote, that *The Poems of Ossian*

> never existed in any other form than that which we have seen. The editor, or author, never could show the original; nor can it be shown by any other. To revenge reasonable incredulity by refusing evidence is a degree of insolence with which the world is not yet aquainted, and stubborn audacity is the last refuge of guilt. . . . He has doubtless inserted names that circulate in popular stories, and may have translated some wandering ballads, if any can be found; and the names, and some of the images, being recollected, make an inaccurate auditor imagine, by the help of Caledonian bigotry, that he has formerly heard the whole.

Except for the first few words, this is, on the whole, a fair statement of the case. But then Johnson went on to utter a judgment which was to arouse the indignation of all good Scotchmen – and to arouse it in more furious form because, if coolly considered, it contains (as Sir Walter Scott himself recognised)[4] an obvious truth:

> The Scots have something to plead for their easy reception of an improbable fiction: they are seduced by their fondness for their supposed ancestors. A Scotchman must be a very sturdy moralist who does not love Scotland better than truth; he will always love it better than enquiry; and if falsehood flatters his vanity, he will not be very diligent to detect it.[5]

In retrospect we must regret that Johnson did not spend a little longer in the Hebrides. Boswell had planned a visit to Benbecula to stay with Clanranald,[6] but this visit would have added a week to the tour, and was omitted. The omission was unfortunate. Clanranald junior, who had lent the manuscripts to Macpherson, was still alive; and at his house Johnson might have corrected his own errors about Gaelic manuscripts. He might also have discovered the facts about the Red Book, and saved later scholars a great deal of fruitless research. As it was, Boswell only heard about Clanranald's manuscripts eighteen months later. He then reported to Johnson that, having dined with a party of Highlanders in Edinburgh, he was beginning to waver on the subject of Ossian. 'I am told', he wrote, 'that Macpherson got one old manuscript from Clanranald, for the restitution of which he executed a formal obligation'; and he added that one Ranald Macdonald from the Isle of Eigg had come to the city with plans to publish several manuscripts of Erse poetry which he possessed. 'This man', Boswell went on, 'says that some of his manuscripts are ancient; and to be sure, one of them which was shown to me does appear to have the duskyness of antiquity' ... Johnson briskly puffed aside these whispers of heresy. 'The dusky manuscript of Eigg', he replied, 'is probably not fifty years old. If it be a hundred, it proves nothing. The tale of Clanranald is no proof. Has Clanranald told it? Can he prove it? There are, I believe, no Erse manuscripts. . . .'[7] Thus, once again, the opportunity was missed to test Macpherson's secret weapon, the Red Book of Clanranald.

While Johnson's book was with the printers, Macpherson, who was in London, learned that it contained some damaging statements about him, and now at last he was roused to action. He did not, even now, offer evidence; but he sought to secure the removal, before publication, of the offending passages. On being told that this could not be done, he suggested that a disclaimer be inserted in the book, and he rashly proposed the terms of the disclaimer which Johnson was to subscribe. Johnson refused. Thereupon followed the most famous incident in the relations between the two literary men. In a letter which does not survive, Macpherson evidently threatened Johnson with violence. Johnson's reaction was to equip himself with a stout oak stick for his defence and to write the best known of his letters:

> Mr James Macpherson
> I received your foolish and impudent letter. Any violence offered to me I shall do my best to repel; and what I cannot do for myself, the law shall do for me. I hope I shall not be deterred from detecting what I think a cheat by the menaces of a ruffian. . . .[8]

When Johnson's book appeared, Macpherson remained obstinately silent. But the controversy had been revived and soon another formidable scholar was drawn in. It happened that Edward Gibbon was then engaged upon the first volume of the *Decline and Fall of the Roman Empire*, and he had to consider whether the poems of Ossian could be regarded as evidence for third-century Scotland. In a letter to John Whitaker – a learned clergyman who had, somewhat inconsistently, refuted the history but swallowed the poet of the Macphersons – he wrote:

> With regard to your old friend Ossian, the dogmatic language of Johnson and the acquiescence or indifference of the Scotch, particularly of Macpherson, seem to have given the bard a fatal wound. It appears at least to be the prevailing opinion, that truth

and falsehood, the Highland ballads and the fancy of the translator, are blended together in such a manner that unless he
himself should condescend to give the clue, there is no power of
criticism capable of untwisting them.[9]

In his book, Gibbon expressed a judicious scepticism. After
describing the alleged battles of Fingal against the Roman army of
Caracalla, he added his own comment:

Something of a doubtful mist still hangs over these Highland
traditions, nor can it be entirely dispelled by the most ingenious
researches of modern criticism; but if we could, with safety,
indulge the pleasing supposition that Fingal lived and Ossian
sung, the striking contrast of the situation and manners of the
contending nations might amuse a philosophic mind.[10]

And he went on to expatiate on that contrast: 'the generous clemency'
of Fingal; 'the tenderness, the elegant genius of Ossian'; the warm,
natural virtues of the untutored Caledonians as against the corrupt,
degenerate cruelty of the Romans.

On reading these words David Hume wrote to Gibbon supporting
and strengthening his apparent scepticism.[11] But Gibbon never
adopted a firm position; to the end he suspended judgment: indeed,
in his third volume, published in 1781, he tentatively used Ossian as
a source. And having once allowed Fingal to live, and Ossian to sing,
even as a hypothesis, he went on to make the great mistake of
choosing, as his guides through the dark age of Scotland, what he
called 'two learned and ingenious Highlanders whom their birth and
education had peculiarly fitted for that office'.[12] These two guides
were none other than the two Macphersons – James Macpherson
himself, and the minister of Sleat – whose historical books, the
*Critical Dissertations on the Ancient Caledonians* and the *Introduction
to the History of Great Britain and Ireland*, had been written, essentially, to support the fraud of Ossian. How Gibbon came to put his
trust in these worthless guides, and thus to continue what has been
called 'a chain of error in Scottish history', is a mystery.[13] But it helps
to show how Ossian distorted not merely the literature but also the

history of Scotland. For if Ossian could even be conceived as a historical figure, then the early history of Scotland had to be adjusted to
contain him; and since the greatest of English historians made that
adjustment, we cannot be surprised that the error was continued, in
Scotland, long afterwards.

Gibbon's acceptance of Macpherson's history might be some
consolation for Johnson's attack; but it could not repel it. For while
Gibbon had allowed a historical context within which Ossian might
live, Johnson had decreed that, whatever his context, Ossian himself
– as a Scottish epic poet – must die. After Johnson's attack, the battle
over the authenticity of Ossian entered a new stage. Hitherto
Macpherson had tried to ignore criticism; and he had tried to silence
it; but he had always refused to answer it. Now, since it would not go
away, he tried a new tactic. While still himself maintaining a haughty
silence, he employed agents to deal with his critics. These agents were
not openly acknowledged by him, but they were in fact indirectly
dependent on him – some, at least, thanks to the patronage which he
controlled in India and could use on behalf of them or their kinsmen.
Directly, they were controlled by his own lawyer and 'most intimate
and confidential friend', John Mackenzie.[14]

John Mackenzie, who from now on was to play a large but dubious
part in the story, was a Highlander who practised law in London, with
chambers at Figtree Court, the Temple. Besides being Macpherson's
agent and accomplice in all his business affairs, he was also secretary
of the Highland Society of London. This Society, of which we shall
hear more, was founded in May 1778 – i.e. in the wake of the revival
by Johnson of the Ossianic controversy – and although its purpose
was more general, to preserve and revive the distinctive virtues of the
Highlanders, emphasis was laid from the beginning on the defence
and assertion of 'the songs of their ancient Bards – the tales of their
former times when FINGAL conquered and OSSIAN sung his
praises'. As the first historian of the Society wrote, the best means of
preserving their ancient virtue was for Highlanders periodically to
meet in the garb of their Celtic ancestors and, on such occasions,
'to speak the emphatic language, to listen to the delightful music, to
recite the ancient poetry, and to observe the peculiar customs of the
country'.[15] Twenty-five members were elected at the first meeting, on

28 June 1778, and another thirty-five, also called 'original members', at a second meeting a week later. The first president was General Simon Fraser of Lovat, the heir of the rebel Lord Lovat, executed after the 'Forty-Five'. Among the 'original members' were James Macpherson and John Macpherson. In due course, all the main supporters of the Macphersons were drawn in. But the essential figure in the Society, as in any society, was the secretary. For the rest of Macpherson's life, and until his own death, Mackenzie ran the Society. In 1794 he would be given a gold medal for his 'able', 'judicious' and 'unwearied' zeal; and after his death he was cited as having been the main cause of the Society's success.[16] Thanks to his double position as Macpherson's confidant and agent, and as secretary of the Society, Mackenzie was able to use the Society, in effect, as an organ of propaganda for Macpherson, an extension of the Macpherson claque in London.

Having thus built up the machinery for counter-attack against Johnson, Macpherson left it to Mackenzie to organise the battle on his behalf. The first champion to be mobilised was the Rev. Donald MacNicol, minister of Lismore in Argyll: a learned clergyman who himself collected Gaelic poems. He was encouraged to write a book against Johnson. But, as he was stuck in his parish in Argyll, he allowed the Highland Society – that is, Mackenzie – to see his book through the press. When the book appeared in 1779, the author was surprised, and not pleased, to discover that his London editors had interpolated passages into it.[17] One such passage ridiculed Johnson's table manners. Another attacked his belief that there were no ancient Gaelic manuscripts, and invited him to correct his errors by calling on 'Mr John Mackenzie, secretary of the Highland Society of London' at the Shakespeare Inn, Covent Garden (the headquarters of the Society), where he would be shown 'more volumes in the Gaelic language and character than perhaps he will be pleased to look at, after what he has said'. These manuscripts, it was alleged, were of great antiquity, up to five hundred years old, elegantly written on vellum; and they included the Red Book of Clanranald, given to Macpherson by the bard MacMhuirich.[18] As a reward for his book, Donald MacNicol, though living so far away, was made an honorary member of the Highland Society of London.

Johnson 'growled hideously' when he read MacNicol's book;[19] but he did not flinch from the challenge. He did not accept it himself – he would not have been able to judge a Gaelic manuscript – but he had a Scottish protégé who was competent for the purpose: a fellow lexicographer and a Gaelic scholar, one William Shaw;[20] and him he now invited to visit the Shakespeare Inn and report on the manuscripts.

Shaw was a native of the island of Arran, who had come to London as a private tutor, and had there become known both to Johnson and to Macpherson. He was then working on a Gaelic grammar.[21] Macpherson at first encouraged him; but when Shaw asked to see the manuscript of Ossian in order to include instances of Gaelic prosody in his work, Macpherson became evasive. The manuscripts were in the country, he said; he had lost the key to the box; perhaps some other time. . . .[22] Johnson gave him more practical support. After publishing his grammar, Shaw decided, with Johnson's help, to compile a Gaelic dictionary. For this purpose he set off to the Highlands. Johnson saw him off with encouraging words: 'Sir, if you give the world a vocabulary of that language, while the island of Great Britain stands in the Atlantic Ocean, your name will be mentioned.'[23]

Up to this point of time, Shaw believed in Ossian; but his northern tour – three thousand miles in the Highlands of Scotland and in Ireland – convinced him, as it had convinced Johnson, that the epic of Ossian had never existed. Now he was back in London; and he gladly accepted the invitation to view, at last, the original manuscripts. He went to the Shakespeare Inn. Mackenzie showed him the manuscripts which, he said, had come from Mr Macpherson. Shaw discovered that they were Irish and Highland genealogies, unrelated to Ossian. So these, he exclaimed, were the original manuscripts of *Fingal* which Macpherson claimed to have exhibited in Becket's shop in 1762! Now that exhibition, no less than this, was shown to be fraudulent. There were no manuscripts of the epic. Shaw published his findings, and Macpherson's case was still further damaged.[24]

Thereupon the claque moved into action again. A close kinsman, perhaps briefly even a pupil of Macpherson in Ruthven, one John Clark,[25] was mobilised by an intermediary – presumably Mackenzie – and indirectly 'authorised' by the great man to make certain statements. The manuscripts shown to Mr Shaw, Clark now stated, were not the same as those exhibited in 1762. Those manuscripts had never been out of Mr Macpherson's hands 'since he withdrew them from Mr Becket's shop, after they had remained there for many months'. The implications of this statement are curious, but were not drawn out. Mr Clark was also indirectly 'authorised' to say that Mr Macpherson would never have shown his manuscripts to Mr Shaw anyway: 'he disliked the manners of the man', saw that he was 'not capable of forming any just judgment on the matter', and therefore had treated him, on his visits, 'with a cold and distant civility'. So that did for William Shaw.[26]

Macpherson's contortions over his manuscripts baffled his defenders as much as his critics. But they were only one part of the problem. For that problem was not merely literary; it was also historical. If Fingal lived and Ossian sang, early Scottish history had to be revised to accommodate that fact; and the historical work of Innes, which was incompatible with it, had to be rejected. We have seen that James Macpherson, following the lead of the Rev. John Macpherson, minister of Sleat, had deliberately made that revision in order to achieve that result; and we have seen that that revision, on the authority of the two Macphersons, had been accepted even by Gibbon, and confirmed by his authority. Fortunately, if Gibbon nodded, he had a disciple who could correct him. That disciple was the greatest of Scottish antiquaries after Innes: John Pinkerton.[27] Pinkerton has already been mentioned in this book. He will recur later, for he has several claims to be noticed. Now is the time to introduce him formally.

John Pinkerton was born in Edinburgh. He was denied a university education and thereby, perhaps, better enabled to resist conformity with the Scottish academic establishment. Escaping from the servitude of the law, he attempted to make a name through literature. The name which he made was bad. He had to admit that he had forged an ancient ballad – the second part of the (also forged) poem of *Hardyknute*. His proposals to improve the English language by adding Italian terminations to English words made him ridiculous. He made impertinent attacks both on Virgil and on Gibbon himself. However, these early follies were overtaken and redeemed, in part at

least – for he never ceased to be eccentric – by his work as an antiquary. His edition of the *Ancient Lives of the Scottish Saints*, published
in 1789, convinced Gibbon of his merit; and his *Enquiry into the
History of Scotland*, which covered the early history until 1056, was
praised by Gibbon as the only work which had given him precise and
authentic ideas on the early history of the country.[28] It did in fact
correct, and correct very emphatically, Gibbon's former guides, the
two Macphersons. In consequence, it caused an outcry in Scotland.

The animating theme of all Pinkerton's work was an antipathy to
the Highlanders. He saw that the constructive part of Scottish
history had been the work of the Lowlanders of the east – the
descendants of Picts and Saxons, Normans and Danes – but that the
Highlanders of the west had, again and again, distorted that history
by imposing on it their own fanciful and self-glorifying interpretation. In the Dark Ages the Scots from Ireland had usurped the Pictish
inheritance. In the Middle Ages they had falsified the national past,
excluding the Picts from any share in it. Now, with Ossian and
the false history which the Macpherson family had constructed in
his support, they were seeking to take over Scottish literature too. To
show that there was indeed an authentic Scottish literature,
Pinkerton hunted out and printed ancient Scottish poems; and he
wrote an essay on the origin of Scottish poetry. His polemical aim
can be seen as the rescue of Scottish literature and Scottish history
from the Highlanders. But that polemical aim, though never
absorbed, was subsumed in a legitimate desire to reconstruct the
authentic history and literature of Scotland, freeing them alike
from Celtic usurpations and the nationalist prejudices of Scottish
antiquaries, with their absurd 'points of honour of Scotland quite
unknown in more enlightened countries'.[29]

A noble task for a scholar! But how could it be done? Before it
could even be begun, the base had to be cleaned of so much rubbish:
first the detritus of the past which Innes had vainly tried to clear
away, and then the luxuriant jungle of fresh weeds which had grown
up in 'this eighteenth century so fatal to real and solid literature': a
jungle which had been watered by a series of Scottish historians and
now 'dunged afresh' by 'that *par nobile*, the Macphersons', and even, 'I
tremble to say', blessed by Gibbon; for Gibbon, 'instead of bestowing

even the slightest examination on the subject', had been led by the
nose by the two Macphersons, 'whose little local designs his large
mind could not even suspect'.[30] Their 'little local designs' were,
presumably, the support of their creation, Ossian.

So just as Innes had had to grub up the deep-rooted tanglewood of
Fordun, Boece and Buchanan, Pinkerton had to hack down the
poisonous new growth of the Scottish Ossian, with its innumerable
new shoots and suckers. And yet, when Pinkerton faces Ossian, his
attitude is always ambivalent. For he too, like so many of his contemporaries, had once been bowled over by that fashionable poetry.
When he had read *Fingal*, at the age of sixteen, his juvenile scepticism
had evaporated. 'The intrinsic style and manner, the imagery of the
poems, with the translator's plausible notes, and the testimonies
given by Dr Blair, a man of the most excellent moral character, made
me a complete convert'. 'With all this *apparent* evidence', how
tempting it was for patriotic Scotchmen 'to shut our eyes and resign
ourselves to the delicious delusion that a Celtic Homer had reached
our times?' Even later, when his own antiquarian studies had
convinced him that *Fingal* was an imposture, anachronistic in
substance and in style, he could not look on its author with undi-
vided contempt. Macpherson, he declared, had no need to fabricate
bogus poems for a mythical Scottish Homer in the third century AD.
He was 'himself the Homer of the Celtic tongue'; he had gilded 'the
mist of Celtic nonsense' with 'the beams of real genius'. Why then
could he not be content to enjoy his just fame which 'will be
immortal? Considered as a man of genius, he is as much to be
admired, as pitied, if beheld as a man of learning'.[31]

When he looked coolly at Ossian, Pinkerton decided that *Fingal*
was not entirely fraudulent: it had some traditional base. Perhaps
half of it was genuine – though not of the third century. Perhaps
some poet or poets of superlative genius had flourished in the
Highlands in the fourteenth or fifteenth century (for it could not be
earlier than that). If only Macpherson would 'descend from the stilts
of his extravagant impudence' and say what he took from tradition
and what he added to it; then, perhaps, the mystery could be solved.
As for *Temora*: that, Pinkerton was convinced, was wholly
Macpherson's work 'save parts of the first book, which he at first

published separately'.[32] In this inference, Pinkerton, as we now know, was quite right.

Having cleared away the distortions and fabrications of the Macphersons, Pinkerton, with exact and delicate scholarship, reconstructed the true history of Scotland in the Dark Ages. He restored the Picts to their rightful place, unravelled the falsifications of the Middle Ages, and left an ancient Caledonia in which Ossian simply could not exist: for his entire Scottish context had been destroyed. As an epitaph on Pinkerton's work we may quote the judgment of the greatest nineteenth-century scholar of Celtic Scotland, W.F. Skene. Skene described Pinkerton as 'the only historian who has estimated correctly the value and superior claims of the earlier documents' as against the later fabrications, 'and saw something of their true bearing upon the early history' of Scotland. Those documents 'were only to a very limited extent accessible to him . . . Still, it is remarkable how near to the truth he came'.[33]

It is unlikely that Pinkerton would ever have converted the Scottish literary establishment which, in the 1780s and 1790s, was still solid in support of Ossian; but he made success almost impossible by the language that he used. Having discovered the continuing antithesis between the Lowlanders and the Highlanders of Scotland, and equated this with the antithesis between Picts and Scots in ancient Caledonia, he discovered a fundamental difference between the two races. While the Highlanders and the Irish were indisputably Celts, the Picts, he decided, were Goths; and having convinced himself of this racial difference (which he argued with great skill and plausibility), he ascribed to the latter all the virtues of a *Herrenvolk*, to the former all the vices of the *Untermensch*. The Goths, he maintained, even as barbarians, had within them the principle of improvement: they were 'always advancing in society'; while the Celts had no such principle: they remained always the same.[34]

In these terms Pinkerton simplified the history of modern civilisation. 'The history of Europe', he wrote, 'is that of the Goths in Europe; that of Ireland is that of the Goths in Ireland'. 'The wild Irish, untainted with Gothic blood, we know to be utter savages at this day'; the Welsh are 'a poor confined race of conquered dastards'; and in Scotland, while 'the Lowlanders are acute, industrious, sensible, erect, free', the Highlanders are 'stupid, indolent, foolish, fawning, slavish'. And yet these savages, he exclaims, through 'their crazy and mercenary bards and senachies', have captured and converted to their use the history of Scotland. Indeed, they very nearly captured the history of England. For think what would have happened to the historiography of England if two little Saxon books – Bede's *Ecclesiastical History* and the *Anglo-Saxon Chronicle* – had not survived from the Dark Ages. As no other English historians arose till the twelfth century, the Welshman Geoffrey of Monmouth would then have been followed in all things . . . and the history of England 'would at this hour have been, like the history of Scotland, a mere Celtic dream'.[35]

What was to be done with the Celtic 'savages' who were now threatening to take over and deform the Pictish inheritance of Scotland? Pinkerton had only one solution to the problem. 'Had all these Celtic cattle emigrated five centuries ago, how happy had it been for our country! All we can do now is to plant colonies among them, and by this and by encouraging their emigration, try to get rid of the breed'.[36] Such was Pinkerton's response to the new cult of the noble savage, the romantic Celt.

Unfortunately Pinkerton's racial theory, though argued with such learning and scholarship, has a serious flaw in it. All scholars now agree that the Picts were not Goths but Celts, like the dastardly and defeated Welsh. Pinkerton's general conclusion could thus be saved only if the Picts were consigned to the same dust-heap as the Scots, and all constructive virtue in Scottish history ascribed to the Saxons, Normans and Danes. This may – or may not – be so; but in any case it would not have suited Pinkerton.

Pinkerton's pathological hatred of the Celtic race could hardly win converts to his real scholarly work. As his friend Lord Buchan – an equally eccentric champion of Scottish nationalism (and of Ossian) – wrote to him, 'I find it has excited violent disgust among my countrymen'. Pinkerton was unabashed: it was the 'violent prejudices' of the Scots, he replied, which obliged him to be so violent in exposing them: 'there is surely no country in which prejudices are so violent as in ours. I am convinced, my Lord, that old John Knox knew us very well, and if he had not reformed us violently, he would never have reformed us at all'.[37]

Against the bogus scholarship of the Macphersons, Pinkerton's reforming iconoclasm beat in vain. Ironically, it was not the scholarship of his critics but the innocent enthusiasm of his admirers which, in the end, forced Macpherson to begin a slow, ungainly, and in the end disastrous descent from his stilts. The enthusiasm came from his 'eastern friends': from that mafia of Highlanders in India who, at this moment – for we are in 1783 – saw that the wicket-gate to prosperity was controlled by the two Macphersons, and deduced that a spontaneous tribute to the national poet would be welcome to them. In this they showed a naivety which was very embarrassing to their patron in London.

The proposal was to refute the calumnies of Dr Johnson by publishing the original Gaelic text of Ossian. In 1762, we may recall, when he published *Fingal,* James Macpherson had hinted at this possibility; but he had never pursued the idea, claiming the cost would be prohibitive. Later, when Johnson's attack had shaken the credit of Ossian, the idea had been revived; and in April 1779 the Highland Society appointed a committee to wait on James Macpherson and propose that it be realised. Macpherson agreed in theory, but once again explained that in practice it was impossible through lack of funds.[38] No doubt he reckoned that that ended the matter, for the generosity of Highlanders has seldom been expressed in cash. If so, he reckoned without the more prosperous Highlanders in the East. In 1783 a group of them, led by John Macgregor Murray, decided to accept the challenge. On their behalf, Murray drew up a manifesto declaring the indignation of all loyal Highlanders against those who denied the authenticity of their sublime Bard, and inviting the Highlanders in India – for only Highlanders, 'men who had Gaelic blood in their veins and Gaelic sentiments in their hearts', were worthy to take part in such a venture – to subscribe money in order that Mr Macpherson might fulfil his long-expressed hope and publish the original Gaelic text of the poems of Ossian. The Highlanders in India responded to the appeal, and nearly £1,000 was sent in instalments to Macpherson through John Mackenzie.[39]

When Mackenzie was informed of the generous gesture of the Highlanders in India, he knew what to do. He acknowledged Murray's letter in rapturous style, welcoming this gallant reaction to 'the unmerited suspicions and aspersions entertained and published by ignorance and prejudice against the greatness and refinement of its ancient genius', and expressing his confidence that 'the elevation of the Caledonian mind in all the undeniable majesty of the venerable Celtic bard', being shown in full in his own words, would 'abash and dissipate' the crowd of envious detractors of his respectable trans-lator.[40] But in fact he did nothing, yet, to advance the project proposed by the Highlanders of India. And Macpherson himself responded in a positively graceless manner to the liberality of his admirers. He tried to avoid receiving a delegation of the Highland Society.[41] He interposed objections. He seemed positively to obstruct the design. At one time he suggested that some of the manuscripts had been lost in Florida. At another, he put off enquiries by saying that the work was proceeding apace: he was preparing the Gaelic text, with a parallel Latin translation. However, he could not delay matters indefinitely. By 1793 he had apparently collected, and handed to Mackenzie, a substantial part of the Gaelic text, and he was prepared to discuss publication.

Discussion duly began; but soon it too ran into difficulties. There were problems, everyone agreed, about the orthography of a language which had so seldom been written. How was it to be printed – in Roman or in Irish characters, in etymological or phonetic spelling? On this subject, the Edinburgh literati – still unshakeable in their belief – were brought into the discussion. Their most active member was Adam Ferguson, the only Gaelic speaker among them, and himself a member of the Highland Society. Blair also, as the chief propagandist of Ossian, was involved. In correspondence with Ferguson, Macpherson proposed that Greek letters be used.[42] Ferguson and Blair found this proposal surprising: there would be few enough readers of a Gaelic text, they observed, but even fewer if it must be read through the medium of the Greek alphabet. It was then suggested that the orthography of the original manuscripts be followed: those nineteen manuscripts which Macpherson had repeatedly offered to exhibit to interested scholars. This was promptly vetoed by Macpherson, who replied to Ferguson (but asking that this be concealed from Blair) that 'there is scarce any manuscript to be followed' except a few which were mutilated and almost unintelligible. Since Macpherson had for years insisted that he had a complete text and numerous manuscripts, and since Blair's Highland correspondents had described these manuscripts, and Macpherson himself had twice put them – though somewhat discreetly – on show, this reply is even more surprising. Perhaps the essential words are 'to be followed'. Macpherson had manuscripts – we know that he had manuscripts – but they gave no guidance for the orthography of *Fingal*, because they did not contain that epic; and Macpherson, under pressure, felt obliged to admit this to his old patron, whom he could not deceive, though not to the naive and, in Gaelic matters, unlearned Blair.

Indeed, by 1793 at least, Macpherson's contempt for the gullibility of 'our friend Dr Blair' was barely concealed; as also for those ranks of reverend helpers who had stood, and continued to stand, so solidly behind their marshal in defence of Ossian. Dr Blair, Macpherson wrote pityingly, 'labours under much want of information on the subject'. He had allowed himself to be deluded by his supposed experts, who were more conspicuous for vanity than real learning. 'With respect to the clergy', Macpherson waxed ironical: 'I would rather take their ghostly advice on matters of religion than accept of their opinion about the manner of printing profane poetry.' But all of this, Macpherson told Ferguson, must be kept from poor Blair: 'for few men wish to *know* that they have been so long deceived, on a point which the smallest attention might at once ascertain'.[43] It is not surprising that such contrary currents of thought impeded progress.

When Macpherson died in 1796, the Gaelic text of Ossian was still unpublished; and by his will the business of preparing and publishing it fell, together with the £1,000, to his friend and executor, John Mackenzie. Mackenzie, as usual, was in no hurry. When he died, in 1803, little had been done. Nor was his executor, George Mackenzie, assistant surgeon to the 42nd Foot Regiment, likely to do more. By now, of course, Sir John Macpherson was no longer a power in India and had been removed from Parliament; and the Highlanders in India, seeing no return on their investment and no advantage in continuing to court the Macpherson family, lost their original enthusiasm. They even threatened legal action to recover their contributions.[44] At this point, the Highland Society of London intervened. It set up a committee to see the matter through. The committee included Sir John Macpherson (who was also one of James Macpherson's executors); John Macgregor Murray, the initiator of the plan, now back in London and a baronet; and Colin Macrae, Mackenzie's clerk in his law office. But the moving spirit in it was its chairman, Sir John Sinclair.

Sir John Sinclair, of Thurso Castle in Caithness, Member of Parliament for the county of Caithness, founder of the Board of Agriculture, editor of the famous *Statistical Account of Scotland*, was a man of prodigious energy and prodigious self-importance. Since we shall meet him again, let us introduce him now. He was not a Highlander – he was a Sinclair of Ulbster, a cadet branch of the Norman earls of Caithness – but he had made a profound study of Highland, as of all Scottish matters. He was indeed the patron – the somewhat oppressive patron – of all Scottish good causes, a champion of enlightenment, improvement, progress: afforestation, enclosure, new roads, new manufactures, new breeds of sheep. Unfortunately he was ludicrously complacent, totally without humour, and oracular on all subjects. Sir Walter Scott, who detested him, regarded him as an ostentatious busybody: describing Sinclair, in a letter, as 'that Great Caledonian Bore'; and deploring, in his diary, 'the ponderous stupidity of the Cavaliero Jackasso'.[45] Thomas Carlyle, who met Sinclair once, described him as 'a lean old man, tall but stooping, in tartan cloak, face very wrinkly, nose blue, physiognomy vague and with distinction, as one might have expected it to be'.[46] That was later, when Sinclair was an old man. Now he was in his prime, ready for any undertaking – agricultural, industrial, commercial or literary. As a parergon, he gladly undertook to preside over the committee of the Highland Society of London which would finally settle the problem of the Gaelic text of Ossian.

Meanwhile, another body also felt impelled to unravel the mystery of Ossian. This was the Highland Society of Scotland, a body which had been founded in Edinburgh in 1784, six years after the Highland Society of London. The proposal to found such a society came from Captain Macdonald of Clanranald, whose family had entertained Macpherson and lent him their manuscripts.[47] Sir John Sinclair, who had been elected to the Highland Society of London in that year, was one of the founding members of this Scottish Society, which, from the beginning, had a somewhat more utilitarian character than its original in London: it was a society for the 'improvement' of the Highlands by the introduction of modern agriculture, manufactures, communications, etc. It would afterwards be renamed the Highland and Agricultural Society. But among its aims it too included 'proper attention to the preservation of the language, poetry and music of the Highlands'; and now, under the impulsion of its most active member, the novelist Henry Mackenzie – known, from his most successful novel, as 'the Man of Feeling' – it also set up a committee under his chairmanship with instructions to investigate, more thoroughly and more objectively than Blair had done in 1763, the methods and materials which Macpherson had used to produce *Fingal*. The committee took its task seriously. It wrote to the surviving lairds and clergy whom Macpherson had visited, or their heirs. It took evidence from Gaelic-speaking peasants in the Hebrides. It obtained the testimony of the Edinburgh literati: for John Home, Alexander Carlyle, Blair and Ferguson were all still flourishing. It sought out such manuscripts as might have been in Macpherson's hands and were now, presumably, in the hands of his executor, John Mackenzie.

The lairds and clergy repeated what they or their predecessors had said thirty-five years earlier, only more emphatically. Macpherson's translation, said the now octogenarian Mr Gallie, was accomplished and faithful as far as it went, but could not do justice to 'some strokes of the sublime and pathetic' in the original – but that, he added, was probably due to the inherent inferiority of the English language.[48] Macpherson, said the now octogenarian Captain Morrison, could no more have been the author of so sublime a poem as *Fingal* than he could have composed the prophecies of Isaiah or created the island of Skye. He could no more have composed it, echoed the septuagenarian Ewan Macpherson, than take wings and fly.[49] The Edinburgh literati, to a man, stood firm. Blair preened himself on the part he had played in the discovery of works which marked 'an important era in the annals of taste and literature'.[50] Only the manuscripts failed to obey the summons. John Mackenzie, approached as Macpherson's executor, replied that 'after a strict search' in Macpherson's papers, no Gaelic manuscripts could be found, and that 'the manuscripts left by Mr Macpherson were not ancient' but in his own handwriting, or that of others whom he had employed as copyists.[51] This statement, in view of John Mackenzie's close connection with Macpherson, and his previous association with the manuscripts, which he had personally exhibited at the Shakespeare Inn, was very curious. It left the committee stumped.

However, in the end, even John Mackenzie's delaying tactics were overcome. In January 1803, six years after saying that no manuscripts could be found, and just before his own death, Mackenzie yielded; and nineteen manuscripts were surrendered by him to the Highland Society of London and by it sent to the committee in Edinburgh.[52] These had belonged to Macpherson and were almost certainly the manuscripts which Macpherson had so often cited and sometimes exhibited, or pretended to exhibit. They were, or included, genuine Gaelic manuscripts which would have refuted Johnson's claim that there were no such manuscripts over a century old. Unfortunately, Macpherson could not produce them for that purpose without at the same time demonstrating that they did not contain a Gaelic text of the epic of *Fingal*. Even now, John Mackenzie did not state that these manuscripts came from Macpherson. To do so would have been too dangerous: it would have revealed their irrelevance. Nor did the Highland Society of Scotland guess their true source, which was first identified after it had published its report.[53]

That *Report*, accompanied by a long appendix of documents, was published in 1805. It declared that Ossianic poetry certainly existed in the Highlands; that Macpherson had undoubtedly collected some of it; but that he had clearly taken liberties with what he had collected; and that, so far, no poem had been found 'the same in title and tenor with the poems published by him'.[54] On the whole, the committee gave Macpherson the benefit of the doubt: for it had not (it thought) seen his manuscripts, and who knew what might still be discovered?[55] Besides, there was the evidence of the Rev. John Smith, minister of Campbeltown in Argyllshire, who in 1780, with the encouragement of the Highland Society, had published a collection of ancient poems collected in the West. These poems not only showed the same strain of 'sublimity and tenderness' as the poems of Ossian, but also 'the same delicacy and refinement of sentiment', and thus implicitly confirmed their authenticity. Mr Smith was himself consulted on the matter, and supported this conclusion in a series of persuasive letters to the committee. Unfortunately, these arguments afterwards lost their force, when Mr Smith's Gaelic poems were found to be fakes, having been composed by him in imitation of Macpherson's Ossian.[56]

Meanwhile Sir John Sinclair's committee had not been idle. John Mackenzie being now dead, the committee had obtained control of his papers and had discovered the one essential document which could prove the authenticity of *Fingal*: the 'original' Gaelic text. This text had been written out partly by Macpherson, partly by another modern hand. The second hand was taken to be that of Macpherson's Hebridean crony, Captain Alexander Morrison; for he assured both committees that the manuscript had been prepared for the press by Macpherson and himself.[57] The London committee at once decided that this document was decisive and that its publication would convince every impartial reader. A prospectus was issued; a native of Sutherland, the Rev. Thomas Ross, then living as a tutor in Edinburgh, was paid £100 to transcribe the text 'agreeably to the established orthography' as used in the Gaelic Bible;[58] and in 1807 the work was duly published in three volumes, with a parallel Latin translation, as Macpherson himself had proposed. It was accompanied by various supporting documents, and introduced by a dissertation by Sir John Sinclair himself. Sinclair's conclusion was that the Gaelic text, now published, finally proved the authenticity of the works of Ossian: the controversy could at last be closed.

In reaching his conclusions, Sinclair made use of the evidence of the Scottish committee, as far as it went; but he also added other arguments. In particular, he remarked on the difference in quality between the Gaelic text, as literally translated for him by Dr Ross, and Macpherson's English version. Wherever they could be compared, he observed, the Gaelic was more vivid, more forceful, terser than the English; and this difference constituted 'the *strongest possible internal proofs* that the Gaelic was the original and Macpherson's prose a loose and in many parts a turgid translation from the original'.[59] He also noted that the imitations from the Bible, Milton, etc., which had been regarded as suspicious in the English text, were absent from the Gaelic. This also suggested that the Gaelic was the original.

Many of Sinclair's arguments were general and subjective; but one was precise and, to him, convincing. Several Scottish Roman Catholic priests had assured him that they had seen a manuscript volume, alleged to contain Ossian's poems, in the hands of a colleague in the Scots College in Douay in the years 1763 to 1773. The volume was a large folio, three inches thick, closely written in small letters. It had been compiled from oral recitations by a Jesuit, John Farquharson, who had been for over thirty years a missionary at Strathglas, and, while there, had learned Gaelic from a Highland lady learned in the literature. When Macpherson's version came to Douay, Farquharson had compared his text with Macpherson's translation, and found the latter far inferior. The Gaelic text, he said, which he alone there could read, was equal to Homer and Virgil. Unfortunately, on returning to Scotland in 1773, Farquharson had left this unique document at Douay, where it was misused by young men ignorant of Gaelic; indeed, one priest said that he had seen leaves torn out of it and used to light fires.[60] This ghost manuscript at Douay would afterwards reappear, along with other ghosts, in a different connection.

Thus in the end Macpherson, it seemed, was vindicated. The Gaelic text – not indeed of the whole works of Ossian, as published by him in English, but of some two-thirds of them – had appeared. The 'Saxon prejudices' of Dr Johnson were refuted; the credit of the discoverer and translator was upheld; the ancient history of Scotland was re-established; the Irish were cut down to size; and the world could rest assured that 'in a rude age, when the southern half of Britain was in a state of total barbarism, the most refined sentiments could be uttered and admired' by the free unconquerable Highlanders of the north.[61] Having completed his work, Sinclair declared that if the Highland Society had done nothing else but publish the poems of Ossian in the original Gaelic, it would have amply justified its existence. His son, a generation later, echoed his confidence.[62] Meanwhile, the expensive three-volume work was distributed gratis in the Highlands so that children might become familiar with their ancient poetry. A cheap pocket edition was published in 1857. A sumptuous, completely new edition, replete with learned commentary, appeared in 1870. Nineteenth-century lexicographers of the Scottish Gaelic language used it as a source for the earliest forms of the language.[63] In 1881 a Principal of St Andrews University could still assume that the poems published by Macpherson were the authentic 'old Ossianic poetry' of the ancient Caledonians.[64]

Unfortunately, one crucial demand of Dr Johnson was not met. He had insisted that the original manuscript of *Fingal* be submitted to the scrutiny of qualified scholars. This was never done. All that the committee had obtained was a fair copy prepared for the press by Macpherson and his assistants. Whatever lay behind that text – if indeed there was anything – had been destroyed. Moreover, even Macpherson's fair copy disappeared without trace after Dr Ross had made his corrected transcript, so that there is no means of knowing what Ross himself may have contributed to the final version. Some fatality, it seems, dogs all Macpherson manuscripts. The negligence of Sinclair and his committee, who allowed such destruction, and their bland indifference to the whole problem of the manuscripts, on which their pretentious book is totally silent, is surprising. In consequence of it, all that scholars have been able to scrutinise is the 'improved' text written by Ross and printed in 1807.[65]

And what is the judgment of scholars on that text? At the time, of course, it was hesitant. In 1807 the scholarly study of the Gaelic language, and especially of the Albanogaelic or Scottish Gaelic, was in its infancy. There were no grammars, no lexicons, except of current usage for practical purposes, no historical study of the language.[66] No work on the literature had been done; and half of the 'ancient' ballads published were, by now, recent forgeries in imitation of Ossian. Contemporary scholars could therefore only point to obvious solecisms, or show that Macpherson's 'original' text, as now 'finalised', varied surprisingly from parts of the 'original' previously published by him or circulated with his apparent authority. But in the following century the scholars took over. Hundreds of genuine Gaelic and Ossianic ballads were collected. The language was historically studied. The literary forms were discovered. And the verdict of modern scholars on the Gaelic Ossian of 1807 is unanimous. 'If one solitary line be excepted, not a single stanza of it' corresponds exactly with any authentic ballad. It keeps none of the rules of prosody in genuine Gaelic poetry: it has 'no fixed number of syllables, no alliteration, no assonance, no rhyme'. Its language is neither ancient nor correct. In short, it is a freak, isolated from 'the whole body of traditional Gaelic poetry'; a modern artefact 'of patent fraudulence', and the work of a writer who thought not in Gaelic but in English.[67] With that conclusion, from which no appeal is possible, all of Sinclair's speculative arguments dissolve. The 'Gaelic text of Ossian', so triumphantly produced as the final vindication of Macpherson, is in fact his ultimate condemnation.

Nevertheless, this does not entirely solve the problem. Indeed, it creates a new problem. For just as the English Ossian of 1762, so authoritatively put forth by Macpherson, had raised the problem of the undivulged material on which it was based, so the Gaelic Ossian of 1807, so authoritatively put forth by Sinclair, raised the problem of its undivulged antecedents. And therein, perhaps, lies the key to the whole mystery.

If the Gaelic 'original' is fraudulent, what of the Gaelic manuscripts which Macpherson had collected, but which he and John Mackenzie had been so reluctant to disclose to competent judges? These at least – or some of them – were now in the hands of the Highland Society of Scotland, although that society had not been told, and did not guess, that they had come from Macpherson. At this point we may digress for a moment and look at the most important of them.

One of these manuscripts, we now know, was the Book of the Dean of Lismore, the earliest and most important collection of Gaelic poems known to us. Whatever his faults, Macpherson deserves the gratitude of scholars for having rescued and preserved this precious manuscript. When and where he obtained it has been conjectured variously in the past;[68] but from the evidence of Ewan Macpherson cited earlier, it now seems clear that James Macpherson acquired it from its current Fraser custodian even before he set out on his journey to the western isles. This manuscript was of great importance to Macpherson, in one way or another. He is on record as referring to it twice. In 1775 Dr Johnson, while expressing his own disbelief in the authenticity of the Fingalian epic, recorded that Macpherson 'has been heard to say, that part of the poem was received by him in the Saxon character'; and Johnson went on to comment, not unreasonably, that 'he has then found, by some peculiar fortune, an unwritten language, written in a character which the natives probably never beheld'.[69] Macpherson himself said something very similar almost twenty years later. In 1793, writing to Adam Ferguson about the difficulties involved in printing a Gaelic edition of *Fingal*, he admitted that he had 'scarce any manuscript to be followed, except, indeed, a very few mutilated ones in a kind of Saxon characters, which was as utterly unknown to the Highlanders as either the Greek or Hebrew letters'.[70] These two descriptions point certainly to the Dean of Lismore's Book, not yet known by that name, or indeed any name.

We must therefore look at the nature of this book, and see what can be learned from how Macpherson used it. The book is unique in several ways; and it was indeed 'by some peculiar fortune' that Macpherson came across it, and was then enabled to tap at least some of its treasures.[71]

The writing of the book began in the early sixteenth century at the prompting of a cultured chieftain of the Macnab clan. He suggested to the head of a learned and literary family of MacGregors, living in and around the village of Fortingall at the mouth of Glen Lyon in north-western Perthshire, that it would be good to compile a collection of Gaelic poetry. So a 'scrap-book' was opened; and over the following thirty years or so it was filled with a miscellaneous collection of writings, most but not all in verse. Much of the verse was composed by members of the MacGregor family and their friends, who included men (and women) not only of Perthshire but also Argyll and the western isles. Ireland, too, was strongly represented. As might be expected from a family with strong clerical associations, there is quite a lot of religious verse. Extracts from secular and non-Gaelic poets were also included, such as Dunbar, Henryson and Lydgate. As usually happens with family scrap-books, extraneous matter sometimes found its way in: so there are jottings of genealogical information, records of horses, even shopping lists. But most important of all, especially from the point of view of this enquiry, the MacGregor compilers wrote down, apparently from dictation, twenty-eight traditional ballads of a broadly Ossianic nature, as sung or recited by 'strolling bards' who came their way. It would be another two centuries before other compilers began seriously to record the repertoire of those historic bards, who by then were on the point of vanishing for ever.

It seems very likely that when Macpherson first got hold of this book, a small quarto of 311 paper pages, he thought he had stumbled across the authentic record, miraculously preserved, of that great Homeric epic of the Scottish race, for which he and others had been looking. Nine of the ballads were clearly marked in the book as having been composed by 'Oisin' himself; the others, some attributed to named authors, were presumably the Caledonian equivalent of the '*Homeridae*': predecessors, rivals, or continuators of the supreme story-teller.

However, there was a problem. Could Macpherson actually read the text of this book, as distinct from merely picking out a few names in it? For the Dean of Lismore's Book, or perhaps more properly the Vicar of Fortingall's Book, is an exceptionally difficult text. It is unique in Scottish literature in that, though written (predominantly) in the Gaelic language, it was not written in a Gaelic script. For some reason which can only be guessed at, the compilers chose to translate the sounds of the Gaelic tongue, with all its inflections and other individual features, into the letters of the alphabet used by Lowland Scots: letters which Macpherson, in his usual muddled and inaccurate manner, called 'Saxon' – meaning 'Sassenach', or associated with Anglo-Saxon culture, as distinct from the Highland Gaels – but which would more normally be known, then and now, as 'Roman'. One can only presume that the MacGregors who compiled this extraordinary book had received a substantial part of their education in Lowland Scotland, and were thus enabled to write in 'a character' which probably was, otherwise, 'utterly unknown' to 'the natives' of the Highlands. Moreover, this attempt at 'phonetic' spelling of Gaelic in Roman letters was carried out in an 'erratic and fluctuating' way across the text, depending (presumably) on which member of the team of scribes was involved in the writing at any point in time. The handwriting style employed in the book is described as 'secretary': that used widely (in Anglo-Saxon circles) in the early sixteenth century; which was, of course, very different from that of James Macpherson's time, over two centuries later.[72] Every Gaelic scholar who has tried to read and edit this book, since Thomas McLauchlan in 1862, has found it 'extremely difficult to decypher' – and when 'decyphered', still 'very hard to interpret'. Each has built, necessarily if not always gratefully, on the labours of his forerunners. Each has peppered his commentary with words like 'exasperating', 'disheartening', and 'disguised'. Even the most recent of them has confessed an inability to decode certain portions of the text.

The condition of the manuscript itself presents a separate set of difficulties. Several pages are missing from both the beginning and the end. 'Many of the leaves are stained and rendered almost illegible from the effects of damp, and several are much worn from use and exposure' – especially at the edges, where line-endings often disappear. All things considered, the task of reading such a manuscript is clearly daunting, even for scholars of long experience and much technical training.

How, then, should we expect James Macpherson to read it: a young man of only twenty-three or twenty-four years of age, and by no means a qualified Gaelic scholar, even though a native Gaelic speaker? For it is now certain that he did use a part of the Dean of Lismore's Book in the construction of his epic. That much was suspected in 1805. For when Macpherson's nineteen old manuscripts came in 1803, via John Mackenzie and the Highland Society of London, to the Highland Society of Edinburgh, that Society's Ossian committee handed this book over for inspection to its senior Gaelic expert, Dr Donald Smith (a man originally from Glenorchy, and later educated at the university of St Andrews). Within a year or so Smith was able to read the manuscript – or at least some of it, if a little tentatively. His conclusions were included in the Society's *Report*.[73] Three passages in the Dean's Book could be said to 'resemble' Macpherson's 'translation': a nineteen-line poem on page 50 of the manuscript, where Oisin complained of being left alone in his old age; a ninety-six-line poem on pages 220–22, composed by Oisin telling the story that Macpherson reproduced as 'the Maid of Craca' in the third book of *Fingal*; and a fifty-five-line poem on pages 230–31, concerning the battle of Gavra where Oscar was killed, said to be composed not by Oisin but by Fergus his brother, which appeared in the first book of *Temora*. In the circumstances of Donald Smith's time these three passages in Macpherson's work could only be seen as parallels with the contents of the Dean's Book, not as derivations.

After almost 150 more years of extensive collection of Ossianic poetry all over the Highlands, and intensive analysis by scholars, Derick Thomson confirmed these parallels, and perhaps one or two others. He pointed out, however, that Macpherson could be shown to have had at his disposal other sources for the same passages, derived from contemporary oral recitations. But he was able to isolate one passage in book four of *Fingal*, the war-song of Ullin addressed to Goll, for which there was no known source dating from before 1762 other than the Book of the Dean. There were, he admitted, 'no strong verbal resemblances' between the Gaelic version in the manuscript and Macpherson's English translation; but he detected in Macpherson's equivalent a distinct attempt at imitation in staccato style of the short lines of the ballad in the Dean's Book. Very cautiously, he put forward his explanatory hypothesis. Knowing that Macpherson had possessed the Book of the Dean, and assuming that he had possessed it before 1762, perhaps Macpherson 'had spotted this poem, with its short lines, in the MS of the Dean's Book, and was unable to derive from it more than a general impression of what it was about'.[74] In the end, summing up his conclusions (still very cautiously) concerning Macpherson and the manuscript of the Book of the Dean, Thomson wrote that 'it is not impossible that either he, or more probably, one of his collaborators, was able to read a part of it, however imperfectly'.[75]

In that last shrewd shot, Thomson was almost certainly aiming at Lachlan Macpherson of Strathmashie. For of James Macpherson's two 'collaborators' in Badenoch in the last three months of 1760, Andrew Gallie and Lachlan Macpherson, Gallie himself was in no doubt that Strathmashie was the superior Gaelic scholar, whereas he personally could only read the old script 'with difficulty'. There is a further clue, moreover, in what Gallie said of Strathmashie's special ability in relation to Gaelic: that he possessed 'a happy facility for writing it in Roman characters'. Strathmashie, that is to say, was good at recognising the essential transliterations between Gaelic characters and Roman characters: just the talent required in someone who was going to try and read the manuscript of the Book of the Dean of Lismore. And was it mere coincidence that the passage in Gaelic from *Fingal* which Gallie preserved in Strathmashie's handwriting, and which he sent to the Ossian committee in Edinburgh forty years later, was a section of book four? More will be said on the rôle of Strathmashie a little later in this chapter.

Before we leave this topic, however, it will be useful to summarise, and then draw out the implications of what we have learned here. Macpherson obtained the manuscript of the Book of the Dean of Lismore before setting off on his journey to the western isles; and he imagined at first that he had obtained all that he really needed: that this book contained, in itself, the great epic generated by his remote ancestors. On his return to Ruthven he settled down to arrange and interpret all the materials which he had acquired. Most of those materials were separate ballads in varying versions in modern Gaelic, acquired directly from oral recitations; and they only needed an organising imagination of an appropriate kind to connect them together into a continuous whole. That turned out to be Macpherson's forte. It required, in unequal proportions, considerable intelligence, some information, and powerful preconceptions (what David Hume would describe, a little later, as 'Highland prejudices').[76]

The historical continuity of the race of Highlanders and islanders, from time immemorial down to the present day, was an article of faith for Macpherson. The Scots of the Lowlands, he knew, had been spoiled by immigration and miscegenation over the centuries: they had lost touch with their roots, both genetically and culturally. But the Highlanders and islanders, owing to the nature of their territory, had remained always 'pure and unmixed'. Genetically and culturally, therefore, they were still the same people, he thought, as the Caledonians who had successfully resisted the power of the Romans, then later the Vikings, etc. The historic memories of the Gaels had always been carried along by their bards, reiterating and reinforcing in every generation the recognised experiences and qualities of their folk. By now the bards had almost died out. However, their stories still remained imprinted on the memories of the older members of the folk: countrymen and blacksmiths, old wives and fishermen. So when Macpherson heard such people singing or reciting the compositions of the great Ossian, who had lived fifteen centuries earlier, he felt himself connected to the still-living, pulsating, essential tradition of his people.

But would those prosy and pedantic Lowlanders and Londoners accept the authentic antiquity of poems collected from the lips of peasants living today in remote and primitive places? Would not Hugh Blair and David Hume in Edinburgh, Thomas Gray and Horace Walpole in London, require some more tangible and demonstrable proof of antiquity? So Macpherson needed old manuscripts to refer to, and to flourish: they would serve as both psychological prop and alibi. Luckily he had the Book of the Dean, which bore within it dates of 1512, 1410, even 1310. The older and more experienced of the Macpherson duo, Strathmashie, struggled hard to make sense of this difficult book inside a mere three-month period, which was all that could be spared. Success was partial. Some of the poems could barely be read at all. Others were a disappointment. They sang of 'Oisin' chatting with, wrangling with, Saint Patrick. That was anachronistic. St Patrick had lived two centuries later than 'Oisin'. Worse still, he was a foreigner: mere Irish. Poems of that kind had to be rejected as later interpolations – false fables, concocted in a dastardly attempt to steal away Scottish heroes. Still, something was left that could be incorporated into the early Scottish epic that was being constructed. The poems in the Book of the Dean might have survived only in a 'mutilated' state. But they played their part, all the same. They gave the future Fingal a great boost.

One more thing should be noted before we leave the Book of the Dean. When Macpherson referred to it in his letter to Ferguson of 1793, and commented on its extraordinary orthography, 'utterly unknown' to Highlanders, he wrote as if it were the *only* old manuscript to which he could appeal.

At the time, however, and indeed later, the most widely trumpeted of Macpherson's manuscripts were those given to him in Benbecula by Clanranald and MacMhuirich. These, of course, being from the archives of a hereditary chief and the hands of a hereditary bard, were important, whatever their contents; and the ceremony of their discovery and the written bond for their return emphasised their value. So Macpherson regularly cited them as the source of his epic. But he never referred explicitly to their contents. All that we know about them comes from others who had been present when they were delivered to him, or had seen them afterwards in his hands. Unfortunately, most of them gave their evidence forty years later; and their evidence is inconsistent and confused.

By all accounts, Clanranald lent to Macpherson one bound manuscript book of some value and several 'parchments'. There was also talk of a manuscript known as *Leabhar Dearg*, or the Red Book, which was described as containing histories of the Highland clans and poems of Ossian. Macpherson evidently thought that he had received the Red Book from Clanranald; but it is almost certain that he was mistaken.[77] His companion Ewan Macpherson, who was his expert and who actually received the manuscripts and could read them, insisted that the book handed over by MacMhuirich was a commonplace book the size of a New Testament, containing accounts of the Macdonald family, the wars of Montrose, and some poems by Ossian. The Red Book, he said, was not in the Hebrides at all. It was in Edinburgh, in the hands of a clansman, Donald Macdonald; and Clanranald gave Macpherson written authority to collect it from him there; but Ewan Macpherson did not know whether he ever obtained it. According to Ewan Macpherson, Clanranald described the Red Book as a folio manuscript, containing some of the poems of Ossian.[78] The minister of South Uist, who was also present on the occasion, described the book that was to be collected in Edinburgh as a partial manuscript, made by Clanranald senior, of an old manuscript treating of the wars of Fingal and Comhal, his father. The original, said Clanranald, had recently been carried off surreptitiously to Ireland by a worthless person, and there irrecoverably lost.[79]

Whatever the manuscripts were which they lent to Macpherson, the Clanranald family never received them back from him. Clanranald senior died in 1766, his son in 1776. Thereafter, the next heir pressed for their return, and finding correspondence ineffectual, began a legal process to recover them; however, his agent delayed action in the hope of a voluntary surrender. When Macpherson died, the manuscripts could not be found in his papers, apart from one document which the committee judged to be of no value, and which was returned to Clanranald.[80] This was, in fact, the manuscript for which Clanranald had exacted the bond: the book of the Macdonald family and the wars of Montrose. The returned book remained in Clanranald's family for most of the nineteenth century, and was then given to the National Museum of Antiquities in Edinburgh. Its contents were published in 1894,[81] and were a fatal blow to the last-ditch defenders of Macpherson, because they include not a single line which can be traced in the works of his Ossian. The other Clanranald papers, the several 'parchments', were not found.

There still remains the Red Book. Although Macpherson undoubtedly thought that he had received this manuscript, we cannot be sure that he was right. But if he did, might not this be the true source of his epic? To this question we can only answer that the Red Book has proved as elusive as the History of Archdeacon Veremund from which Boece derived his pre-historic kings. Undiscovered in Macpherson's papers, or in Clanranald's archives, it – or rather its ghost, or will-o'-the-wisp – has been pursued by zealous Gaelic scholars over half the globe. It has been whispered that it is in the Antipodes, carried thither in the nineteenth century, its richly illuminated vellum leaves – well over a hundred of them, and of folio size – stitched into the petticoats of a female member of the Clanranald family.[82] The long sea-journey through the tropics must have been a distressing experience for manuscript and lady alike. Thanks to that whisper, the whole continent of Australia has been combed. But it has been combed in vain.[83] That central manuscript, the last hope of the faithful, remains invisible. Macpherson's secret weapon, if he ever possessed it, is secret still.

Thus the only identifiable Gaelic text which corresponds to Macpherson's Ossian remains the fraudulent text published by Sir John Sinclair in 1807. The question, therefore, naturally arises: who perpetrated this fraud? For there can be no escaping the fact that it is a fraud, a laborious and conscious fraud; and whoever perpetrated it is the real deceiver in the story. All other fabrications can be extenuated – at a pinch – as mere 'liberties' taken in the course of translation, poetic licence, concessions to the spirit of the age. But this cannot: this is an imposture; and behind it stands, somewhere, concealed in the shadows, the impostor. Who can that impostor be?

In seeking to answer this question, a crucial dilemma at once faces us. When was the Gaelic text written: before or after the English text? However we answer this question – and we must answer it one way or another – the implications are interesting. Let us consider them.

If the Gaelic text was written after the English text, an innocent explanation is quite impossible. The retrospective fabrication of an 'original' text can be seen only as a 'cover-up': a second and more elaborate fraud, belatedly perpetrated to protect a previous fraud from exposure. In that case, the perpetrators can only have been Macpherson himself, or his successors, the committee of the Highland Society of London. Both these explanations have been seriously advanced; but both, on examination, break down. The latter requires us to believe that Sir John Sinclair, in the interest of Macpherson's reputation, connived at a fraud which included: the construction of a bogus text; the false statement that this text was partly in Macpherson's hand; the fabrication of false testimony ascribed to Captain Morrison (who was then still alive); and finally the destruction of the evidence of his own fraud. A conspiracy theory on such a scale breaks down under the weight of its own implications. It would be much simpler to say that Macpherson must have forged the document himself in retrospective self-defence against the consequences of the naive enthusiasm of his 'eastern friends'. In that case we can only say that the Macpherson mafia in India produced a very agreeable nemesis.

However, even this interpretation entails difficulties. First of all, could Macpherson have done it? He was never a Gaelic scholar. All those who escorted or met him on his famous journey of research agree on that. The Gaelic poet John McCodrum ridiculed 'the incorrectness or inelegance' of his language. Ewan Macpherson and Alexander Morrison both emphasised his weakness in this respect.[84] Could he, after twenty or thirty years in London, busy with the affairs of Parliament, the Nabob, the East India Company, government propaganda, patronage, the Cluny estates, and the stock market, have translated an epic poem into even a poor semblance of ancient Gaelic?[85] Would it not have been much easier merely to continue his proud silence, or to say that this manuscript, like so many others, had disappeared?

So we are forced to consider the only other alternative, viz. that the Gaelic text was written not after, but before the English version. And indeed, quite apart from the difficulties of any other theory, there are reasons for thinking that this must be so. For all Celtic scholars, however they may disagree in their conclusions, agree that in structure, form and content the Gaelic text does not correspond with the English and cannot be a translation from it. Moreover, they also agree with Sinclair that the Gaelic text, in spite of its philological inexactitude, is more vigorous, more colourful, more concrete than the English text: in short, that it reads more like an original than a translation. If this is so, we must assume that the Gaelic text was written in the last three months of 1760, when Macpherson had returned from his Highland tour, armed with manuscripts and recitations, and before he arrived in Edinburgh to translate it, under the eye of Blair, into its English form.

Forty years later, the Highland Society of Edinburgh sought evidence on this point, as on all other matters Ossianic. One of its committee members, Lord Bannatyne, obtained very specific testimony relating to it from what looked like an unimpeachable source. Dr Hugh Macleod, professor of church history in the university of Glasgow, had been a friend of James Macpherson from undergraduate days at Aberdeen. Macleod scouted the idea that *Fingal* had existed in any *old* manuscript. He said firmly that 'the original Gaelic Ms, in verse, from which Mr Macpherson made his translation' – from which Macpherson had, indeed, read a considerable portion aloud to him, and would have read more if Macleod had had the time to listen to it – before translation and publication in English 'was of no older date than his own handwriting'. For Macpherson's *Fingal* was, Macleod continued, 'literally a Rapsodia, digested and patched together according to his own best judgement, out of the huge mass of detached pieces of Fingallian poetry communicated to him by every gentleman who happened to have any such, taken down by his father, or grandfather, or by himself, from the time that the Bards, Recitators and Genealogists began to grow rare, and threatened to be soon extinct; as, in fact, they soon became, though the oldest only within my memory.' He himself, he added, had learned many 'such poems' in his youth, long before he met Macpherson; and he could still repeat 'many broken scraps' of them 'even at this long and late hour' (for he was then seventy-one years old).[86]

Macpherson thus arrived in Edinburgh with what sounds like a fair copy in modern Gaelic of the epic which he would then translate and publish as *Fingal*. Could he, given what we know of his limited expertise in Gaelic, have produced that fair copy on his own? It seems unlikely. For shortly after his arrival in Edinburgh he received from the Rev. James Maclagan of Amulrie a letter sent on to him after he had left Badenoch. That letter accompanied copies of some Gaelic poems, as Macpherson had requested. In acknowledging receipt of these poems on 16 January 1761, Macpherson regretted that he found some of them, at least, obscure – and made doubly obscure by being written in the 'uncouth way of spelling' of the old Irish orthography. Unfortunately, he said, he could not find anyone in Edinburgh to whom he could turn to help him read them.[87]

Who, then, could have assisted Macpherson in producing that fair copy of *Fingal* in modern Gaelic, derived in part from ancient materials as it allegedly was, before he had come to Edinburgh earlier in that month? Only one candidate for that honour presents himself: the laird of Strathmashie.[88] In the cohesive Macpherson family combine, he was undoubtedly the best Gaelic scholar. He was also a Gaelic poet. He had accompanied James Macpherson on that famous expedition – was, perhaps, its initiator – and had taken down recitations, and interpreted and translated texts. He was present, and played a most active part, in the redaction of the manuscripts at Ruthven in those three months. He presided, in fact, over what has been called 'the mysterious laboratory of Ruthven'.[89] The one other person, besides Strathmashie and James Macpherson, who took part in those alchemical sessions, was the minister, Andrew Gallie. But Gallie was not in the secret. He was shown the Gaelic manuscripts which had been brought back from the west. He was asked occasionally to help in interpreting a word. But he was not a scholar: he could read the Gaelic characters only 'with difficulty'. His comments

1 Hector Boece, humanist historian: imaginative, gullible, or both.

2 George Buchanan: poet, revolutionary agitator and historian in extreme old age.

3 James Macpherson strikes a poetic pose for Sir Joshua Reynolds in 1772.

4 A Celtic tragedy: Oscar's end, as sketched in the early 1770s by Alexander Runciman (who had trained in Rome).

5, 6 & 7  The Romance of Scotland is exported: Napoleon, his generals and his painters are inspired by Ossianic legend.

5  Ossian conjures up spirits in a rugged and romantic landscape. Painted by Gérard in 1801.

6 Phantoms in the clouds, envisioned by Ossian as he rests on his harp, and dreams. Painted by Ingres in 1813.

7  Ossian presides at the glorification of France's conquering heroes. Painted by Girodet in 1801.

**8** *Sir Walter Scott* in 1822 by Sir Henry Raeburn. Scott did more than any other person to bind Highlanders and Lowlanders together, creating an image of the modern 'synthetic Scotsman'.

## 9, 10 & 11 Tartan Mania.

**9** Sir Henry Raeburn, *Colonel MacDonell of Glengarry* in 1812, a direct descendant of the first Highland chief to wear a modern kilt less than a century earlier.

**10** Hanoverian King George IV, converted into a Highland warrior chief in 1822. By David Wilkie.

11 The fantastical 'Sobieski Stuart' brothers at Eilean Aigas: a self-portrait, painted in the 1840s.

on the manuscripts are largely external: their size and shape, texture and illuminated capital letters. And 'as to copying for Mr Macpherson, I never did'.

And yet, did Mr Gallie never suspect? Forty years afterwards, he would be questioned by the Edinburgh committee, and would write in defence of *Fingal*, sending, as evidence of its authenticity, 'a few stanzas taken from the manuscript ... by a friend' whose Gaelic scholarship he praised highly, but whom, rather coyly, he did not name.[90] Questioned about the identity of the learned friend who had supplied it as 'original', Gallie admitted, rather curtly, that it was Strathmashie, who had been dead for thirty-two years.[91] Pressed for further details, he shrank from the suggestion – presumably a hint from the Edinburgh committee – that Strathmashie might have helped 'his friend to impose on the publick in the affair of Ossian's poems'. If he had, Mr Gallie would surely have known. . . .'[92]

The hypothesis that Strathmashie was at least part-author of the Gaelic Ossian, and that James Macpherson later translated from that production, can be supported by other evidence. Most of the Gaelic texts which have been put forward as 'originals' of Macpherson's poems can be traced back to Strathmashie.[93] A Gaelic version of part of the seventh book of *Temora* is said to have been found, at his death, among Strathmashie's papers, corrected in his hand and headed 'First rude draft of 7th book of Temora'. This piece of information might, indeed, be considered doubtful. For it was transmitted by oral report to W.F. Skene, when he was staying in the neighbourhood of Strathmashie's house, perhaps eight decades after Strathmashie's death; furthermore, when Skene committed his recollection of the story to writing in 1862, in the introduction to McLauchlan's edition of *The Book of the Dean of Lismore*, he could no longer remember who had been his informant.[94] But this long-known and apparently questionable testimony can, in fact, be buttressed by other evidence that is rather more solid, and which extends further. For, as we shall see shortly, when James Macpherson announced to his friend and agent John Mackenzie in 1793 that he had finally managed to find in various receptacles in his house at Putney all of the sections of *Temora*, which had become separated from each other over the previous thirty years, and described the result as reuniting 'the original copy' of the poem, it was in Gaelic, and the second book (at least) was in Strathmashie's handwriting.[95]

Was it only *Temora* in which Strathmashie had been so extensively involved, or *Fingal* too? Earlier, in chapter four, we noticed instances of Strathmashie's copies of the Gaelic *Fingal* turning up at a later date to inform, or confuse, subsequent enquiries. Old Mr Gallie sent to the Edinburgh committee in 1799 a section of book four of *Fingal* in Gaelic in Strathmashie's handwriting; without quite realising initially, it seems, the potential implications of such a production: for he became noticeably defensive when those implications were made clear to him. We have seen that Strathmashie himself, in answer to Blair's questions in 1763, stated that he personally had compared *Fingal* carefully with 'copies of the originals in my hands' and found the English version remarkably accurate, even preserving the cadence of the Gaelic.[96] This implies that Strathmashie had these 'copies' in his hands before December 1761, when *Fingal* first appeared in print.

We must therefore ask the question: what exactly did Strathmashie mean when he referred to these 'copies' and 'the originals'? We cannot be totally sure; for his expressions are ambiguous, and susceptible of more than one interpretation. We must make the effort, however, to elucidate his meaning and its implications. It is certain, at least, that he was claiming a major part for himself in the enterprise of bringing 'the poems of Ossian' to light. He it was who, during the journey with James Macpherson, 'took down from oral tradition, and transcribed from old manuscripts, by far the greatest part of those pieces he has published'. It looks as if, by 'originals', Strathmashie meant the original recitations and the original manuscripts from which he had taken down and transcribed 'the copies' – which remained with him, and in his own handwriting. At that point there is a gap in our reconstruction of what must have happened until we reach the English translation, which clearly was produced by James Macpherson, not Strathmashie. That translation, Strathmashie certified, was 'amazingly literal' when he compared it with the Gaelic 'copies' still in his hands. Since we now know for certain, as a result of 150 years of subsequent scholarship, that whatever else Macpherson's translation was, it assuredly was not 'amazingly literal', we are left with a dilemma. Did Strathmashie not know what he was talking about?

That is implausible. Alternatively, the gap in our reconstruction has to be filled by assuming that Strathmashie had, at the very least, collaborated with James Macpherson in building up a Fingalian construct which contained the elements 'taken down from oral recitation, and transcribed from old manuscripts', and which James could later translate in a way that was 'amazingly literal'; and that Strathmashie was concealing this step in the process. In short, we are envisaging the production of an 'intermediate' Gaelic version, cobbled together from bits and pieces of the old Ossianic ballads in precisely the manner indicated by Professor Macleod. If we make this assumption, we must hold Strathmashie guilty of part-fabricating a Gaelic epic (or two), but we can save him from the otherwise inevitable charge of bare-faced and gratuitous mendacity, which is the only other possible explanation for the terms used in his letter to Blair.

Having come this far, let us push on a little further. Let us examine briefly, so far as we can, whether the surviving poetry of Lachlan Macpherson bears any resemblance to that of *Fingal* and *Temora*, the translated offspring attributed to James Macpherson. Not in strictly poetical terms – that must be left to those who read Gaelic and possess technical skills – but in terms of ideas, attitudes, and general tone. Thus we turn to the English translations of Strathmashie's verse which were published by the Rev. Thomas Sinton in 1906 in *The Poetry of Badenoch*.[97]

To facilitate our task, we must first boil down to their essence what we find in the epics. *Fingal* and *Temora* are stories of the ancient heroes of the Highland race. Those heroes lived for hunting, and especially for fighting. Deer and dogs provided their sport. Valour in battle was the primary measure of their quality as men. Their virtues lay in loyalty to the code of their tribe; and it was tested in conflict with other tribes. As hunters and warriors they lived in an intense affective relationship, not only with each other, but also with their natural surroundings of mountains, mist, heath and sea. That was the environment in which they drank and sang, fought and died. As Smart pointed out perceptively in 1905, all of this can quite easily be seen as a mythicized version of life in the Highlands before the 'Forty-Five'. And the sadness which suffused the epics? – that 'melancholy passion and revolt against the tragedy of life', which is felt behind such lines as: 'They went forth to the war, and they always fell.' That was a poetical reflection of the prevailing mood among Highlanders following the catastrophic defeat of 1746, and the enforced undoing of the old structures and habits of Highland society in its aftermath.[98]

There is no doubt, in the first place, that Strathmashie was a Jacobite. We need not assume as much from his membership of the Macpherson clan, or from his presumptive part in the prolonged concealment of his chieftain, Cluny. For he avowed it openly in his poetry. It appears casually in the background of a funny, hard-hitting poem on the power of whisky. Whisky can fell heroes to the ground, he tells us, without even a sword being drawn. But while the heroes are still upright and in tongue, they will boast that a score of them will suffice to set the crown on fair-headed Charlie for the rest of us. Speaking for himself, and in another mood, Strathmashie appears the angry Jacobite. Creeping out of his house early one morning, feeling heavy and sad because he is now obliged (by law) to wear breeches and a long clumsy coat instead of his customary belted plaid, making him look 'like a Lowland beggar' instead of a Highland gentleman, he climbs a nearby mountain and encounters a stag. The stag taunts him for his breeches, and threatens to call the red-coated soldiers if he produces a gun. Infuriated, the hunter-bard swears that he would like to shoot both stag and [King] George with the very same bullet – along with every great man in the country hostile to Prince Charles. At least, he says, he still has the power to set his dog to kill the stag. In another poem he resents being called 'a rogue' simply because he believes that King James should be on the throne.[99]

Strathmashie's Jacobitism was not merely a matter of personal affiliation. It was a proclamation of his adherence to a way of life: the Highland way of life. That way of life was now threatened by more than repressive legislation and harsh enforcement. It was being corroded by other forces. Honest men were going down, he proclaimed; men of trickery were rising. At the root of it was the power of money. Commercial values were corrupting the social order. A rich old brewer, able to dress up in fine clothes, could now presume to consort with a duke. Even the learned professions – the lawyers, doctors and clergy – were thinking less about truth, and more about the money that might be jingling in their pockets.[100]

Strathmashie's deep feelings of anguish at what had happened in the Highlands, and was still happening, were mournfully expressed when his chieftain, Cluny, died in January 1764, still an exile in France. His elegy for the departed chief begins with a lament at the tribulations of the age, and the enduring 'defects in Alban'. So many 'well-hitting warriors' who had risen for the Stuarts had died on the battlefield; the gallows and the axe had despatched others; still more had had to leave their country. Then follows the eulogy of the departed hero: small in size, but great of heart. He personified the qualities of the Highland race, and of his own high station therein: 'He was the famous energetic Gael'. His character had been that of a force of nature:

> Like was he to waves against an ocean rock;
> Like a seagull and the tempest darkening over it;
> Like fire on the heather of the rugged grounds;
> Like the terrible swirl of water in spate.

He had been a fierce and fearless fighter: 'like a keen scythe under the green grass' – mowing down his enemies in the field. Yet, when not in battle, the chief had been a wise guardian of his people, maintaining harmony, without false leniency, but with pity and humanity for the needy. Now he has gone to his Maker in peace, 'despite King and Parliament'. His people remain oppressed, with his protection gone.[101]

Strathmashie's lament for Cluny, and through him for the fate of the old Highland society, was composed just two years after the publication of *Fingal*, and one year after the publication of *Temora*. In the dissertation prefixed to *Fingal*, the dissolution of the old Highland society is pointed to explicitly in explaining both the difficulty and the urgency of collecting and preserving these treasures of the Gaelic past. 'The genius of the highlanders has suffered a great change within these few years.' Communications with the rest of Britain had been opened up; trade and manufactures had been introduced. Many Highlanders had left their mountains to seek their fortunes elsewhere; even those who later returned had learned 'enough of foreign manners to despise the customs of their ancestors'. The new emphasis on 'property' made people more individualistic, more materialist, more present-minded. 'Men begin to be less devoted to their chiefs, and consanguinity is not so much regarded.' Bards had been cast aside; the spirit of genealogy was greatly diminished. There was less leisure, and generally less interest in continuing the old culture. 'Hence it is, that the taste for their ancient poetry is at a low ebb among the highlanders.'[102]

This was the background against which we see both Lachlan Macpherson and James Macpherson announcing the motives of their involvement in publishing works of the old Gaelic bards, set in very similar terms. In October 1760 James wrote from Ruthven to another Highlander, the Rev. Mr Maclagan of Amulrie in Perthshire, asking him to contribute as much as he could of 'the ancient poetry in the Gaelic': proclaiming that 'it will be for the honour of our ancestors how many of their pieces of genius are brought to light'.[103] In October 1763 Lachlan wrote from Strathmashie, 'as a Highlander', to Hugh Blair, a Lowlander in Edinburgh, volunteering information on the joint labours of James and himself in collecting and transcribing for publication the works of Ossian, 'which do so much honour to the ancient genius of our country'.[104]

Bringing together all these fragments of evidence, it seems only reasonable to suppose that Lachlan Macpherson of Strathmashie must have played a considerable part in the construction of *Fingal* and *Temora*. On this assumption, we can also explain the behaviour of James Macpherson: the discrepancy, so obvious to his contemporaries, between his character and his achievement; his insistence that there was an 'original' manuscript of the epics which he had 'translated'; his reluctance to produce that original, which, of course, being modern, would only have involved him in further difficulty; and also his refusal to discuss Ossian when he was out of reach of his mentor. *Fingal* was cooked up in the course of animated discussions, with manuscripts, recitations and recent experience to give it substance and momentum. *Temora* (as Macpherson admitted) was sent to him through the post:[105] the post, no doubt, from Badenoch to London. And after *Temora* there was nothing. James Macpherson was away in America from 1763 till 1766. When he returned, Strathmashie was in the 'severe and long continued illness' which ended in his death in August 1767. On his deathbed he gave orders that all his papers, except those on business and family affairs, should be put in a bag and burned; 'which', we are told, 'was accordingly done'.[106]

There is no doubt that Strathmashie experienced, at the end, a classic 'death-bed repentance'. His most intimate friend, the Rev. Mr Gallie, ministered to him, and recorded of him later: 'For months before he died, he became most serious and devout indeed, and deeply lamented how much he had wasted of his time and talents in amusements that diverted him from views and projects more worthy of both.' He confessed 'with great contrition and freedom' to 'crimes and follies less serious' than having 'engaged in helping his friend to impose on the publick in the affair of Ossian's poems'. But on that subject, he had dropped not a hint.[107] Yet we may think it suspicious that Strathmashie had made a holocaust of all his literary papers. Why did he choose to burn those 'copies' of the Gaelic original of *Fingal* which he had had in his own hands in 1761, and of which he had still been so enthusiastically proud in 1763? Did he, perhaps, have something to hide when death drew near: something that might, if it survived, besmirch 'the honour' of his country – and himself? Strathmashie's remaining papers, relating to 'business and family affairs', passed on his death into the custody of his brother-in-law, Mr Butter of Pitlochry. Forty years later, Sir John Sinclair sent one of his Ossianic bloodhounds, the Rev. Alexander Irvine, in search of Strathmashie's papers, which by then had descended to Colonel Butter of Fascally. Irvine sniffed hopefully among the papers, but drew a blank. Disappointed, he reported back to Sinclair that he had found not a trace of Ossianic scent remaining in them.[108] Strathmashie had blown it all sky-ward on a fiery wind.

With Strathmashie's death, it seems that Ossian died too. If we make this connection, we can also explain the deviousness of Macpherson's later actions in relation to the old manuscripts which he had collected – the Book of the Dean, the Clanranald papers, etc. Macpherson undoubtedly had these manuscripts. Why did he never bring them fairly into the open? Why were they exhibited so furtively in 1762? Why did Mackenzie behave so oddly at their second exhibition in

1779? Why did Macpherson, in 1793, seem to deny to Ferguson almost that any relevant manuscripts existed? And why, even after Macpherson's death, was Mackenzie so reluctant to produce them? Why, in the end, did he send them to the Highland Society with no indication that they had come from Macpherson: that these were the famous manuscripts which had been so often referred to, but never convincingly shown?

The answer to these questions can hardly be in doubt. James Macpherson could not read the old manuscripts. He could understand and speak Gaelic in its contemporary Highland form; but he was no scholar in the language. It was not he who, in 1760, had taken down the recitations.[109] Even for that he had relied on others: on Strathmashie, Morrison or Ewan Macpherson. And before an ancient manuscript he was helpless. A little over a decade later, in 1773 or 1774, he was humiliated by being shown, in the Bodleian Library at Oxford, a fourteenth-century Gaelic manuscript of a dialogue between Ossian and St Patrick, of which, he had to admit, he could not read a word.[110] Although he possessed Clanranald's manuscripts, he never referred to their contents. His recoverable references to the Book of the Dean of Lismore are solely to the mutilated and obscure state of the manuscript, written in a peculiar script unknown to all Highlanders. Twice he exhibited – or claimed to have exhibited – his ancient manuscripts; but always he saw to it either that they were not seen, or that their identity was wrapped in protective ambiguity. The inference is clear: he did not himself truly know what was in those manuscripts and was terrified lest a real Gaelic scholar should read them and cause trouble. It was safe to invite a visit of inspection from Dr Johnson, who could not read Gaelic; but when the visitor turned out to be William Shaw, who could, up went the smokescreen. Similarly, in 1793, Macpherson was forced to admit the irrelevance of the manuscripts to Ferguson, who knew Gaelic. If we assume that Macpherson had based his Ossian not on the old manuscripts, which he could not read, but on an intermediate Gaelic text, whose relationship to those old manuscripts was unverifiable by him, then his difficulty becomes clear. His Gaelic manuscript containing *Fingal* was the modern manuscript cooked up imaginatively at Ruthven or Strathmashie, mostly out of a series of contemporary oral recitations. That would convince no one of its authenticity. On the other hand, his genuine old manuscripts – those manuscripts which had been silently accumulated in Badenoch, or fetched with such triumph from the Hebrides – were dynamite. He could have used them to blow up Dr Johnson (who had denied the existence of any ancient Gaelic manuscripts) – but only at the risk of blowing himself up too. The safest course was to lock them away, even to deny their existence. At all costs, they must not be submitted to scholars as the Gaelic originals of Ossian.

So, when the Highlanders in India forced the issue, and Macpherson could hold out no longer, he decided to dig out, not those real ancient manuscripts, but the intermediate text, either supplied by Strathmashie, or concocted by himself and Strathmashie. It had evidently fallen into disorder; but in the end a number of pieces were discovered and handed to Mackenzie, who was now his agent for all Fingalian affairs. Of this process there is clear evidence, both in a private note written in Macpherson's own copy of *Fingal*, afterwards discovered in his house in Badenoch,[111] and in extracts from Mackenzie's private diary, transcribed by his clerk Colin Macrae on 7 December 1807 for Sir John Sinclair.[112] Both sources agree in noting that, of one poem, *Carthon*, only a part could be found. It is unreasonable to suppose that Macpherson and Mackenzie were engaged in independent exercises of elaborate private deception. The notes in Mackenzie's diary confirm this interpretation of how the process of searching and handing-over had gone. In meetings at his house in Putney in September and November of 1792, Macpherson told Mackenzie that he had 'searched everywhere' for the missing part of *Carthon*, but could not find it. In April of the following year Macpherson announced to Mackenzie that he had found the original Gaelic version of *Temora*, which he now needed a clerk to copy. At least part of the text that Macpherson had found, book two, as Mackenzie recorded, was in Strathmashie's handwriting.

The role ascribed here to Strathmashie is admittedly a hypothesis; but it is a hypothesis which explains the known facts and, incidentally, reduces the charge against the principal accused – Strathmashie, Macpherson, Mackenzie – from machiavellian fraud to lower and more human proportions. If it is objected that Strathmashie's known poetry is not in the high style of *Fingal* – that, as his friend Andrew Gallie wrote, 'wit, humour and merriment was his line, not the solemn, sedate and plaintive',[113] we have seen that this description, though generally true, is belied by at least one major exception; and that darker thoughts could surface occasionally even in his lighter-toned pieces. Moreover, it would be unwise to ignore other indications of Strathmashie's versatility. Sinton recorded that Strathmashie wrote poetry in English as well as Gaelic, and mentioned one such poem in particular: 'a sort of parody on the Homeric style', written after a devastating flood on the river Spey.[114] Strathmashie actually published this poem in English. Unfortunately, concerning himself in his book solely with the Gaelic poetry of Badenoch, Sinton chose not to reprint this English poem of Strathmashie's, so it is not available for comparative analysis here. But in any case, it can equally well be argued that there is little in James Macpherson's other work to suggest that he was capable of writing the works of Ossian: as his own friends said, he could as soon have taken wings and flown, or created the island of Skye. Gallie also protested that if Strathmashie had been 'engaged in helping his friend to impose on the publick in the affair of Ossian's poems', he, Gallie, being his 'intimate acquaintance and friend', would surely have known.[115] But did not Blair make an identical protest in respect of James Macpherson?[116] There is no reason to suppose that the minister of Laggan was more perceptive than the Regius Professor in Edinburgh. And yet someone composed the works of Ossian. Perhaps, as was once thought of the works of Homer, they were composed by a committee. If so, it was a committee of two.

With this hypothesis in mind, we can now turn to the second great question: the personality of James Macpherson. He was not an attractive character. Other literary adventurers – we shall come to some of them – reconcile us to their innocent frauds by personal charm, amiable eccentricity, or inspired fantasy. No such quality redeems the narrow calculating spirit of Macpherson. He seems to have been entirely without charm. In the years of his literary success, he knew the literati of Edinburgh: David Hume, John Home, Blair, Ferguson, Carlyle. That success carried him into the literary world of London, where he lived for thirty years. We find him dining in the company of

Johnson, Boswell, Sheridan, Garrick, Goldsmith, Gibbon.[117] And yet he made no impact, or an unfavourable impact, on all these men. No interesting or entertaining conversation of his is recorded: only sullen silence, or provincial bêtises, or positive malevolence (he made trouble between Johnson and Sheridan). In the world of letters he was isolated, for he refused to discuss the only subject which had made him interesting. He was a member of parliament for seventeen years, but he never spoke there. Nathaniel Wraxall, who has left such a vivid account of parliamentary life at that time, and who must have known him well, for he was his colleague as agent for the Nawab of Arcot, gives a striking and favourable account of Sir John Macpherson but barely mentions James. His letters reflect an overbearing spirit: something of a bully.[118] They also lack any literary grace, sometimes even syntax. From them, Gray thought him grossly uncultured; and his few recorded utterances on literary matters would surely have confirmed Gray in that view. Boswell tells us that one evening at Lord Eglinton's house, someone praised Gray's *Elegy* in Macpherson's presence. '"Hoot!" cried Fingal' (as Boswell recorded) '"to write panegyrics upon a parcel of damned rogues that did nething but plough the land and saw corn!" He considered that fighters only should be celebrated,' as Eglinton observed; going on to describe Macpherson as 'really a Highland claymore. If you was to scour him, you would spoil him':[119] in other words, an *ingénu*, a barbarian whose only point of interest was his naivety. Boswell called him 'the Sublime Savage'; but the savagery was more apparent than the sublimity, at least in his manners. David Hume began by thinking him 'modest and sensible' but soon found him 'perverse and unamiable', and wrote of his 'effrontery and absurdity'. Hume told Boswell that Macpherson was 'full of Highland prejudices', and illustrated for him the perversity and absurdity of Macpherson's talk: 'he hates a Republic and he does not like Kings. He would have all the Nation divided into Clans, and these clans to be always fighting.'[120] Boswell himself, on first meeting Macpherson, described him as 'a man of great genius and an honest Scotch Highlander'; but he, too, soon changed his mind. One day he observed to Johnson 'what a strange mortal Macpherson was, or affected to be, and how he railed at all established systems'. Johnson's reply was contemptuous: 'so would he tumble in a hog-sty as long as you look at him and cry to him to come out. But let him alone, never mind him, and he'll soon give it over.'[121]

Johnson was right. Macpherson, in himself, was utterly uninteresting and, apart from the mystery of *Fingal*, nobody could find much to say about him. There is no adequate contemporary account of him as a person. Alexander Carlyle states that he came to know him 'intimately'; but all that he can tell us about him is that, when they met at Moffat, he was tall and good looking; that he wore boots, 'though not then the fashion', to hide the thickness of his legs; and that he showed himself 'proud and reserved and shunned dining with us on some pretence'.[122] John Ramsay of Ochtertyre, who met him in Edinburgh two years later, describes him as 'a plain looking lad, dressed like a preacher: what he said was sensible, but his manner was starch and reserved'.[123] Blair similarly described Macpherson, after his death, as stiff, proud, irritable and morose.[124]

What lay behind the handsome presence and the irritable pride? Apparently nothing except discontent with himself and the world. Boswell, who met him often in London during 1762 and 1763 – the time of his greatest fame – describes him 'railing against the human species in vast discontent', cursing all established opinions and 'all reserve and dignity of behaviour', declaring that there was no distinction between virtue and vice, and professing that he had 'no relish for anything in life except women, and even these he cared but little for'. 'I hate John Bull,' he told Blair, who wondered what kept him in London, 'but I love his daughters.' Blair once declared 'that Macpherson must be miserable, because he was absolutely void of curiosity'.[125]

Boswell observed Macpherson as a young man in London; but the character which he observed did not change substantially in later life. After 1763 Macpherson put Ossian behind him and sought prosperity by other means. He accepted his fame but refused all discussion, ignoring or overbearing his critics. His historical works, his translation of Homer, were received with contempt. In literature, as in politics and finance, he was a lonely, selfish figure, outwardly proud, sullen, reserved; inwardly devious. He drove ostentatiously to Parliament in his flamboyant yellow coach; but, once there, was silent except in alcoves and corridors. At home, his bachelor establishments

– his house in Fludyer Street, his villa in Putney – welcomed only the *clientèle* of Highlanders who fought his underhand battles in literature or politics. In these battles he was quite unscrupulous. We find him, on one occasion, secretly proposing to puff his own work over the pseudonym 'Impartial'.[126] His political propaganda for the government was described by Walpole as a 'daily column of lies'.[127] His business associates, and his business methods, were questionable. But he grew rich. The pursuit of wealth filled the void and supplied him with a driving force. Financial independence, he more than once admitted, was the only motive, 'the uniform pursuit of my life'.[128]

Even in his native county in his last years, where he was at ease among his own people, he failed to win real friends. He liked to impress the natives. A ferryman on the Spey described him as 'a great man from London and the Court, bedizened with rings, gold seals and furs'.[129] He was a hospitable and, latterly, a generous laird. By his fame he brought distinction to that remote valley. But a neighbour who was not ill-disposed towards him wrote that, though a local hero, he was shunned by the best society: he was excluded from polite social intercourse by unhappy connections, kept only tavern company, and was the prey of toad-eaters and designing housekeepers: the northern equivalent of his Highland mafia in London. Anne Grant was not only a literary lady, but also the wife of a minister, and she did not like to speak ill of the dead. But in writing a letter to convey the news of Macpherson's last days, she contrived, by indirect expression, to let her correspondent know that she had found him 'gross, callous, and awkward': owing, she supposed, to his deeply ingrained habits of life. He had not been a happy man, and he had not made others happy either.[130]

Between this pushing philistine and the 'sublime', 'refined' Ossian there is, as Paul van Tieghem wrote, 'an abyss'.[131] But if we insert the character which we have described into the history of the poems as we have surmised it, the problem becomes soluble. When James Macpherson set out from Ruthven to Moffat with the family of Graham of Balgowan, he was a young man of frustrated literary ambitions. He had a genuine interest in Gaelic poetry, now becoming fashionable; and he had the encouragement of his more prosperous kinsman and neighbour at Strathmashie. He had evidently acquired at least one Gaelic manuscript containing poems ascribed to Ossian. But he lacked originality, his talent was slight, and his published poems had fallen flat. So he saw himself condemned to a humble profession which he disliked, and to a remote valley in which he could not prosper. He saw no escape. Then, at Logierait, he met Adam Ferguson and, through him, at Moffat, John Home.

What a vital part in the history of Scottish literature was played by Adam Ferguson! At his house the young Walter Scott would meet Burns; and through his patronage both the Macphersons would make their prosperous careers. But for him Ossian might never have been created, and John Macpherson might never have found his way into the labyrinth of politics. Rightly did they both revere him as their earliest patron. For Ferguson introduced James to Home as he would afterwards introduce John to the Earl of Warwick. And once James had met Home, the magic door was open which might lead, through Gaelic poetry, to fame and wealth.

To Home, who was fascinated by Gaelic poetry but knew no Gaelic himself, Macpherson was a means of tapping that mysterious mountain spring. To Macpherson, Home was a link with the literary establishment, with the world of high patronage. When Home asked him to produce a Gaelic ballad, Macpherson had nothing to hand. So, after some hesitation, he fabricated. It was not a great crime. Lady Wardlaw had fabricated. Chatterton would fabricate. Pinkerton would fabricate. Robert Surtees, the historian of Durham, would fabricate a ballad which would deceive Sir Walter Scott. Hawker of Morwenstow, a beneficed clergyman, would similarly deceive Macaulay. Anyway, Macpherson's innocent fraud succeeded marvellously. He found himself carried up to Edinburgh, fêted by the literati, told by them that his poems – nine-tenths of which he knew to be forged – were probably the dwindling relics of a great epic still to be found, and that he was the man whom Providence had chosen to find it. Perhaps he himself believed in this epic – he had, after all, studied under the shadow of Thomas Blackwell.[132] In any case, he could see that his new patrons were not over-critical. If he could produce the epic, they would swallow it. They did.

So now his course was set. If he were to exploit his good fortune, if he were to preserve the goodwill of the men of letters, and capture the patronage of the men of power, he must not draw back; he must go on. Perhaps he had been rash, perhaps he had speculated beyond his own intellectual resources; but he knew that he could rely on the interest and support of his cousin at Strathmashie, who was older than him, who was a Gaelic scholar and a Gaelic poet, and who, as a laird, could introduce him into the houses of men of authority in the Highlands and islands. Lachlan Macpherson of Strathmashie accepted the challenge, and the opportunity. As he saw it, his young kinsman, by lucky connections in Edinburgh and London, might be the channel through which Gaelic literature might at last claim its rightful due. He accompanied James to the west: to the minister of Sleat, to the lairds and chieftains of the isles. He took down recitations for him, helped him to discover manuscripts; and then, when James returned to Ruthven with his haul, he undertook to make sense of those disconnected notes and unintelligible old manuscripts: to discover the epic of which they were the broken and corrupted relics. So the two cousins worked together, in an exciting collusive work of imaginative reconstruction; and occasionally the local minister, Andrew Gallie, dropped in, to be flattered by consultation on a difficult phrase, or dazzled by the sight of an ancient text – fetched, he was told, from the Outer Hebrides.

Strathmashie's part must have been vital in those three months of literary concoction; for he alone could read the texts fully, if anyone could. By age, social standing and command of the language, he exercised authority. In the circumstances of time and place – in Ruthven in the last months of 1760 – only he could have carried out some of the essential work of constructing the 'complete epic' which James claimed already to possess when he arrived in Edinburgh in January 1761. There the translator took over from the author. The text had been gone through, and the meaning cleared, in Ruthven. Now it was to be put into the appropriate style and form. The style was determined, in part, by Blair, who had such clear ideas on 'rhetoric and belles-lettres'. Almost every day, at dinner, Macpherson read his work, and surely the professor commented. As for the form, that had already been determined by their previous common venture, the *Fragments*. The day of the disciplined heroic couplet which Pope had used for his translation of the *Iliad* – and which Macpherson himself had used in his juvenile verses – had now passed. Only a few years ago, Dr Lowth, the Professor of Poetry at Oxford – Blair's opposite number – had delivered his famous lectures on the sacred poetry of the Hebrews, presenting the Old Testament not as divine revelation but as national poetry. If the national poetry of the Hebrews had captured the minds of men through translation into poetic prose, why should not the national poetry of Scotch Highlanders do the same? The argument proved sound by the event, and Macpherson, as the translator, found himself, at the age of twenty-seven, suddenly famous, patronised by the prime minister, courted by men of letters, a London lion.

It was a remarkable success story. But could such success be maintained and consolidated in the slippery metropolis? The more he savoured his triumph, the more Macpherson became inwardly aware of its unreality. He could not avow the truth about the poems which were making his fortune. He could not live on equal terms with the wits of London: how could he talk freely to men so much more learned and sophisticated than himself, who might, at any time, press him about *Fingal*? If he was challenged, he could not simply produce the modern 'intermediate' Gaelic text, without being denounced instantly as a forger. Nor did he dare to produce the old manuscripts which he could not read himself, whose contents were largely unknown to him, and which, if read, might so easily be the beginning rather than the end of controversy. He was temperamentally unfitted for controversy, even for dialogue, as Blair made plain.[133] He was still a crude provincial, secretly aware of his own inner emptiness, which he concealed behind postures of bravado and vulgar self-assertion, and – when in the company of a sympathetic fellow Scot like Boswell – breaking out in abject self-pity and denunciations of the world. In the end, he recognised that he could not sustain the part. The carefree excitement of the mysterious laboratory at Ruthven could not be recaptured. After *Temora*, most of which lacked any genuine basis, he was on the defensive. So was Blair. And when Strathmashie died, no impetus was left. So Macpherson, having already, through Ossian, established himself in the antechambers of power, changed direction. The quest, and then the defence, of Ossian had brought him into contact with his namesake, the minister of Sleat; and the minister's son, John Macpherson, would replace the Celtic Homer as the means of realising his essentially philistine ambitions: wealth, status, the deference, if not of the literary world, at least of clan Macpherson.

But for our purposes the important question is not so much how *Fingal* came to be forged, but why the Scots continued for so long to insist that it was genuine. In England the forgery was regarded as self-evident by 1763; and Walpole thought it indecent to revive a dead controversy in 1774. But in Scotland Johnson's incursion in 1775 was generally resented, not as an indelicate reminder of an old error, but as an outrageous attack on an unquestionable truth. That truth continued to be asserted for another generation. Neither the doubts of the English, nor the challenge of the Irish scholars, could shake the conviction not merely of the Highlanders, soon to be organised in the Highland societies of London and Edinburgh, but even of Lowlanders, like the cosmopolitan 'philosophers' of Edinburgh; and the informed criticism of Scottish dissidents like Pinkerton and Shaw was dismissed as the work of anglicised traitors. Even after Macpherson's death, Blair, Carlyle, Home and Ferguson refused to admit that the poems could have been forged. The most that they would allow was that Macpherson might perhaps have taken some liberties in piecing together what was found in separate or broken fragments; which, they hastened to add, was no more than 'Homer is said to have done when he collected the songs of the bards of Greece'.[134]

After the publication, in 1805, of the *Report* of the Highland Society of Edinburgh, the Scottish supporters of Ossian became more cautious. That report brought them some comfort, indeed; but the failure of the committee to discover a single line of authentic Gaelic poetry which corresponded exactly to anything in *The Poems of Ossian* was undoubtedly inconvenient. Moreover, in the same year, Malcolm Laing, who had already expressed his views in a dissertation appended to his *History of Scotland* in 1800, published a critical edition of the *Poems of Ossian*, roundly declaring them, in the title, to be the works of James Macpherson. In his commentary Laing cited numerous passages to show that Macpherson had repeatedly borrowed language and concepts from the Bible, Homer, Milton, etc. However, the Scottish believers, though shaken, were not routed by such revelations. The publication of the Gaelic text in 1807, and Sir

John Sinclair's *Dissertation*, were held to refute the negative conclusions of the *Report*. Laing was conveniently discovered to be an Orkneyman, and so, like the English and the Irish, naturally biassed against the Scots. Perhaps, as the octogenarian Andrew Gallie put it, the severe checks given by the ancient Caledonians to Laing's predatory Scandinavian ancestors had 'raised prejudices not yet extinct'.[135] An even more intemperate attack on Laing's 'Teutonic bile' would later be made by a Regius Professor in Edinburgh.[136] Pinkerton was not alone in introducing racial criteria into Scottish criticism. Thanks to such arguments, the case for Ossian continued to be made in Scotland long into the nineteenth century. It was not till the close of the century that the researches of Gaelic scholars, by collecting and studying a vast corpus of genuine Ossianic literature, and establishing the fraudulent character of the Gaelic text of 1807, settled the matter for all but a few pockets of Old Believers.

But if Scottish belief in the authenticity of Ossian weakened in the course of the nineteenth century, that was not because the Scots, however belatedly, yielded to reason. Like Boece's kings and Buchanan's ancient constitution, Ossian's poems lost their authenticity, not when they were disproved, but when changing circumstances made them no longer necessary – and when another myth was available to supersede them. The myth of Ossian had been accepted because it filled a need – the need for a purely Scottish literature. In 1760 there had been no such literature, and Ossian had come to fill the void. To jettison it, to deny its authenticity, was to re-create that void. But by the early nineteenth century that was no longer true. In 1802 appeared the *Minstrelsy of the Scottish Border*; in 1805 the *Lay of the Last Minstrel*; *Marmion*, *Rokeby* and *The Lady of the Lake* followed. With the rediscovery of genuine traditional Scottish poetry and the creation of genuine modern Scottish poetry, Scott had filled the void, and Ossian was no longer necessary. He had anyway, by now, been monopolised by the national enemy, Napoleon. With Napoleon he would die: die in Delphine Gray's *chant ossianique* for the dead Emperor. Meanwhile the new myth which was to replace the cult of Ossian had already taken root. Next year it would celebrate its triumph in Edinburgh. The organiser of that triumph would be – appropriately – Sir Walter Scott.

*Part III*

# THE SARTORIAL MYTH

# The Coming of the Kilt

The several races of the British isles have contributed unequally, but distinctively, to our common culture. Political and intellectual initiative has come mainly from the Anglo-Saxons or Anglo-Normans. Myth, fantasy, and the traditions that are the crystallisation of such myth, have been supplied by the Celts. No halo of romance surrounds the misty figures of Hengist and Horsa. Norman blood and the Norman yoke survive only as the symbols of a proud or hated *Herrenvolk*. But King Arthur and Camelot have been adopted into English legend and literature; the Irish language and Irish mythology have been accepted by the descendants of Strongbow and the English ascendancy; and in Scotland the apparatus of Celtic tribalism has been assumed, and formalised, by those whose ancestors regarded the Highland dress as the badge of barbarism, and shuddered at the squeal of the bagpipe.

The re-creation of legend requires a continuing capacity for legend; and its formalisation can be seen as a ritual adjustment, a formal accommodation of barbarism to civility. The process therefore entails a necessary element of fantasy, often indistinguishable from fraud. Geoffrey of Monmouth, Hector Boece, James Macpherson, 'Iolo Morganwg', the lesser-known Sobieski Stuart brothers, stand out as great artists in this continuous history of innocent fraud, whose deposit – Glastonbury Abbey, the annual Eisteddfod, the tartan industry of Scotland – is still with us. Perhaps we should venerate these men for having, as it were, domesticated a dangerous process. After all, that same process was less innocent in some other countries.

Herder, like Macpherson, extolled the virtues of the ancient barbarians of his nation. A later generation of Germans took his message seriously. Ritualisation would have been better.

My theme in this, and the following chapter, is the history of this process of innocent ritualisation in Scotland: the process whereby the customs and costumes of the Scottish Highlanders, previously despised as barbarous, and at one time formally extinguished, were resumed, elaborated and extended. Thus, today, the kilt and the tartan are regarded as the traditional dress of historic Scotland: Lowland Scots imagine themselves as members of 'clans', and visitors from England are welcomed by the noise of bagpipes, and must struggle to read road signs in Irish lettering.

The process was the work of a well-defined era: the century from 1745 to 1845. Before 1745, the Highlanders and all their customs were disowned and despised by every articulate Scotchman. After 1845 the Highland takeover was complete. The voice of protest, and of historical truth, was often raised; but it was always powerless. Romanticism might lose its power; but then tourism and commercialism would take over its legacy, extending and vulgarising it in detail. Today it is fixed in the elaborate rituals of Scots abroad, and in the well-stocked souvenir shops of Lowland Scotland.

The Celtic takeover in Scotland is particularly dramatic, because in Scotland alone the Celts had no claims to a native civilisation. Lost in almost complete darkness, broken only by occasional flickers of light from Celtic Ireland or Saxon Northumbria, authentic Highland society had almost no history, till it was invented by Hector Boece in the sixteenth century, almost no literature till it was invented by Macpherson in the eighteenth. On the rare occasions when the Celtic tribes of Scotland were noticed by those Saxons or Normans who established themselves in the country and gradually created some kind of government there, it was merely as savages. When the Anglo-Norman baron, King David of Scotland, invaded England in 1138, he was met by a fellow Anglo-Norman baron, Robert Bruce, the grandfather of the later Scottish hero, who remonstrated with him for using native mercenaries: 'Picts' of Galloway. To involve the blacks in customary colonial competitions was not gentlemanly. The same crime was committed, five centuries later, by Montrose, who was never forgiven for leading Highland tribesmen against the civilised towns of the east. Royalism might be a respectable cause; but to introduce Highlanders into constitutional struggles was going too far. 'The Highlanders', said James VI summarily, in describing his own subjects for the enlightenment of his son, are 'barbarous for the most part', the islanders 'utterly barbarous'.[1] A century later, the great Scottish patriot, Andrew Fletcher of Saltoun, looked upon them in the same way: to him they were the 'wretched Highlanders': few, worthless, and contemptible.[2]

In general, the attitude of the Lowlanders to the Highlanders was that of the Romanised Britons to the Picts. They relied on a *limes*, a 'Highland line', beyond which the inaccessible barbarians, who were not worth conquering, were left to themselves. The function of government was not to penetrate, or transform, or even chart those inhospitable wastes, but simply to seal them off.

All this was changed by the rebellions of 1715 and 1745, when the local resentments of the Highland clans were fused with the political cause of Jacobitism. Thereby they threatened, not merely the political party in power in Edinburgh, but the government of Britain itself. After the first rebellion, which was soon crushed, the British government passed laws to disarm the Highlanders,[3] and sent General Wade to Scotland to 'secure' the Highlands by building new forts and new roads. These were the time-honoured methods which had been begun by Oliver Cromwell and continued by William III. They were not very effective. In 1745 the Young Chevalier, Prince Charles Stuart, arrived in the western Highlands, rallied the clans, collected an army in the Jacobite north-east, occupied the unresisting city of Edinburgh, and led a victorious army into the heart of England. For a moment there was panic in London. Suddenly it seemed possible that the whole structure of central government, perhaps of society, might be overthrown by these inner barbarians while the forces of the state were distracted in a serious foreign war. When the rebellion was over, that government decided that it should never again be put to such risk. It would tackle the problem at its base. Fortunately, it now had the means to do so. United with England, Scottish Lowland society now had new strength, new energies, and a new philosophy of 'improvement'. With such resources, it was possible to carry out a wholesale transformation of that archaic Highland society, which neither James VI, nor Oliver Cromwell, nor William III had done more than contain.

So, in the wake of the rebellion, the Hanoverian government enacted a series of laws, whose purpose was to 'open up' the Highlands: to dissolve the relics of their archaic social structure; to 'improve' those barren lands; to break the inveterate habits of that tribal society. It was an attack in depth: an attempt to transform a whole social system; and it necessarily entailed an attack on the symbolism as well as the substance of that system. Hereditary jurisdictions were at last to be abolished. Sound religion was to be propagated. Chieftains were to become British aristocrats; their retainers should be industrious peasants, artisans, or soldiers in the British army. And all were to wear civilised clothes. The tartan was outlawed. Trousers were to replace the distinctive Highland dress.[4]

But what was the distinctive dress of the Highlander before 1745? This is a subject which has been widely and profoundly argued; but the argument has been obscured by prejudice. The essential facts, however, are not in dispute, and can be set out briefly.

Before the sixteenth century there is no evidence of distinctive Highland dress. Medieval writers, like Froissart, who refer to the *sauvages d'Écosse*, say nothing about any peculiarity of garb. But in the sixteenth century evidence of such peculiarity begins to accumulate. The earliest such evidence comes from the French-educated Scottish theologian John Major, whose *Historia Maioris Britanniae* was published in Paris in 1521. Later accounts are by Major's pupil, George Buchanan, and by Buchanan's contemporary and rival, John Leslie, bishop of Ross, the political agent of Mary Queen of Scots. There are also accounts by Frenchmen who served in Scotland; and there is an illustration published in Paris in 1562. All of these sixteenth-century accounts are in substantial agreement. They show that the ordinary dress of the Highlanders was a long 'Irish' shirt (in Gaelic *léine*), which the higher classes – as in Ireland – dyed with saffron (*leni-croich*); a tunic or *failuin*; and a cloak or plaid, which the higher classes had woven in many colours or stripes, but which in general was of a russet or brown effect, as protective colouring in the heather. In addition, the Highlanders wore shoes with a single sole (the higher classes might wear buskins) and flat soft caps, generally blue. In battle, the leaders wore chain mail, while the lower classes wore a padded linen shirt painted or daubed with pitch, and covered with deerskins.

This was the normal Highland dress. However, there was also a variation used, probably, only by the chieftains and great men who had contact with the more sophisticated inhabitants of the Lowlands. This was the trews, a combination of breeches and stockings. The trews could not be used conveniently out of doors in wild country and all weathers except by men who had attendants to protect or carry them. It was therefore a mark of social distinction. Both trews and, probably, plaid were made of tartan. The origin of tartan – both name and substance – is disputed. The name is generally supposed to be of French origin – *tiretaine* – and the substance, or the method of weaving it, to have been imported from France or Flanders. If so, it presumably acquired its peculiar character in the Highlands. It is first mentioned in Scotland in the 1530s, and was by then already associated with the Highlands. In 1538 King James V ordered a hunting suit of Highland tartan. This consisted of a velvet Highland suit of various colours, tartan trews and a low-hanging tartan shirt.

In the course of the seventeenth century the Highland costume was modified. The principal modifications were three. First, the long shirt was gradually disused. Secondly, the trews gained in popularity among the upper classes. Finally, for ordinary purposes, the plaid was converted, from a loose cloak, into part of the normal dress by being belted round the waist.

These changes occurred irregularly over the century. The long shirt was evidently laid aside in the islands early in the century, and replaced by coat, waistcoat and breeches, as in the Lowlands.[5] On the other hand, as late as 1715, a Scottish minister – the father of the enlightened philosopher Adam Ferguson – noted that the wild Highlanders in the Jacobite army which passed through his parish wore 'neither plaid nor philibeg', but merely a home-made close-fitting coat of one colour, stretching below mid-leg, with a belt:[6] in other words, the old *léine*. The Highlanders, it seems, were by then less sophisticated than the islanders. But this is the latest evidence, so far as I know, of the survival of the *léine*.

The growing fashion of the trews among the upper classes was no doubt due, in large part, to the influence of the Lowland breeches. This was particularly apparent in the Highland armies which, from the time of the Puritan Revolution, increasingly appeared in the Lowlands and sometimes, by their intervention, turned the fortunes of war. On all these occasions it was noted that the officers wore trews while the common soldiers had their legs and thighs bare. Both officers and men wore the plaid, which formed a cloak over their shoulders; but whereas, to the officers, the plaid was an upper garment complemented, at a lower level, by the trews, to the common soldiers it was the main covering for the whole body. It was belted round the waist, and the part below the belt formed a kind of skirt or petticoat. The essential fact is that, as yet, there was no mention of the kilt, as we know it today. At the end of the seventeenth century, as far as the written evidence goes – and we have some explicit accounts[7] – the alternative was simple. A Highlander wore either the plaid and the trews, or the 'belted plaid' ending, below the belt, in a skirt. The former was the dress of an officer, or a gentleman; the latter of a common soldier, or peasant.

Against this clear conclusion of the literary sources, certain pieces of pictorial evidence have been advanced to suggest that the kilt, as a separate garment, was worn in Scotland before the Union with England. The most important is the coat of arms of the family of Skene of that Ilk as matriculated in 1672 and drawn by Alexander Nisbet. The supporters then added to that coat of arms are two Highlanders: of whom one is a gentleman 'in proper garb', i.e. in trews – and the other a plebeian, described in the official matriculation as 'in servile habit'. This servile habit has been interpreted by some as a modern kilt. However, the illustrations used are a nineteenth-century representation of a worn stone carving and cannot be implicitly trusted. In any case, they do not necessarily show a kilt. Close examination suggests that the servile habit is, in fact, the belted plaid.[8]

The name 'kilt', in its early form of 'quelt', first appears twenty years after the Union; but even then, only as a term for the belted plaid, not for a distinct garment. The author who first uses it is Edward Burt, whom we met earlier. Burt was an English officer posted to Scotland in the reign of George I as chief surveyor, under General Wade, for the making of roads in the Highlands. While there he wrote, mainly from Inverness, a series of interesting and intelligent letters to a friend in England, describing critically, but not unsympathetically, the character and customs of the country. These letters were not published till 1754, the last year of the author's life, when the great rebellion of 1745 and its aftermath had again drawn popular interest to the Highlands; but internal evidence shows that they were written at the time of his service there in 1725 and 1726.

According to Burt, the elegant trews were only used by the upper class of Highlander, and then only when in the Lowlands, or on social visits, or when riding; but 'those among them who travel on foot, or have not attendants to carry them over the waters', use 'the quelt', which is 'the common habit of the ordinary Highlands' – and, he added, 'far from being acceptable to the eye'. This 'quelt', he explains, is not a distinct garment but simply a particular method of wearing the plaid, a small part of which is

> set in folds and girt round the waist to make of it a short petti-
> coat that reaches half-way down the thigh, and the rest is
> brought over the shoulders and then fastened before, below the
> neck, often with a fork, and sometimes with a bodkin or sharp-
> ened piece of stick, so that they make pretty near the appearance
> of the poor women in London when they bring their gowns over
> their heads to shelter them from the rain.

This 'petticoat', says Burt, was normally worn 'so very short, that in a windy day, going up a hill, or stooping, the indecency of it is plainly discovered'.

Burt was explicit about the Highland dress because already, in his time, it was a subject of political controversy. After the suppression of the Jacobite rebellion of 1715, proposals had been made to ban this dress, as the Irish dress had been banned in the reign of Henry VIII.[9] So the 'Disarming Act', presented to the British Parliament by Duncan Forbes of Culloden, had originally included such a ban. However, it had been resisted, and – since the rebellion had been so easily dispersed – had not been pressed. But the discussion had continued, and Burt records the arguments used on both sides. The advocates of the ban argued that the Highland dress distinguished the Highlanders from the rest of British subjects and bound them together in a narrow introverted community: that the plaid, in particular, encouraged their idle way of life, 'lying about upon the heath in the daytime instead of following some lawful employment'; that, being 'composed of such colours as altogether in the mass so nearly resemble the heath on which they lie, that it is hardly to be distinguished from it until one is so near them as to be within their power', it facilitated their robberies and depredations; that it made them, 'as they carry continually their tents about them', ready to join a rebellion at a moment's notice; and, lastly, that in Ireland it had already, for these reasons, been suppressed long ago by Act of Parliament, 'and no complaint for the want of it, now remains among the mountaineers of that country'. To these arguments it was answered that the Highland dress was convenient and necessary in a wild and inhospitable country, where a traveller must 'skip over the rocks and bogs' and may often have to lie all night in the hills, and that it was very cheap: 'a few shillings will buy this dress for an ordinary Highlander' who could never afford 'a lowland suit, though of the coarsest cloth or stuff, fit to keep him warm in that cold climate'.[10] Cheapness and the rigours of a savage life were the arguments which, in the end, saved the peculiar dress of the Highland peasantry after the defeat of 1715.

It is ironical that, if the Highland dress had been banned after the 'Fifteen' instead of thirty years later, after the 'Forty-Five', the kilt, which is now regarded as one of the ancient traditions of Scotland, would probably never have come into existence. It came into existence a few years after Burt had made his observations – and very close to the area in which he had made them. Unknown in 1726, it suddenly appeared a few years later; and by 1745 it was sufficiently well established to be explicitly named in the Act of Parliament which forbade the Highland dress. Its appearance can, in fact, be dated within a few years. For it did not evolve; it was invented. Its inventor was an English Quaker from Lancashire, Thomas Rawlinson.

The Rawlinsons were a long-established family of Quaker ironmasters in Furness. In the early eighteenth century, in association with other prominent Quaker families – Fords, Crossfields and Backhouses – they controlled 'a wide meshwork of furnaces and forges' in Lancashire. But they faced a problem: an increasing shortage of charcoal. How their attention was drawn to the Highlands, we do not know. But, in March 1727, only a year after Captain Burt left Inverness, and partly, no doubt, because of the opening up of the Highlands in which Burt was employed, Thomas Rawlinson made an agreement with Ian MacDonell, the chieftain of the MacDonells of Glengarry, near Inverness, whereby MacDonell leased to him and his partners, for thirty-one years, a wooded area of Glengarry, running from Loch Garry to Loch Ness, including the castle of Invergarry. The sole value of Glengarry to Rawlinson was the abundant birchwoods which supplied him with charcoal for a furnace. The furnace was duly built on the spot, and the iron ore was shipped thither from Lancashire for smelting. Rawlinson was himself in charge of the Scottish operations. Unfortunately the enterprise was not an economic success. It was wound up after seven years. But during those seven years Rawlinson came to know the area, had regular relations with the MacDonells of Glengarry, and, of course, employed 'a throng of Highlanders' to fell the timber and work the furnace.[11]

During his stay at Glengarry, Rawlinson became interested in the Highland costume; but he also became aware of its inconvenience. The belted plaid might be appropriate to the idle life of the Highlanders – for sleeping in the hills or lying hidden in the heather. It was also conveniently cheap, since, as all agreed, 'the lower classes could not afford the expense of the [belted] trousers or breeches'. But for men who had to fell trees or tend furnaces, it was 'a cumbrous, unwieldy habit'. Therefore, being 'a man of genius and quick parts', Rawlinson sent for the tailor of the regiment stationed at Inverness and, with him, set out 'to abridge the dress and make it handy and convenient for his workmen'. The result was the *felie beg*, philibeg, or 'small kilt', which was achieved by separating the skirt from the plaid and converting it into a distinct garment, with pleats already sewn. Rawlinson himself wore this new garment; and his example was followed by his associate, Ian MacDonell of Glengarry. After that, the clansmen, as always, obediently followed their chief; and the innovation, we are told, 'was found so handy and convenient that in the shortest space the use of it became frequent in all the Highland countries and in many of the Northern Lowland countries also'.

This account of the origin of the kilt was first given in 1768 by a Highland gentleman who had known Rawlinson personally. It was published in 1785 and excited no dissent. It was confirmed by the two greatest authorities on Scottish customs then living, Sir John Sinclair and John Pinkerton, as we shall see a little later. Independent testimony from the Glengarry family to the same effect was later given to the Sobieski Stuart brothers, as we shall observe in the next chapter. It was not challenged for another forty years. It has never been refuted. All the evidence that has been accumulated since then is consistent with it. Pictorial evidence also comes to its aid: for the first person to be painted wearing a recognisable modern kilt, as distinct from a belted plaid, appears in a portrait of Alexander MacDonell of Glengarry, the son of the chief who was Rawlinson's associate. It is interesting to note that, in that portrait, the kilt is worn not by the chief himself but by his servant – thus emphasising, once again, its 'servile' status. On all this evidence, the best modern authorities accept the story as true.[12] We may thus conclude that the kilt is a purely modern costume, first designed, and first worn, by an English Quaker industrialist; and that it was bestowed by him on the Highlanders, not in order to preserve their traditional way of life, but to ease its transformation: to bring them off the heath and into the factory.

But if this was the origin of the kilt, another question immediately forces itself on the mind. What tartan did the kilted Quaker wear? Was a distinctive 'sett' or pattern of colours devised for a Lancashire Rawlinson, or did he become an honorary member of the clan of MacDonell? Were there, indeed, any such 'setts' in the eighteenth century? When did the differentiation of patterns by clans commence?

The sixteenth-century writers who first noticed the Highland dress clearly did not know any such differentiation. They describe the plaids of the chiefs as coloured, those of their followers as brown: so that any differentiation of colour, at that time, was by social status, not by clan. The earliest evidence to be adduced in support of differentiation by clan is a remark in the book of Martin Martin, who visited the western islands at the end of the seventeenth century. In the second edition of his book (published in 1716), he stated that 'every isle differs from each other in their fancy of making *plads* as to the stripes, in breadth and colours. The humour is as different through the mainland of the Highlands, in so far as they who have seen those places are able at the first view of a man's *plad* to guess the place of his residence'.[13] In this statement Martin merely assigns different patterns to different localities; he does not differentiate them by clans. And although chieftains no doubt clothed their personal retainers in similar material, in fact the evidence against a more generalised clan-based differentiation is strong. Thus, a carefully painted series of portraits of the different members of the Grant family by Richard Waitt in the early eighteenth century shows all of them in different tartans. The portraits of the Macdonalds of Armadale show 'at least six distinct setts of tartan'. Contemporary evidence concerning the rebellion of 1745 – whether pictorial, sartorial, or literary – shows no differentiation of clans, no continuity of 'setts'. The only way in which a Highlander's loyalty could be discerned was not by his tartan, but by the cockade in his bonnet. Tartans were a matter of private taste, or necessity, only.[14] Indeed, in October 1745, when the Young Chevalier was in Edinburgh with his army, the *Caledonian Mercury* advertised a 'great choice of tartans, the newest patterns'. As D.W. Stewart reluctantly admits, 'this is a great stumbling-block in the way of those who argue for the antiquity of the patterns; for it seems peculiar that, when the city was filled with Highlanders of all ranks and many clans, they should be offered not their ancient setts but a great choice of the newest patterns'.[15]

What can be said of the period from 1707 to 1745 is that, owing to the Union, the manufacture of tartan received a new impulse: for tartan rugs, hangings, etc., could now be freely imported into England. At the same time tartan became popular in Scotland among opponents of the Union; Jacobite ladies wore tartan scarves and other items to emphasise their opposition; and sophisticated Highland gentlemen exercised their ingenuity in designing fancy tartans for themselves to wear on ceremonial occasions. Thomas Rawlinson could thus please himself. As a good Quaker, who also wished to set

an example to his workmen, he probably chose a simple and inex-
pensive tartan such as was being ordered not only by Highlanders in
Scotland for their own use, but also by Scottish settlers in Jamaica for
their negro slaves.

This was the situation in 1745. Then came the great rebellion and
its consequences: the series of punitive measures designed to put an
end to the isolation of the Highlands, to break down the barriers,
physical and traditional, behind which they had hitherto preserved
their 'idle', 'useless' life, and integrate them into modern, 'improving'
Lowland society. As this second rebellion had been far more serious
than that of 1715, so the 'disarming' bills put before Parliament
after it were more severe; and the omissions of the earlier acts were
now repaired. In vain Duncan Forbes of Culloden, the man who, as
Lord President, had done more than any other Scotchman to defeat
the rebellion, sought to save the threatened Highland dress. He
urged that it was non-political, practical and cheap. But his opposition was overruled. The bill became law, and from the date of its
passage, any man or boy who wore 'plaid, philibeg, trews, shoulder-
belts ... tartans or parti-coloured plaid or stuff' was liable to be
imprisoned without bail for six months and, for a second offence, to
be transported for seven years.

This draconian law remained in force for thirty-five years. It was
evidently effective. Possibly it was less generally resented than later
writers have supposed. Highland society, in those years, was anyway
in rapid decay. The pressure of Lowland 'improvement', the building
of roads and the penetration of commerce were undermining it; and
emigration was draining it of life. When Johnson and Boswell made
their famous tour in 1773, they found that the old social organisa-
tion was already dissolved: the rebellion and its consequences had
merely quickened its dissolution. 'We came hither', Johnson wrote,
'too late to see what we expected: a people of peculiar appearance
and a system of antiquated life'. Johnson regretted the change, and
thought the ban on Highland dress unnecessarily severe; but he
recognised that it had been passively accepted. In the whole of their
tour, he remarked, he and Boswell had never seen the tartan worn:
'the law has in all places that we have visited been universally
obeyed'. Even the bagpipe, he noted, 'begins to be forgotten'.[16] The

analogy with Ireland seemed correct; and when the proposal was put forward in 1782 to repeal the Act, it met no resistance – probably because the work done by the Act now seemed irreversible. As a Highlander wrote forty years later, 'breeches, by force of habit, had become so common that it is remarkable how the plaid and philibeg were resumed at all'.[17] After an interruption of thirty-five years, no rational man could suppose that the obsolete habits of a primitive people could be revived.

However, history is not rational; or at least it is rational only in parts. The Highland costume did indeed die out among those who had been accustomed to wear it. After a generation in trousers, the simple peasantry of the Highlands saw no reason to resume the belted plaid or the tartan which they had once found so cheap and serviceable. They did not even turn to the 'handy and convenient' new kilt. On the other hand, the upper and middle classes, who had previously despised that 'servile' costume, now picked up with enthusiasm the garb which its traditional wearers had finally discarded.[18] During the years when it had been banned, some Highland noblemen had taken pleasure in wearing it, and being portrayed in it, in the safety of their homes. Now that the ban was lifted, the fashion spread. Anglicised Scottish peers, improving gentry, well-educated Edinburgh lawyers and prudent merchants of Aberdeen – men who were not constrained by poverty, and would never have to skip over rocks and bogs, or lie all night in hillside heather – would exhibit themselves publicly, not in the historic trews, the traditional costume of their class, nor in the cumbrous belted plaid, but in a costly and fanciful version of that recent innovation, the philibeg or small kilt.

Two causes explain this remarkable change. The first, in importance, was the romantic movement. The second, which served as a support to the first, was the formation of the Highland regiments.

By a pure coincidence, those thirty-five years from 1747 to 1782, which should have marked the extinction of the Highland dress and the Highland way of life, happened to be the formative years of the new romanticism, which arose just in time to preserve them. It was in those years that poets and philosophers began to protest against 'reason' and 'progress', and to discover the virtues of primitive peoples and the equal, if not superior, claims of their authentic, autonomous culture, literature and way of life. And where in Europe was any people so primitive as the 'wild Highlanders' of Scotland, whose distinctive 'culture' was now being deliberately exterminated in the name of 'improvement' and 'progress'? Continental Europeans knew little of Scotland and nothing at all of the Highlands. But their imaginations had been struck by the dramatic adventure of the 'Forty-Five'; and after 1762 they beheld a picture of Highland society which satisfied all their desires. This picture was, of course, James Macpherson's 'Ossian'.

In vain did sceptics in Britain denounce Ossian as an impudent forgery. Scottish culture had always been sustained by forgery. Had not Hector Boece, by appealing to the documents of an imaginary twelfth-century archdeacon, created a golden age of Scottish history in the third century BC, with Scotch philosophers reading Aristotle in Greek at the royal capital of Berigon in the western Highlands? And was not Scotland, even in the eighteenth century, as Lord Hailes remarked, 'though reformed from popery, not yet reformed from Boece'? To drive one myth out of Scotland what was needed was not reason but another myth. So now, at the ideally chosen moment, Boece and his mythical kings melted away. A new and more modern impostor had taken over, and was to reign in his stead.

'Ossian' convinced few in England. He moved Scotland, however. Many even of the non-Celtic Lowlanders were persuaded into acceptance, indeed enthusiasm, by nationalist sentiment. Those who resisted, like David Hume and Sir Walter Scott, had to swim hard against the current. And the Highlanders, who had so long been despised as barbarians, grasped eagerly at this phantom hero, quickly exploiting the new mood in their own favour. Foreigners, who saw the Highlands of Scotland only through a romantic mist, were bowled over by Ossian. To Herder, the founder of German romanticism, the Highlanders of Scotland were the very type of those 'primitive' peoples whose authentic culture was being trampled underfoot by an arrogant and complacent modern 'civilisation'; and the sublime poems of Ossian were their authentic voice. In his anthology of the spontaneous poetry of Europe, Ossian, the Homer of Celtic Scotland, held an honoured place; and he poured his irony and scorn on those 'progressive' Anglo-Saxons, those fashionable 'improvers', who were forcing a noble Celtic people to discard their ancient native costume and wear the artificial trousers of an alien civilisation.[19] In Italy, the poet Alfieri, the lover of Louise von Stolberg, wife of the Young Chevalier, would translate the *Poems of Ossian*. In France, Ossian would become the legendary hero of a greater man.

The literary imagination of poets and philosophers, intoxicated by Ossian, peopled the Scottish Highlands with romantic heroes. The political imagination of a great statesman drew the real Highlanders from their homes and created an army which would make their strange new costume famous throughout Europe. As early as 1725 the British government had begun to recruit Highlanders into the army which, under whig officers, was used to police the disaffected areas of Scotland. By 1740 a Highland regiment had been created, which would serve abroad, and would take part, in 1745, in the battle of Fontenoy. This regiment was at first called the Black Watch, from its original duties of controlling Highland 'blackmail'. Then it became the 43rd, and afterwards the 42nd line regiment. It was the nucleus of the series of Highland regiments which William Pitt, later Earl of Chatham, would form in the years 1757 to 1760, and send out to Canada and the West Indies to fight against the French in the Seven Years War. In forming them, Pitt diverted the martial spirit of the Highlanders from Jacobite adventure and directed it, instead, to imperial purposes. As he would afterwards claim, 'I sought for merit wherever it was to be found; it is my boast that I was the first minister who looked for it, and found it, in the mountains of the North. I called it forth, and drew into your service a hardy and intrepid race of men.'[20]

These Highland regiments wore, as their uniform, either the belted plaid or the 'little kilt', the philibeg; but gradually the kilt, through its convenience, prevailed. In the years when the Highland dress was banned, an exception had been made for 'such as shall be employed as officers or soldiers in His Majesty's forces'; and it was those regiments which kept the kilt, and perhaps the tartan industry itself, alive in those years when its normal outlet was legally blocked. They may also, indirectly, have furthered the idea that distinct clans had distinct 'setts' of tartan. The different regiments naturally were distinguished by different uniforms. But these were not 'clan' uniforms. They could not have been so, even if such had existed in the Highlands. For although chieftains who became officers in these regiments were followed into the army by their clansmen, the regiments were not confined to particular clans: the Highlanders were enlisted promiscuously; and to impose upon them a clan uniform (had such existed) would have been to divide, not to unite, the regiment. It was simply a uniform, like any other regimental colour. In fact there was a 'government' tartan, which was varied, from regiment to regiment, 'by the simple expedient of adding small lines of different colours to the basic pattern' worn by the original regiment, the Black Watch.[21]

Thus in 1782, when the tartan, the plaid, the trews and the philibeg were again legally allowed to be worn by civilians, these obsolete garments had acquired a new character. The romantic movement had given them a new charm; and the Highland regiments, which had preserved their continuity, had both transformed and sophisticated them. They had established the wearing of the novel kilt, and they had set a new fashion of distinguishing particular patterns as the uniform of particular groups of men. To the civilian, the old Highland costume, if he remembered it, was the costume described by Burt: the trews and the belted plaid. In 1743, on the eve of the rebellion, these were still cited as the only forms of Highland dress;[22] and in 1782, when a Gaelic poet crowed over the defeat of compulsory trousers, he naturally cherished the memory, not of the now established philibeg, but of the old belted plaid.[23] But in the meantime a generation had grown up which knew not the belted plaid, nor even the trews; and to which the new 'small kilt' of the Highland regiments was the only visible form of the Highland dress. Indeed, from now on, the word 'kilt' comes to mean the philibeg: the qualification 'small' had become unnecessary, for the large kilt, or belted plaid, had become extinct – so extinct that, by military men at least, the philibeg was now generally assumed to have been the peculiar Highland dress from time immemorial.

It was on this promising basis that the romantic movement, aided by the Napoleonic wars, revived and inflated the cult of a supposedly ancient tribal dress. One of the first symptoms of this revival was the foundation of the Highland Societies in both Scotland and England. The Highland Society of London was founded in 1778, perhaps at first informally as a dining club for Highland gentlemen. In 1783, after the repeal of the ban on Highland dress, it was legally incorporated; and its aims were defined as 'the preservation of the martial spirit, language, dress, music and antiquities of the Caledonians and rescuing from oblivion the valuable remains of Celtic literature'. It would contribute to these purposes by offering prizes and patronising the publication of learned works; and it managed funds which it applied to charitable uses and in illustrating the Gaelic language.[24] It would soon have branches in Glasgow, India and Jamaica. The Highland Society of Scotland was founded in Edinburgh in 1784, and from the beginning had a more utilitarian character: it was a society for the 'improvement' of the Highlands by the introduction of modern agriculture, manufactures, communications, etc. It was later renamed the Highland and Agricultural Society. But among its aims it included 'proper attention to the preservation of the language, poetry and music of the Highlands'. In pursuit of this aim, in 1792 it appointed a teacher of Gaelic and undertook to manage an annual competition for bagpipers (the prize to be given by the London Society); and in 1797, on the death of James Macpherson, who by his will had directed that the Gaelic 'original' of the *Poems of Ossian* be published, it carried out its famous inquiry into the authenticity of those poems.[25]

For by 1797, though Macpherson was dead, Ossian was not. Far from it. Thanks to his foreign admirers, he had become a cult-figure in Europe. Napoleon himself adopted Ossian into the pantheon of his new imperial religion. In his palace of Malmaison an artist represented the souls of his dead warriors being welcomed into a romantic non-Christian paradise by a venerable white-robed sage, who was none other than our Celtic poet-hero.

Meanwhile, to fight against Napoleon, the Highland regiments were being expanded and multiplied; and the tartan kilt, as worn by them, was made familiar on the battlefields of Europe. Military traditions are quickly formed, especially in times of action; and soon the soldiers of the Highland regiments came to believe in the immemorial antiquity of their new uniform. The philibeg, unknown in 1725,

and still recognised as a novelty in 1745, was by now the distinguishing mark of the Highland soldier – and so came to be thought
of as the traditional costume of the nation, essential to its very identity. In 1804, when the War Office, possibly influenced by Sir John
Sinclair, contemplated replacing the kilt by the trews, and duly
sounded out serving officers, Colonel Cameron, of the 79th regiment, was outraged. Was the High Command, he asked, really
proposing to stop 'that free congenial circulation of pure wholesome
air' under the kilt which 'so peculiarly fitted the Highlander for
*activity*?' 'I sincerely hope', protested the gallant colonel, 'that His
Royal Highness will never acquiesce in so painful and degrading an
idea . . . as to strip us of our native garb and stuff us into a harlequin
tartan pantaloon.'[26]

By 1815, thanks partly (we must suppose) to the free circulation of
pure air under Highlanders' kilts, Napoleon was at last defeated; and
kilted regiments in occupied Paris showed the world that the French
Enlightenment was over: the romantic past ruled the present.

This gradual revival of kilts and tartans after 1782 was not entirely
unresisted in enlightened Scotland. Its most notorious opponent was
an eccentric but learned Scottish antiquary who, on this account, was
to have a very bad press in the following century. This was John
Pinkerton: a man who, having incurred some ridicule and some
enmity by his early absurdities, nevertheless, by his genuine scholarship and his readiness to yield to evidence – a quality not so common
among Scotch antiquarians – won the friendship and the patronage
of the greatest of his victims, Edward Gibbon, as we saw earlier.

Pinkerton's views on the ancient dress of the Scots were first
advanced in his *Dissertation on the Origin and Progress of the
Scythians or Goths*, published in 1787. In this he argued that the
Goths and Scythians were the same race, and that the Picts were a
branch of that race; and he insisted that 'the braccae, or breeches,
were in all ages the grand badge of the Scythae or Goths'.[27] From this
it followed that the indigenous inhabitants of Scotland were
trousered, not kilted. Two years later, in his *Enquiry into the History of
Scotland*, Pinkerton became more radical. Observing that no
medieval writer had noted the philibeg, or anything like it, he
declared it a modern invention. Tartan also he declared to be 'a late

invention, and it is believed passed from the Lowlands to the Highlands. The Highland dress is not ancient but singular, and adapted to their savage life'.[28] The mere fact that Pinkerton, in 1789, thought it necessary to deny the antiquity of the philibeg shows how quickly the generality of his compatriots had forgotten – what English scholars could have told them[29] – its recent origin.

Pinkerton was the first scholar to document the early history of the Highland dress, and his observations led to an interesting exchange of letters with the great Panjandrum of Scotland, Sir John Sinclair, whom we have already met. In 1794 Sinclair patriotically raised the Rothesay and Caithness Fencibles, the first such corps to be raised for foreign as well as domestic service; and, after careful research, he dressed them not in kilts, but in tartan trews, which, he had satisfied himself, was the correct ancient costume. The next year he decided to appear at court himself in Highland dress – although, of course, he was not a Highlander at all, or a member of a clan: being the descendant of a family of Norman earls, as we have noted earlier. He thereupon ordered tartan trousers, and designed a special tartan for himself. But before committing himself he wrote to Pinkerton, as the leading Scottish antiquary, soliciting his support. In his letter he justified his own decision by referring to the modern invention of the philibeg by the Quaker Rawlinson. 'It is well known', he wrote, 'that the philibeg was invented by an Englishman in Lochaber about sixty years ago, who naturally thought his workmen could be more active in that light petticoat than in the belted plaid, and that it was more decent to wear it than to have no clothing at all, as was the case with some of those employed by him in cutting down the woods in Lochaber'.[30]

In his reply, which was amply documented, Pinkerton expressed his approval that Sir John, in assuming Highland dress, had substituted 'trousers or pantaloons for the philibeg': for that supposed ancient Highland dress 'is in fact quite modern and any improvement may be made without violating antiquity. Nay the trousers are far more ancient than the philibeg'. The philibeg could not be traced – either word or thing – among any of the ancient Celtic nations; nor indeed could the plaid – the early references were all to a mantle. Tartan had evidently come to the Lowlands from Flanders in the fifteenth century, and passed thence to the Highlands. Having thus denied both to the kilt and to the tartan any medieval origin, Pinkerton went on to express his own view of their appearance. The philibeg, he declared, 'is not only grossly indecent, but is filthy, as it admits dust to the skin and emits the *foetor* of perspiration'; it is absurd because, while the breast is twice covered by vest and plaid, 'the parts concealed by all other nations are but loosely covered'; it is also effeminate, beggarly, and generally disreputable. As for the colours used, 'nothing can reconcile the tasteless regularity and vulgar glow of tartan to the eye of fashion, and every attempt to introduce it has failed'. Sir John's personal design, however, managed to escape Pinkerton's censure. By using 'only two tints of a colour proverbially mild and without glare', he declared, Sinclair had avoided all such objections and secured a very pleasing general effect.[31]

So spoke 'the celebrated antiquary', Mr Pinkerton. Sir John Sinclair evidently approved of Pinkerton's views, for he afterwards published the letter, with fulsome praise of its writer. Others, on reading it, were less pleased. Few Scottish writers of the nineteenth century could touch on this subject without a condescending sneer at the man who was perhaps the ablest of Scottish antiquaries after Thomas Innes – 'sour old Pinkerton'.[32]

They could afford to sneer, because in the meantime the tide had turned. A great tartan mist had rolled over Scotland. Pinkerton had sunk from sight – our last glimpse of him is in Paris as a little wizened figure with green spectacles bent over a desk in the Bibliothèque Nationale – and a far greater man, 'the Antiquary' par excellence, having taken over the whole past of Scotland, was setting it out, in bold seductive colours, to an admiring Europe: Sir Walter Scott.

Scott was a scholar as well as a poet and a novelist. His vast reading included everything that he could find on Scottish history and Scottish life. He collected the trophies of the Scottish past and published its literary and historical remains. Within him there were two – at least two – souls. At one time he would be the Augustan man of letters, the practical Unionist, the well-balanced, scholarly heir of the eighteenth-century Enlightenment who edited Dryden, saw through Ossian, and brought gas to Abbotsford; at another he would be the romantic Jacobite, the poet who would allow himself to be carried away by his own too sympathetic vision of an archaic Highland past. His first novel, *Waverley*, was published in 1814, in the year following Napoleon's first great defeat in battle at Leipzig. It was a Jacobite novel, a novel of the 'Forty-Five', and it was marvellously well timed. It struck, at exactly the right moment, the new mood of romantic conservatism which had been encouraged by the successful resistance of ancient societies to French modernising conquest, and which now set the tone for the age of 'Restoration' and 'Legitimacy'. When the Scottish regiments appeared in Paris, in their kilts and tartans, Scott's writings linked them with the historical imagination of Europe. For the next decade, kilts and tartans were all the rage. They appeared on the stage, in the opera of Paris, in the ballrooms of Berlin. At Abbotsford, Scott transformed himself from a new Border laird into an imaginary Highland chieftain. Thanks to him, all Scotland, Lowland and Highland alike, was suffused with a new distorting tartan glow.

One symptom of this tartan mania was the foundation, in January 1820, of the Celtic Society of Edinburgh. This was a society of young civilians whose first object was 'to promote the general use of the ancient Highland dress in the Highlands'. To do so, they wore it themselves in Edinburgh, where they dined together regularly, 'kilted and bonneted in the old fashion, and armed to the teeth'. Scott himself, though a Lowlander, was President of the Society and attended its dinners. He dressed more staidly, in trews; but he declared himself 'very much pleased with the extreme enthusiasm of the Gael, when liberated from the thraldom of breeches'. This enthusiasm seems to have expressed itself in agility and noise rather than in discussion of Celtic philology or literature. As Scott recorded after one of the dinners, 'such jumping, skipping and screaming you never saw'.[33]

Scott was a first-class passenger in the Celtic club; its driver was Colonel David Stewart of Garth. Stewart had spent almost his whole adult life hitherto in the army. Having joined the 42nd Highlanders at the age of fifteen, he had served abroad throughout the war with France. After the final victory, he had been retired on half-pay, and had devoted himself to a study of the Highland regiments. This led him to a more general study of Highland life; and he showed himself an enthusiast for the Highland traditions which he had discovered – though more often, perhaps, in the officers' mess than out in the straths and glens. These traditions included both the kilt and the clan tartans. The idea that the kilt had been invented by a pragmatic Englishman seemed to this loyal and romantic Scotchman too preposterous to be entertained. He dismissed it impatiently, preferring what he called 'the universal belief of the people that the philibeg had been part of their garb as far back as tradition reaches'. Unfortunately, he made no attempt to document either this 'universal belief' or this ancient tradition – or even, it seems, to read the evidence against it.[34] He also declared that tartans had always been woven in 'distinctive patterns (or setts, as they were called) of the different clans, tribes, families and districts'. Of this too he gave no evidence.[35] His book was completed in 1821 and published early in 1822 under the title *Sketches of the Character, Manners and Present State of the Highlanders of Scotland*. It was immediately popular and, as we are told, 'has been the foundation of all subsequent works on the clans'.[36] It can therefore be regarded as the origin of the new orthodoxy concerning the antiquity of the kilt and of distinctive clan tartans.

Stewart's book was timely; for only a few months after its publication, King George IV announced that he would follow up his recent visit to Dublin by a long-promised visit to Edinburgh. This announcement caused a thrill of excitement in Scotland. It was the first time that a Hanoverian king had set foot in the country. The last Stuart pretender, Henry Cardinal of York, was now dead; Jacobitism was therefore without a claimant; and Scottish loyalty could be united at last in the person of the reigning monarch. The task of orchestrating that loyalty was given, naturally enough, to Walter Scott. It was he who, by his writings, had given to Scotland its renewed sense of history and historic unity; he had himself seen his novels as a means to confirm the Union with England; and he was also, as George IV would himself say on landing, the man in all Scotland whom he most wanted to meet. Scott accepted the responsibility gladly, and named as his assistant – his 'dictator' in all matters concerning Highland ceremony and dress – the animator of the Celtic club, Colonel Stewart of Garth.

Thanks to Scott and Stewart, the royal visit was planned, from the start, almost exclusively as a Highland affair. It was to be, as Scott wrote, 'a gathering of the Gael', with 'cocking of bonnets and waving of plaids'. In order to ensure success, he wrote to his Highland friends urging them to 'sort out their tartans'; and he pressed the Highland chiefs to come with their 'tail' of followers to pay homage to the king. 'Do come, and bring half-a-dozen or half-a-score of clansmen', he wrote to a Hebridean chief, 'so as to look like an island chief as you are. Highlanders are what he will best like to see'.[37]

The Highland chiefs responded. They went to their tartan-weavers and chose, or were offered, a suitable fancy dress. Many of them went to the old-established firm of William Wilson and Son of Bannockburn, who had long dominated the industry, sending their products all over Scotland, and supplying both the Scottish regiments and the markets abroad. The vast correspondence of this firm survives, an invaluable source for historians.[38] In the late eighteenth century the trade had not been brisk; but with the new century things had improved; and in 1819, when the royal visit was first suggested, the firm had prepared a 'Key Pattern Book' in expectation of much new business. When the visit was finally announced, the firm was 'snowed under with orders' and could not meet the demand. 'To cope with the orders which flowed in, all hands were switched from other forms of textile to tartan; forty new looms were installed'; but even so, 'every piece of tartan was sold as it came off the loom'. At the same time, the firm set out to simplify their problem by both specialisation and standardisation of the product.

They devised tartans for each clan, and had these tartans 'certificated' by the clan chiefs – who, no doubt, obediently certified whatever was submitted to them by these self-constituted experts. The Highland Society of London also entered into the game, and began to build up a collection of such tartans, so certified – almost all of them supplied by Wilson and Son.[39] In this way the Highland chiefs were supplied with 'proper' tartans for the royal visit. Cluny Macpherson, for instance, heir to the chief of 'Ossian', was given a tartan off the peg. For him it was labelled 'Macpherson'; but previously, having been sold in quantity to a Mr Kidd, the same tartan had been labelled 'Kidd'; and before that, it had been anonymous, simply described as

'No. 155'. Sir Evan MacGregor arrived in Edinburgh similarly fitted out 'in his proper Highland tartan, with his tail, banner and pipers'; and also Colonel MacDonell of Glengarry, heir to the second oldest kilt in Scotland, now doubtless more sophisticated for the occasion.[40] Thus equipped, a number of minuscule tartan armies converged in Edinburgh.

Altogether some three hundred 'wild Highlanders' followed their chiefs to Edinburgh, 'armed *cap-à-pie*'. Since none of them would accept orders from chiefs of other clans, all were put under the command of the Lowlander, Walter Scott. Scott paraded them daily in Castle Street, and his house 'rang with broadswords and targets and pipes from daybreak to sunset'. Meanwhile another tartan army had sprung up within Edinburgh: for those 'enthusiasts for the philibeg', the members of the Celtic club, had formed four companies, 'dressed in proper costume', to act as a bodyguard for the king, the hereditary office-holders and the regalia of Scotland, with mysterious Gaelic inscriptions woven or picked out in pearls on loyal banners and votive crosses. The king himself, at last, appeared in a kilt of the so-called 'royal Stuart' tartan, in which, as Lockhart drily remarked, 'certainly no Stuart except Prince Charles had ever before presented himself in the salons of Holyrood'. George IV was somewhat put out to find himself, on one occasion, face to face with an equally portly alderman of London, wearing exactly the same incongruous dress. The alderman was Sir William Curtis, MP for the City, who, as a sugar-baker from Wapping, had even less claim to Highland blood than the king. This 'portentous apparition', says Lockhart, 'cast an air of ridicule and caricature over the whole of Sir Walter's celtified pageantry'. Assuredly it gave great pleasure to irreverent caricaturists. But the king was not amused.

The climax of the farce came at a civic dinner in the royal honour, when the king invited the assembled dignitaries to drink a toast to 'the chieftains and clans of Scotland' – those formerly predatory outer barbarians whom the citizens of Edinburgh had always despised and sometimes feared. This was too much for some of Scott's fellow Lowlanders, who afterwards complained that 'the whole land was *tartanised*, in the royal eye, from Pentland to Solway'. But at the time the magic worked. Reason and sense were numbed by the potent mixture of myth and *snobisme*. 'So completely had this hallucination taken possession', wrote Lockhart, that nobody seemed startled by the suggestion that 'the marking and crowning glory of Scotland' consisted in those Highland clans and their chieftains who had, in truth, 'always constituted a small and almost always an unimportant part of the Scottish population'.[41]

# 8

# The Tartan

The charade of George IV's visit to Edinburgh has an important place in the mythology of Highland dress. Designed to complete the victory of 1746 by reconciling the minds of Celtic Scotland to Hanoverian rule, it ended by reversing that victory. The Celtic clans, conclusively defeated at Culloden, and thereafter subjected effectively to Anglo-Saxon rule from London and Edinburgh, now asserted their claim that all Scotland was really theirs; and their claim – in the realm of myth – was allowed. For the next century, scholars and historians might protest; but they protested in vain. Even the greatest and most popular historian of that century, who established a new orthodoxy in the interpretation of political history, was powerless against this particular fallacy. The historian was Lord Macaulay, and he wrote a full generation after the royal visit, when the 'hallucination' of that event might have been thought to have passed into historical perspective. His comments were made, in the course of his *History of England*, when he came to compare the relations between Saxon and Celt in Scotland and Ireland since the decisive events of the reign of William III.

Macaulay had some special qualifications for writing about Highland history. He was himself, by origin, a Highlander. His grandfather had been minister on the remotest of all the western islands of Scotland, now totally uninhabited: St Kilda. The family, like so many Highland families, had since emigrated; and the minister's grandson had no romantic illusions about the life from which they had escaped. Romanticism he regarded as an intellectual luxury, parasitic on the body of economic progress. Highland life before 1745 was, in his eyes, as in those of Hume and all previous writers, merely barbarous; and he insisted that it was only since roads and inns had been built, regular law enforced, and personal safety ensured, that soft-headed modern writers could invest that barbarism with retrospective romance: so that, in the present century, 'thousands of clerks and milliners' could be 'thrown into raptures by the sight of Loch Katrine and Loch Lomond'. From his rational, utilitarian, progressive whig viewpoint, Macaulay was particularly contemptuous of the tartan revival, which he ascribed, not unjustly, to the genius of Sir Walter Scott. Scott, argued Macaulay, was not a historian but a poet; and by his poetic interpretation of the old Highland life, Scott had created a picture of it which, by now, had

> superseded history. The visions of the poet were realities to his readers. The places which he described became holy ground, and were visited by thousands of pilgrims. Soon the vulgar imagination was so completely occupied by plaids, targets, and claymores, that, by most Englishmen, Scotchman and Highlander were regarded as synonymous words. Few people seemed to be aware that, at no remote period, a Macdonald or a Macgregor in his tartan was to a citizen of Edinburgh or Glasgow what an Indian hunter in his war paint is to an inhabitant of Philadelphia or Boston. Artists and actors represented Bruce and Douglas in striped petticoats. They might as well have represented Washington brandishing a tomahawk, and girt with a string of scalps. At length this fashion reached a point beyond which it was not easy to proceed. The last British King who held a court in Holyrood thought that he could not give a more striking proof of his respect for the usages which had prevailed in Scotland before the Union, than by disguising himself in what, before the Union, was considered by nine Scotchmen out of ten as the dress of a thief.[1]

'Beyond which it would be difficult to proceed' . . .. Difficult indeed, but not impossible. In the years after 1822, in fact, the folly proceeded apace; and, even before Macaulay wrote, had been carried to quite unpredictable lengths by two brothers who can claim, as myth-makers, to rank with Boece and Macpherson. Unlike Macaulay, a Scot whose family had left the Highlands for England and sober sense, these brothers were Englishmen who had moved from England and common sense to the Highlands and romantic folly. Their name – at the beginning of their lives – was Allen.

They came from a well-connected naval family. Their grandfather, John Carter Allen, was related to the Hill family, marquises of Downshire and earls of Hillsborough, and had ended his career as Admiral of the White.[2] The admiral's two sons were also both naval officers. The elder of them, Thomas, left the service after a few years. His father may have disapproved of him, for he left the bulk of his property to the younger son, John, who continued in the navy and would also become an admiral. Thomas Allen evidently lived at Egham in Surrey, where he married the daughter of a local cler- gyman, the Rev. Owen Manning, vicar of Godalming. By her, he was the father of our next two heroes. His father-in-law, the vicar, was a learned antiquary: his *History of Surrey* is one of the best of English county histories; and perhaps his antiquarian scholarship was the modest seed which, in his grandsons, was to ripen into such exotic blooms.

Of the early life of the brothers John and Charles Allen nothing at all is known. The time and place of their birth, their education, their home: all are wrapped in mystery, made more impenetrable by their own later embellishments. But in 1822 they suddenly appeared before the world. In that year John, the elder of them, who seems throughout to have been the dominant personality, published a volume of forty-two romantic Highland poems, faint echoes of Sir Walter Scott, with learned annotations;[3] and one of them – probably the younger – celebrated the royal visit to Edinburgh with 'stanzas for the King's landing'. It appears that he, and his father, were in Edinburgh at the time.[4] The two sons had now Scoticized their names, changing them from John and Charles Allen to John Hay Allan and Charles Stuart Allan. The name of Hay reflected a family tradition that they were descended, in the direct male line, from the last Hay, Earl of Erroll, who had died a bachelor in 1717. Presumably they supposed a secret marriage.[5] For the name of Stuart they could offer no justification – as yet.

Having taken this first step, they soon took a second. From Allan they became Allan Hay, and then simply Hay. They did not crudely assert their nobility; they merely acted the part with complete self-assurance. Sir Walter Scott afterwards recalled seeing the elder of them wearing the badge of the High Constable of Scotland – the hereditary office of the earls of Errol – 'which he could have no more right to wear than the Crown'.[6] There is a certain prophetic irony in that remark. Later, the brothers themselves would recognise its logic. What Scott called their 'exaggerating imagination' would expand to encompass the Crown.

For the next quarter-century the two brothers flitted through the noble houses of Scotland, dressed (said an English eyewitness) 'in all the extravagance of which the Highland costume is capable – every kind of tag and rag, false orders and tinsel ornaments'.[7] They were strikingly handsome, and with their courtly manners and personal charm they were able to seduce or persuade Scotchmen of every kind: aristocrats, antiquaries, romantically inclined ladies, supposedly hard-headed men of affairs. Wherever they went, they moved easily into high society. They stayed in castles and attended routs. They had dedicated their first poems to the Duke of Argyll. In Edinburgh, the learned publisher and scientific writer Dr Robert Chambers was their constant friend. In the north, where they established themselves at Logie House, Elgin, all doors opened to them. Their neighbour Sir Thomas Dick Lauder, a solid whig Lowlander, busy with manufactures and fisheries, welcomed them to his wife's estate at Relugas. They stayed with the MacDonells of Glengarry at Inverie. A young Russian aristocrat observed them, resplendent with orders and knighthoods, at Altyre. The Earl of Moray gave them the run of Darnaway Forest, where they built themselves a mossy hunting lodge behind the river Findhorn and spent whole days – always in elaborate Highland costume – stalking the wild deer. Whatever they did, they did thoroughly, and with style. They were proficient huntsmen, deeply learned in the life and lore of the forest and the chase.[8]

They were also learned in the arts and human sciences. They seem to have been largely self-taught, and to have had some of the usual qualities of the autodidact: a lack of proportion, a crudity of synthesis and an obstinacy in their own theories.[9] But their talents were extraordinary. Both of them were skilful draughtsmen and painters, wood-carvers and furniture-makers. They could quote Greek and evidently knew Latin well. They were fluent in Gaelic as well as in French and Italian. They would cite Welsh and Old Norse. Their familiarity with arcane Highland literature and Scotch antiquities was remarkable. When they were not stalking the deer, or drawing the eyes of all in great houses, they were, it seems, bent over old folios: copying family portraits, old armour or sculpture; collating ancient manuscripts; or taking down Gaelic poetry from the lips of nonagenarian *senachies*.

By 1829 these antiquarian studies had borne their first fruit. In that year the two brothers Hay (as they now called themselves) revealed to Sir Thomas Dick Lauder that there was in their family a document of great interest for Scottish history. This was a manuscript which had once belonged to John Leslie, bishop of Ross, the confidant of Mary Queen of Scots, and which had been given to their father by none other than the Young Chevalier, Bonnie Prince Charlie. The manuscript was entitled *Vestiarium Scoticum* or *The Garde-robe of Scotland*, and declared itself to be the work of one Sir Richard Urquhart, knight. It carried the date 1571, but could, of course, be much earlier.

According to 'the Messrs Hay', this document showed that, at the time of its composition, not only all the Highland clans but also all the Lowland families – Scotts, Kerrs, Armstrongs, etc. – had worn tartan costume; and it described and illustrated in colour the distinct 'setts' by which each clan and each family had distinguished itself. The original manuscript, the brothers explained, was with their father in London; but they had in their own hands a somewhat crude copy, dated 1721, which they had obtained (they said) in 1819 from an old Highlander whose ancestor had been a tutor in the Cromarty family, i.e. of Urquhart. This copy they now lent to Sir Thomas. Sir Thomas was so excited by it that he transcribed it himself; and the younger brother, 'with very great politeness', gave up three weeks of his time to illuminate the transcript with coloured drawings of all the tartans: 'by which labour', as Sir Thomas said, 'he has made me a most beautiful book'.[10] Sir Thomas was eager that so important a document should be published, in order to correct the numerous 'uncouth, spurious, modern tartans which are every day invented, manufactured, christened after particular names, and worn as genuine'. He thought that such a publication might be sponsored by some learned antiquarian society such as the Bannatyne Club. So he wrote a long and enthusiastic account of it to the great oracle of Scottish antiquarianism and tradition, Sir Walter Scott.[11]

By now Scott had recovered his balance after the euphoria of 1822, and his reply shows him at his best as a historical scholar and a man of sense. Like Dr Johnson, faced with the claims of 'Ossian', he would concede nothing till the original manuscript had been produced and scrutinised by an expert. Prima facie, he believed that it was bogus: for 'the general proposition that the Lowlanders ever wore plaids is difficult to swallow'. After all, the great Lowland families were mainly Norman; and those Norman colonists used to speak of the wild Scots of the west, who had come over from Ireland, 'as a British officer would do of Cherokees'. Even the ordinary natives of southern Scotland, though Celts, were not of Irish origin but 'British, Welsh if you please, with the language and manners of that people, who certainly wore no tartan'. There were so many objections to the thesis, said Scott, that even if the manuscript itself were proved authentic, he would not accept its authorship: 'I had rather suppose the author had been some tartan-weaver zealous for his craft, who wished to extend the use of tartan over the whole kingdom'. As for the two brothers, they were no doubt agreeable and talented men, amusing companions in the country; but their authority in such matters was nil. And how, anyway, did they come to possess such a manuscript? Their father, Scott had heard, was a naval officer, known to and contemporary with 'an old acquaintance of mine, Captain Watson of the Navy'. 'What chance was there that either from age or situation he should be receiving gifts from the Young Chevalier of Highland manuscripts?'

Sir Thomas dutifully pursued the matter. He invited the brothers to submit the original manuscript to expert inspection. They 'displayed every possible readiness' to do so, and wrote (as they said) to their father in London begging him to send it 'without delay', or at least himself to submit it to the experts of the British Museum. Unfortunately, they had to report failure. In due course the elder brother presented to Sir Thomas a letter which, he said, he had received from his father. It was signed 'J.T. Stuart Hay', and it reproved 'my dearest Ian' for having divulged the secret of the manuscript, which could never be published on account of certain 'private memorandums on the blank leaves' – no doubt in the hand of the Young Chevalier. This veto was 'unalterable' and 'absolute'. Anyway, wrote the supposed owner, it was by now too late to revive the authentic tartans of Scotland: the age of their reality had gone irrecoverably with the glory of the Scottish past. Finally, the writer of the letter turned the tables on Scott, who had presumed to deny the antiquarian authority of the two brothers: 'As to the opinion of Sir Walter Scott, inasmuch as I never heard it respected among antiquaries as of the least value, it is quite indifferent to me'. That put the great oracle in his place – and stopped any further inconvenient enquiry after the original manuscript.[12]

However, if they could not produce the original manuscript, 'the Messrs Hay' were at least able to satisfy Sir Thomas by producing further indirect corroboration of its authenticity. This was 'a traced facsimile' of a signed autograph note by the bishop of Ross, which, they said, was inscribed in the manuscript. Sir Thomas duly sent this to Sir Walter, suggesting that he might be able to compare it with an authenticated signature. If he had done so, Sir Walter would have found it a remarkably accurate copy.[13]

Sir Walter did not do so. His scepticism was not to be shaken by a mere facsimile. The whole basis of the *Vestiarium Scoticum*, he insisted, was fraudulent. 'The idea of distinguishing the clans by their tartans is but a fashion of modern date in the Highlands themselves; much less could it be supposed to be carried to such an extent in the Lowlands'. Here the tory romantic, Scott, showed himself more critical than the whig realist, Dick Lauder, whose last words on the subject were: 'I confess, I am still a believer'. How could anyone fail to believe persons of such high character, dignity, veracity, modesty, etc., as 'the Messrs Hay'?

The voice of Scott was the voice of reason and scholarship. But had reason or scholarship prevailed against the bogus kings of Boece or the bogus poems of Ossian? Of course not. Nor would they prevail against the bogus manuscript of 'the Messrs Hay'. Thirteen years later, though their father was still alive, they would have forgotten his 'absolute', 'unalterable' prohibition. They could afford to do so; for Scott was now dead, and they were in a position to give a knock-out answer to his impertinent doubts. For by now they had once again changed their name, and appeared openly in a new character. From Hay they had become Stuart. Their father, it was now revealed, was not, after all, the son of the admiral (and therefore could not claim his supposed Hay ancestry). He had moved up higher. He was the only legitimate child, and they were the only legitimate grandchildren, of the Young Chevalier. This, of course, made the gift of the manuscript quite natural.

This new transformation of the Hay brothers had been slow and cautious. It had begun, it seems, about 1825.[14] It had been hinted in the correspondence of 1829. Thereafter it continued in the seclusion of the far north. Then, in 1836, the news began to spread. In that year the two brothers decided to pursue their Gaelic studies in Ireland. They arrived in Glasgow in 'royal Stuart' tartan; and they were piped aboard ship by their own piper, drawn from their 'clan'. They had now improved their names by appropriate royal additions: John had become John Sobieski Stuart, after John Sobieski, king of Poland, the maternal grandfather of the Young Chevalier; Charles was Charles Edward Stuart, like the Young Chevalier himself. In keeping with this new identity, they had declared themselves Roman Catholics; and they did not disdain the title of Princes. Their father, now a total recluse in Clerkenwell but a necessary link in their genealogy, was described by them as the Comte d'Albanie. *De jure* he was, of course, King Thomas I of Great Britain.

After their return from Ireland, 'the Sobieski Stuarts', as they were now called, found a new patron. This was Lord Lovat, the Catholic head of the Fraser family, whose ancestor had died on the scaffold for his support of the Young Chevalier in 1745. On a romantic islet in the Beauly river, beyond Inverness, this benevolent patron now built for the two brothers a delightful house, Eilean Aigas; and there they settled, together with the aristocratic wife of the younger brother, their four children (all bearing royal Stuart names),[15] her sister and an adequate staff. The house was a miniature court; and a formidable etiquette was imposed upon the household.[16] The royal arms of

Scotland were carved on the pediment. Indoors, the 'princes' sat on thrones in their antlered hall. Men bowed and women curtseyed before them. Visitors were shown Stuart relics and a great chest, which was said to contain important title deeds. On Sundays, when they were rowed upstream to the Catholic church at Eskadale, the royal pennant flew above their boat. Their seal was a crown.

It was from their court at Eilean Aigas that the brothers published the *Vestiarium Scoticum* in 1842. It did not come out now under the aegis of a learned society; nor did it need the blessing of any patron. It issued from the press in royal magnificence: in a sumptuous edition limited to fifty copies. John Sobieski Stuart, as editor, supplied a learned commentary. The numerous coloured illustrations of Highland, Lowland and Border tartans were the first such series to be published. The designs themselves bore witness to the marvellous ingenuity of the editor;[17] and the production was worthy of the design. The tartans were illustrated by a new process of 'machine printing', and (in the words of a scholar writing fifty years later) 'for beauty of execution and exactness of detail, have not been excelled by any method of colour-printing subsequently invented'.[18] Only a pedant would point out that the 'setts' of the tartans illustrated were materially different from the versions so faithfully copied, from the same original manuscript, for Sir Thomas Dick Lauder thirteen years earlier.

The history of the manuscript had also been improved during that same interval. From the preface, which described the document in great detail, it now appeared that after the death of Bishop Leslie, its first recorded owner, the manuscript had passed to the Scots College in Douay; and that the college had subsequently given it to the Young Chevalier. Moreover, from the archives of Douay, the editor had now acquired still further confirmation of its authenticity: in the form of a transcribed extract from a personal diary kept by Bishop Leslie himself. In this document the bishop acknowledged receipt of 'the buke clyppit *The Garde-robe of Scotland*' by Sir Richard Urquhart, knight. This transcript, the editor said, had been supplied to him by a distinguished antiquary who had been familiar with the Douay archives before their unfortunate dispersion in the French Revolution, viz. 'the late Mr Robert Watson'. This Robert Watson –

'the chevalier Watson' as he was called – was a worthy ally of the Sobieski Stuarts. A radical and a republican, he had been the Principal of Napoleon's reconstituted and secularised Scots College in Paris; and he had played a curious and not very creditable part in the process whereby the papers of the exiled Stuarts, saved from destruction in Rome, had found their way to the royal archives at Windsor. Unfortunately, once again, the original document could not be produced, or the facts checked; for the chevalier Watson was now beyond reach. He had committed suicide, a few years earlier, by strangling himself in a London tavern at the advanced age of ninety-two.[19] Thus the authenticity of Bishop Leslie's copy, itself still invisible, was now doubly demonstrated: first by a 'traced facsimile' of his autograph note in it, and secondly by a transcript of his own receipt for it. Moreover the text itself was now confirmed by another early manuscript of the same work, with which (it was said) it had been 'carefully collated' by the editor. This additional manuscript, the editor explained, had been discovered by an unnamed Irish monk in the monastery of St Augustine in Cadiz. It was unfortunate that this monastery had recently been secularised, and its treasures scattered: so that the manuscript could not now be produced in evidence. But other copies were known to exist. One, for instance, had belonged to the family of Lord Lovat. Unfortunately, it had been carried to America, and there lost; but it was being actively sought. . . .

Two years after the publication of the *Vestiarium*, the Sobieski Stuart brothers published an even more sumptuous volume, for which that document could now be seen as a preliminary *pièce justificative*. This new book was a stupendous folio, lavishly presented, with numerous illustrations – copies of portraits and sculptures – by the two brothers themselves. Clearly they had been working on it for many years. It was dedicated to the King of Bavaria, as 'the restorer of the Catholic arts of Europe'; it was addressed, in a high-flown epistle in both Gaelic and English, to 'the Highlanders'; and it was published, according to the title page, in Edinburgh, London, Paris and Prague. It was entitled *The Costume of the Clans*.

*The Costume of the Clans* is a remarkable work, in content as in form. For sheer erudition, it makes all previous work on the subject seem thin and trivial. It cites the most arcane sources, Scottish and

European, written and oral, manuscript and printed. It draws on art and archaeology, as well as on literature. A careful and scholarly Scottish antiquary, writing half a century later, when the authors were dead and discredited, could still say of it that, 'considering the period at which it was written, and the difficulty of access to the widely scattered material of which it is composed, [it] is a perfect marvel of industry and ability. It has been the productive quarry of all successive writers on the Highland dress';[20] and the best modern writer on the subject has described it as 'one of the foundation-stones on which any history of Highland dress is built. It cannot be ignored, and it is surprising how little it has been consulted by writers on the subject. We can think what we like about the ancestral claims of the Stuart brothers, but this does not reduce the value of their monumental book'.[21]

On the other hand, something of a doubtful mist hangs over this magnificent display of erudition. Among many genuine documents now first put in evidence, there are some whose credentials are less persuasive. Thus, evidence is drawn from the poems of Ossian and other Gaelic literature of dubious origin and date. The authority of the eleventh-century archdeacon Veremund, the alleged source of Boece's fabulous kings, is gravely cited. The *Vestiarium Scoticum*, now assigned, 'on internal evidence', to the late fifteenth century, is used as a historical source. Reference is made, once again, to 'Douay papers recently in the possession of Mr Watson', but now, alas, untraceable: papers which contained, we learn, 'a large copy of the original poems of Ossian and many other valuable Gaelic Mss'. Much play is made with a Latin manuscript account of the expenses of John, Lord of the Isles, dated 1355 and found, with other important documents, in that same (now unfortunately dissolved) monastery in Cadiz, in which the authors had found the second (now unfortunately unavailable) manuscript of the *Vestiarium*. With the aid of such evidence, stirred as seasoning into their rich and effervescent brew, the authors served up their exciting new thesis; in which the errors of all previous writers, and particularly the 'frequent ignorance and universal presumption' of Pinkerton, were exposed and refuted.

What was that thesis? Briefly, the Sobieski Stuarts argued that the Highland dress, as it was when first noticed by the outer world – that is, in the late sixteenth century – was the fossil relic of the universal dress of medieval Europe, artificially preserved. In the early Middle Ages, Celtic Scotland, they said, was a rich, polished, cosmopolitan society – and they drew a picture of a great Catholic civilisation, in which the splendid courts of the tribal chiefs were nourished, thanks to the advanced Hebridean manufactures, by the luxuries, and the enlightenment, of continental Europe. At that time, they explained, the Highland dress was merely a local form of the universal dress of Europe, and, as such, excited no comment. Hence the silence of the medieval writers, which Pinkerton had so misinterpreted. But in the fourteenth century there was a general revolution in European dress. The 'bonnet, tunic and square mantle' gave way to the hat, cloak and close-bodied jerkin. Only the remote Highlanders and islanders of Scotland, and their Irish kinsmen, were not reached by this sartorial revolution, but remained faithful to their ancient garb. So, by the sixteenth century, visitors from the outside world began to comment on their eccentricity. But they were not really eccentric, only conservative. The Highland dress now seemed peculiar, 'not because it was a novelty in itself but because the novelties of the world had left it solitary and strange'.

So far, so good. But why, we naturally ask, was the Celtic fringe of Britain exempt from this otherwise general change? The answer given is that, by the end of the Middle Ages, the rich, cosmopolitan civilisation of the Highlands – those humming Hebridean factories, those brilliant island courts, and 'the high intellectual sophistication' of Mull, Islay and Skye – was going into decline. From now on, the Highlands were cut off from the world, introverted and impoverished. Their costume remained fixed in its superannuated form – but at the same time became meaner. So, among other signs of decay, the old tartan setts of the clans, so faithfully recorded in the *Vestiarium*, were gradually obscured and forgotten. There was still room for changes of fashion – changes which the authors traced with genuine learning. But the changes occurred within a shrunken context; and by the eighteenth century the decay of the Highland costume was final. The *Vestiarium*, said the Sobieski Stuarts – echoing the supposed voice of their father in 1829 – was the authentic record of a past which could never now be revived.

Modern tartans were no longer the expression of a living Highland society. They were mere fancy dress.

Thus the Sobieski Stuarts altogether repudiated the thesis of Pinkerton that Highland dress was an innovation of the sixteenth century. Highland dress, they argued, was the most ancient dress in Europe. While other societies had changed, the Highlanders had remained steadfast in their ancient habits; and although, in the dark centuries after the Reformation, their civilisation had shrunk and their dress degenerated, its continuity was still recognisable. Even in its deformation it reflected a medieval Catholic civilisation.

On the other hand, there was one subject on which the Sobieski Stuarts were entirely in concert with Pinkerton. The philibeg, or short kilt, they agreed with him, was a modern innovation, unmentioned by any writer, undocumented in any picture, before 1724. They did not, indeed, repeat Pinkerton's strictures on the garment. They allowed that it was an 'elegant and beneficial novelty'. But they agreed with him in ascribing its invention entirely to two Englishmen; and they told, with added circumstantial detail supplied by the family of Glengarry, the story of the English iron-founder at Lochaber and the English regimental tailor, whose practical genius had given the Scots 'that commodious abridgement of the belted plaid'. Since the Sobieski Stuarts were naturally inclined to claim originality for the Highland dress in general, their firm conclusions on this particular subject must be respected.

Such was the bold thesis which the Sobieski Stuarts supported by their massive display of unequal evidence. It leaves us asking a question. If the ancient Highland dress could not now be revived, since the civilisation which had provided its natural context had perished, why did the Sobieski Stuarts themselves wear that dress in so purist a form? The answer must be that they alone wore it (as they supposed) in its real context: a context which they consciously revived. Their lives of make-believe were a re-creation of the authentic Highland way of life; and, as such, justified incidental archaisms which, outside that context, would be an impertinence. In other words, they were true romantics. Their romanticism was not a spare-time luxury; it was total. They went the whole hog. Therein lies their charm.

Whatever its elements of weakness, or even fraud, their book deserved a reasoned notice. Unfortunately it did not receive it. In fact (so far as I know) it never has been critically reviewed. This was not owing to any inherent fault in the work, however, but to an external accident.

For soon after the book's appearance, the two brothers committed a grave imprudence. Hitherto, in respect of their royal claims, their policy had been that of all successful mystery-men: never assert, never argue, never explain. They simply played their part as if they believed it, and left others to speculate – and by their speculation to build up the myth. But in 1847 they attempted to give that myth a helping hand. The result was disastrous: for the hand was at last something palpable, something which their critics, hitherto helpless, were able to grasp; and, by grasping, pull its owner down.

The first public assertion of their claims was made not by them, but by a fashionable French novelist and poet, the 'vicomte' d'Arlincourt, who, while visiting the north of Scotland in pursuit of romantic Jacobite tales, heard of the two brothers and visited them at Eilean Aigas. D'Arlincourt published an account of his visit; and his account was soon supplemented, or rather diffused, by two new works published by the brothers themselves. These were *Lays of the Forest*, a collection of poems, learnedly annotated, concerning the hunting of deer; and a prose work, entitled *Tales of the Century*. The century covered the period from 1746 to 1846: from Culloden to the current year. The tales were a series of short stories which, under the cover of romantic but transparent names, revealed – or professed to reveal – an important historical truth.

From these sources, through a thin veil of allegory, the reader could learn that the royal line of the Stuarts was not, after all, extinct; that a legitimate son of the Young Chevalier had been secretly born to his wife Louise von Stolberg; that soon after his birth the infant had been secretly conveyed, lest he should be murdered by Hanoverian agents, to the safe custody of an English admiral who, it was hinted, was rightful earl of Errol and High Steward of Scotland; that this son had grown up in England and married a well-born English lady; and that these two had become the parents of two sons who, after fighting for the Ossianic conqueror Napoleon at Dresden,

Leipzig and Waterloo, and being personally decorated by him for bravery, had retired to their ancestral land to await their destiny. These two sons, it was discreetly intimated, were the same two brothers who were now maintaining Highland traditions, hunting the Highland deer, and recreating the true Highland dress. Learned notes to the *Tales*, based on arcane published texts, on the still uncatalogued 'Stuart papers', on unverifiable German and Polish sources, and on 'manuscripts in our possession', amply documented this history.

So far, none of the works of the two brothers had been critically reviewed; and their pretensions, which floated innocently and impalpably on the breath of mere gossip, had not seemed worthy of attack. But with the publication of the *Tales*, opportunity was given; and it was taken. In the *Quarterly Review* an anonymous writer moved to the attack. Ostensibly, his essay was a somewhat belated review of the *Vestiarium Scoticum*. But the reviewer did not stop there. Having referred – inaccurately – to the proposed publication of the *Vestiarium* in 1829, and to its condemnation by Sir Walter Scott, he went on to draw out, from the *Lays* and the *Tales*, the royal claims of the two brothers. Then he destroyed them, both by showing the impossibility of such claims, and by setting out the true genealogy of the claimants. The hatchet job was very effective. By the end of the essay, the *Vestiarium* and the royal claims had both been gravely mauled.

To this formidable attack, the elder brother promptly replied.[22] His reply was olympian, but weak. He was able to challenge some details in the reviewer's account of the episode in 1829, but they were details only; they did not touch the heart of the matter. It was not enough to point out that Scott had not seen the original manuscript of the *Vestiarium*: that, after all, had been Scott's chief complaint. To the demolition of the royal claims, John Sobieski Stuart made no reply. He simply consigned his critic's arguments to 'silent contempt' on the assumption that the critic was committed to the interest of a rival Jacobite pretender. In fact, his assumption was wrong.[23] Though the article contained some errors, its main points were, and are, unanswerable. The claims of the Sobieski Stuarts were thereby permanently discredited; an attempt to publish a cheaper edition of the *Vestiarium* a year later came to nothing;[24] and their great work, *The*

*Costume of the Clans*, though untouched by the reviewer, was discredited by association. From a challenging original work, it sank to being the unacknowledged but 'productive quarry' of other, less ambitious, and, one must add, less scholarly writers.

In the wake of this unfortunate episode, the ménage at Eilean Aigas broke up. Soon it was reconstituted abroad, in Prague. There, in the ephemeral and long-lost kingdom of their supposed ancestor, the Winter King of Bohemia, the two pretenders established themselves and majestically gave their address as 'the Hradshin', the ancient royal palace of Bohemia. Similarly, in France, their address had been 'Versailles'. They lived abroad, mainly (it seems) in Prague, for the next twenty years. How they lived, we do not know. But how had they ever lived: these mystery-men, of whom no private correspondence survives, no intimacy has been revealed? All that we are told is that, in the Austrian Empire, their claims were always respected: they were received as royalty; the military saluted them as such; and those who were 'presented' to them 'kissed hands'. Finally, in 1868, they returned to London, where, though now very poor, 'they went into society and, with their orders and spurs, were well-known figures in the British Museum Reading Room' – studying, no doubt, royal genealogy, Jacobite history, and Scottish tartans. A table there, we are told, was reserved for their use; and 'their pens, paper-knives, paperweights, etc., were surmounted with miniature coronets, in gold'.[25] In 1872 an appeal was made to Queen Victoria to relieve their poverty on the ground of their supposed kinship; but the review in the *Quarterly* was cited against them, and the appeal failed.[26] Of them, as of John Keats, it can be said that they were killed by the *Quarterly*. They died in 1872 and 1880 respectively, and were buried in Eskadale, the church which they had attended from their romantic island home at Eilean Aigas. Lord Lovat, it seems, like Sir Thomas Dick Lauder and many others, remained 'still a believer'.

The relevance of the Sobieski Stuarts to our story consists in the *Vestiarium Scoticum*. The original of this document has never been seen; and there can be no doubt that both it and all the documents invoked, quoted, or 'copied in facsimile' in its support – the Cadiz manuscript, the Douay manuscript, the notes of Bishop Leslie, the letter of 'J.T. Stuart Hay' to his dearest son, the numerous unspecified 'manuscripts in our possession' – are either fictions or forgeries: the products of the 'exaggerating imagination' or the artistic ingenuity of the two brothers. And yet how can we withhold a tribute of admiration from these engaging charlatans? They had at least one of the qualities of their supposed grandfather, Bonnie Prince Charlie. He, by some mysterious charm, and by belief in himself, raised up an army of men who believed in him, fought for him, and, after defeat, never betrayed him. The 'Sobieski Stuarts', thanks to similar qualities, never lacked believers, friends, patrons. Any sense of the absurdity of their pretensions dissolved in their presence. They lived their unreal life so completely that it was accepted, even respected, by real people. Their inconsistencies triumphed over criticism and exposure. And by the scholarship which they applied to their forgeries they continued, even after their deaths, to bewitch even the most learned of antiquaries.[27] Or at least they bewitched Scotchmen; for no Englishman seems to have taken them seriously. Like Boece and Ossian, they could be persuasive to Scots and Europeans; but their charm ceased to work among the sceptical Anglo-Saxons beyond the Cheviot hills.

The psychology of the Sobieski Stuarts is one thing. Their significance and results are another. In order to put them in their context, it is convenient to recall certain dates, and to look behind them to certain material facts: these concern Queen Victoria and the tartan industry.

First the dates. The Sobieski Stuarts surfaced in 1822, the date of George IV's visit to Scotland. They began to feel their way towards Stuart ancestry about 1825. In 1829 they tried to publish the *Vestiarium*, but withdrew when Scott insisted on production of the original manuscript. They finally published it, independently, in 1842, and *The Costume of the Clans* in 1845. Now these were not only the years of neo-Catholic gothic romanticism – the years when Pugin's vision of the higher civilisation of the Middle Ages was becoming popular – they were also the years when Queen Victoria was discovering the Highlands. Her first visits were in 1842 and 1843. In 1847 she leased, and in 1848 she bought Balmoral. It is appropriate that the Sobieski Stuarts should have flitted from their phantom court in the Highlands, like ghosts at cock-crow, when the real Hanoverian court moved in.

Meanwhile the tartan industry had been growing apace. Throughout the nine years after the visit of George IV – the years from 1822 to 1831 – the correspondence of Wilson and Son shows a continuous increase in the demand: a demand encouraged by the book of Colonel Stewart of Garth, and by the propaganda of the Highland Society. These were the years in which the Sobieski Stuarts were compiling the *Vestiarium Scoticum*, which was first seen in 1829, but which had evidently been in their hands earlier. In the same years, a rival propagandist was preparing to continue the work of Colonel Stewart. This was James Logan, an Aberdonian settled in London. In 1831, after an extensive walking tour through Scotland, he published his book *The Scottish Gael, or Celtic Manners as preserved among the Highlanders*, which he dedicated – since George IV had just died – to his successor William IV. In this work Logan swallowed all the Highland myths. He accepted the reality and authority of Archdeacon Veremund and of 'the sublime bard' Ossian. He denounced the infamous Pinkerton as 'an author notorious for his anti-Gaelic spirit'. He asserted the antiquity of the kilt, and deplored the fact that the Seaforth Highlanders unaccountably wore trousers – 'a source of great vexation to their clan and country'. And he declared that 'the particular *setts* or patterns of tartan appropriate to each clan must have been long fixed'. He admitted that, since George IV's visit, the rage for tartan had been fed with some fraudulent speculations; but he announced that he intended to correct that: he was, himself, 'preparing a work expressly on tartans and badges, with illustrative plates'. Meanwhile he published in his book a table of clan tartans, and one illustration: the tartan worn by H.R.H. the Duke of Sussex as Earl of Inverness.

In consequence of this work, Logan was elected President of the Highland Society of London; and the Society undertook to sponsor his promised new book. Meanwhile the Highland Society offered a prize for the best history of the Highland clans. The prize was won by W.F. Skene, whose work *The Highlanders of Scotland* was published at the instance of the Society in 1836. Skene was an able scholar, who would go on to become the great authority on Celtic Scotland; and although he was, as his later editor would write, 'weak in the critical faculty' (he too swallowed Ossian), his observations on kilts and tartan are generally sensible. He admitted that both were modern inventions, 'or, at all events, that the trews is the only ancient form' of Highland dress. Six years later, in 1842, came the published version of the *Vestiarium Scoticum*. Then, the next year, Logan published his promised book. It was called *The Clans of the Scottish Highlands*, and it was lavishly illustrated by seventy-two paintings of clansmen in their distinctive tribal tartans. These illustrations were by R.R. McIan, and the book is generally known by his name. In the text, Logan paid tribute to 'the recent splendid work of John Sobieski Stuart' – i.e. the still unexposed *Vestiarium* – on which it clearly drew. Though occasional differences were explicitly mentioned in order to justify a separate publication, many of the tartans illustrated by McIan were 'unacknowledged reproductions from the designs in the *Vestiarium Scoticum*'.[28]

Logan's *Clans of the Scottish Highlands*, like his previous work, was dedicated to the reigning monarch. He observed, in his dedication, that Queen Victoria had 'graciously deigned to visit the country of the Clans and patronised their manufactures and costume': than which, he added, 'no branch of home manufacture has so long received the public patronage'. The Wilson correspondence shows that Logan himself was in touch with the firm, which was eager to patronise, and to correct, his work.[29] Thus the romance of the clans, and the controversy about tartan and kilt, had its economic side; and we naturally wonder what were the relations of the Sobieski Stuarts and this growing industry. In general, the two brothers, with their royal airs, seemed to stand far above vulgar commerce; but in the course of controversy they made certain admissions which suggest that they, too, were responding to the pressure of the market as well as to the requirements of scholarship.

Already in 1829, we know from Dick Lauder, the two brothers were advising clan chieftains about their tartans; and these chieftains – Cluny Macpherson, McLeod, McLauchlan, Comyn – were acting on their advice and wearing 'correct' tartans drawn from the still unpublished *Vestiarium*. At the same time the brothers were evidently in direct touch with Messrs Wilson, who made for them – it can only

have been for them – a 'Hay Stuart' tartan, no doubt to their specifi-
cations. There is also evidence that in February 1819, when the royal
visit was first mooted, Wilson and Son were in touch with a
gentleman 'who is writing on the subject of the Highland clans in
Italy', and who wished for 'specimens of all coloured tartans used by
these clans'.[30] Since Thomas Allen, the father of the two brothers, was
living in Italy about that time, this evidence points towards them; and
since 1819 was the year in which Wilson and Son drew up their 'Key
Pattern Book', which was the basis of their specialisation, it is possible
that the two brothers were already in alliance with the manufacturers
at the very beginning of the new boom in 'clan tartans'. Later evidence
is more explicit. In 1848, in his reply to the *Quarterly Review*, the
elder brother, referring to the proposed publication of the *Vestiarium*
in 1829, stated that his sole motive in that matter had been 'to gratify
the repeated importunity of manufacturers, who, having derived
great advantages from its resources, were solicitous for its general
use'. In other words, in the 1820s, not only the chieftains but also the
manufacturers were using the brothers as their advisers. The brothers
had agreed to the proposed publication, they said, only 'in consideration of the advantage which it was expected to convey to Scottish
manufacturers'. A year later, John Sobieski Stuart repeated the statement when seeking to promote a cheap edition of the *Vestiarium*. He
had always intended a wider distribution, he then said, so that the
book might be available 'to manufacturers and the trades in general
concerned in tartan. It was at the long and anxious solicitation of
many manufacturers that . . . I consented to publish the volume'.[31] We
may be sceptical of the royal claims of the Sobieski Stuarts; but we
must surely respect their admissions as to economic motives. Perhaps
Scott had not been wrong when he scented, behind the *Vestiarium*, a
tartan-weavers' publicity stunt. Whether the Sobieski Stuarts derived
any financial benefit from their association with industry, we cannot
say. Their finances, like everything else about them, are mysterious.[32]

However that may be, the *Quarterly* ruined all for them. In the
middle years of the nineteenth century, tartan manufacture, differen-
tiated by clans, prospered hugely: together with Highland scenery,
Highland cattle, Sir Edwin Landseer and the ghillie John Brown. But
the *Vestiarium* was discredited; and its contents, mythical as they

were, were transmitted to the manufacturers through the sterilising medium of less adventurous works. The failure of the *Vestiarium* lay behind the success of Logan's *Clans;* and that success in turn inspired other works. In 1850 no fewer than three works on the subject were published, all of them visibly, though silently, indebted to the *Vestiarium.* They were: *Authenticated Tartans of the Clans and Families of Scotland* by William and Andrew Smith, Scotch snuff-box makers to his late Majesty, with sixty-nine plates supplied by the manufacturers, 'machine-painted' as in the *Vestiarium*; Thomas Smibert's *The Clans of the Highlands of Scotland,* with fifty-five coloured lithographic plates of tartans copied partly from the *Vestiarium* and partly from Logan's work (itself partly based on the *Vestiarium*); and James Browne's *History of the Highlands and the Highland Clans*: a useful work of history, which incidentally reproduced twenty-two lithographic plates of tartan in colour taken from the *Vestiarium* without comment. For the rest of the century, books of tartans continued to pour off the presses, all based on these books, and so all indebted, directly or indirectly, to the *Vestiarium.* The *Vestiarium* itself sank from view; but its work was done. *The Costume of the Clans* was reprinted in 1892, and Logan and McIan's book in 1893. These various works have provided the standard 'setts' for tartan manufacturers ever since; and so today the imaginary tartan 'setts' of the *Vestiarium* supply the skirts and carpets of Scots, and supposed Scots, from Texas to Tokyo. It is sad to think, however, that the Sobieski Stuarts, who did so much to enrich the manufacturers of their adopted country, should have died so poor themselves.

# Notes

Material within square brackets has been added by the editor.

## Chapter 1 Scotia's Rise to Glory?

1. The cannibalism of the Scots – a very sore point with later Scotch antiquaries – rests on a single statement of Jerome in his *Adversus Jovinianum*. For the discomfort which this text caused later, see, for example, the several pages of intellectual writhing over the topic by Sir Thomas Craig in his *de Unione Regnorum Britanniae Tractatus*, 1605, ed. and trans. C. Sanford Terry (Scottish History Society, Edinburgh, 1909), pp. 132–8, 383–90.

2. In Europe 'Scotus' continued to mean 'Irish' till the eleventh century, when the Irish chronicler Moelbrigte, having become a monk of Cologne in 1056, was known as Marianus Scotus. But by that time it had come to mean 'Scottish' in Scotland.

3. Edited by W.F. Skene as *Chronicles of the Picts, Chronicles of the Scots, and other Early Memorials of Scottish History* (Edinburgh, 1867).

4. John of Fordun, *Chronica Gentis Scotorum*, ed. W.F. Skene, trans. F.J.H. Skene (Edinburgh, 1871–2), I, 294–5, [II, 290, in English].

5. The Scots of the fourteenth century, who repeated the story of the destruction of their documents, had, of course, no means of knowing it: they only knew that the documents had disappeared. On the whole, it seems improbable that Edward I, that legalistic king, would have destroyed any Scottish public documents: for they were potentially too useful a weapon, provided that he kept them under his own control. In 1789 John Pinkerton, in *An Enquiry into the History of Scotland preceding the Reign of Malcolm III, or the year 1056*, p. xxxiv, argued that no such destruction had happened, and that the surviving records of Scotland, between the eleventh and thirteenth centuries 'present a series of original history equal to that which could reasonably be expected for a country so remote and so lately civilised'. In his view, Scotland was no worse off for records of that period than most other northern nations, such as Ireland, Denmark, Sweden, Bohemia, Prussia and Poland; England and France were better supplied only because they were richer and had more centres of learning.

6. Fordun, *Chronica Gentis Scotorum*, I, 88, [English version, II, 79].

7. Ibid., I, 147, [English version, II, 138].

8. Arthur H. Williamson, in *Scottish National Consciousness in the Age of James VI* (Edinburgh, 1979), p. 101, cites, as a 'most notable' sign of Major's scepticism, that he reduced the number of kings before Fergus mac Erc 'from 40 to 15'. But in Major's time the number was not forty but forty-five (it was Boece who reduced them to forty); and I suspect, with Innes (*Critical Essay*, p. 344), that the change from forty-five to fifteen is one of the many typographical errors in Major's book, which was printed in Paris while the author was away (see Robert Freebairn's preface to the Edinburgh edition of 1740).

9. Williamson, *Scottish National Consciousness*, p. 120.

10. Thomas Innes, *A Critical Essay on the Ancient Inhabitants of the Northern Parts of Britain or Scotland* (London, 1729); the edition used here is the second, prepared by George Grub for the 'Historians of Scotland' series (Edinburgh, 1879), p. 143.

11. So the rumour ran in Aberdeen in the 1590s, when Robert Gordon, later of Straloch, was a student there: recorded in his letter of 4 August 1649 to David Buchanan on the writing of Scottish history, cited in William Nicolson, *The Scottish Historical Library* (London, 1703), p. 75.

12. This was suggested by W.F. Skene in his edition of Fordun. But Fordun's explicit statement that he had found no accounts of the early kings is decisive. Innes, *Critical Essay*, pp. 128–9, 136–7.

13. Geoffrey's phrase is: 'quendam britannici sermonis librum vetustissimus, qui a Bruto rege usque ad Cadvaladrum filium Cadvalonis actus omnium continue et ex ordine perpulcris orationibus proponebat'. Boece's phrase is: 'Veremundi archidiaconi olim Sancti Andreae de nostris rebus, etse rudi quadam vetustate conscripta historia, a Scotorum gentis origine usque ad Malcolmi Canmor regem omnia abunde complectens'.

14. On Chambers and his evidence, see Innes, *Critical Essay*, pp. 171–6.

15. Chambers was a partisan of Mary, and fled abroad after her escape into England. He lived first in Spain, then in France; and the work in which he quoted Veremund, *Abrégé des histoires de tous les roys de France, Écosse et Angleterre*, was published at Paris in 1569. Innes excuses John Leslie, bishop of Ross, for pretending to quote Boece's original sources, whereas he had only read Boece himself, on the ground that a life of business and exile had confused his memory (*Critical Essay*, pp. 169–71). Exactly the same could be said of Chambers.

16. Shakespeare took the material of Macbeth from Holinshed; but Holinshed had taken it from Boece. Fordun had indeed given some account of Macbeth's reign; but Fordun's chronicle, though circulated in manuscript in Scotland, was not printed till 1722. We can, therefore, say that without Boece Shakespeare would not have known about Macbeth.

17. Craig, *de Unione Regnorum Britanniae*, pp. 113, 135; [in English 357 and 370].

18. See Gordon's letter of 4 April 1655 on Archbishop Spottiswoode's *History*, printed in the preface to *Joannis Lelandii Antiquarii de rebus Britannicis Collectanea*, ed. Thomas Hearne (Oxford, 1715), I, xliii.

19. John Leslie, *De Origine, Moribus et Rebus Gestis Scotorum* (Rome, 1578).

20. Sir George Mackenzie, *A Defence of the Antiquity of the Royal Line of Scotland* (against William Lloyd, bishop of St Asaph), 1685; *The Antiquity of the Royal Line of Scotland further cleared* (against Edward Stillingfleet), 1686.

21. Pinkerton, *Enquiry into the History of Scotland*, I, 239–40.
22. Innes, *Critical Essay*, pp. 2, 109.
23. David Dalrymple, Lord Hailes, *Annals of Scotland from the Accession of Malcolm III surnamed Canmore to the Accession of the House of Stewart*, vol. I (Edinburgh, 1776), pp. 102, 105; vol. II (Edinburgh, 1779), p. 224.

## Chapter 2 George Buchanan

1. Craig, *de Unione Regnorum Britanniae Tractatus*, pp. 132, 382.
2. Boswell's *Life of Johnson*, ed. G.B. Hill, revised L.G. Powell (Oxford, 1934), IV, 185–6.
3. Ninian Winzet, *Velitatio in Georgium Buchananum* (Ingolstadt, 1582), p. 197. This tract against Buchanan's *de Jure Regni apud Scotos* was added to, and paginated following, two others of a more general anti-Protestant nature, entitled *Flagellum Sectariorum*. Though a Catholic exile in Germany when he wrote, Winzet referred back to a conversation which he had had with Buchanan in Edinburgh some twenty years earlier.
4. G.J.G. Henriques, ed., *George Buchanan in the Lisbon Inquisition* (Lisbon, 1906), p. 32; [also in English translation in James M. Aitken, ed., *The Trial of George Buchanan before the Lisbon Inquisition* (Edinburgh and London, 1939), pp. 38–9].
5. It is curious that, during a period of military service in Scotland in 1523, he enlisted with French troops campaigning there, rather than with native Scottish troops, in an ill-fated assault on the English border.
6. P. Hume Brown, *George Buchanan, Humanist and Reformer* (Edinburgh, 1890), pp. 135–41, excused Buchanan's obscenity by describing it as a literary fashion, and comparing it with Theodore Beza's early verses, afterwards regretted. But there is no just comparison between the coarseness of Buchanan's poems and the conventional amorous exercises of Beza.
7. Some time after his return to Scotland he would start to conceal the embarrassing evidence of his earlier admiration for the Guise family: altering the names of the persons to whom he had dedicated his poems.
8. See his poem *Adventus in Galliam*, cited by Hume Brown, *George Buchanan*, p. 160.
9. His reference to the pope as 'pater romanus', in his poem celebrating the French capture of Calais in that year, is also Catholic orthodoxy: see *Buchanani Opera Omnia*, ed. Thomas Ruddiman (Edinburgh, 1715), II, 102 (in the miscellaneous poems).
10. In his *Vita sua* he wrote of the five years, 1555–60, which he spent in the Maréchal de Brissac's household in France, Piedmont and Italy, 'quod tempus maxima ex parte dedit sacrarum studio, ut de controversiis, quae tum maiorem hominum partem exercebat, exactius diiudicare posset': ['he gave most of his time in these years to studying theology, in order that he might pass a more exact judgment on the controversies which were then occupying most people's thoughts': English translation given in Aitken, *Trial of George Buchanan*, p. xxvii].

11. Sir James Melville of Halhill, *Memoirs of his own Life* (Bannatyne Club, Edinburgh, 1827), p. 262.

12. For the Scots to rise from rusticity and barbarism to culture and civilisation, he explained, it would be necessary for them to exchange the uncouth sounds of their ancient tongue for the more melodious tones of the Latin language: in this way they could cancel the disadvantages of their native background. *Rerum Scoticarum Historia* in Buchanan, *Opera Omnia*, I, 4. [*History of Scotland*, trans. William Bond (London, 1722), I, 8.]

13. [Reference not found. Marc-Antoine Muret (1526–85), an able and independent-minded young French humanist, a friend of Buchanan in 1552, fled from France a year or two later, pursued by accusations of heresy and homosexuality. Sheltering first in the more tolerant environment of Venice, he later found sanctuary in the bosom of the Roman Church. There, in order to continue his work as a scholar unmolested, he adopted the camouflage of fanaticism. Ultimately he would shock his earlier associates by delivering on behalf of the Pope, at a grand welcome for the French ambassador, a formal panegyric on the Massacre of St Bartholomew, which he then published. See Charles Dejob, *Marc-Antoine Muret: un professeur français en Italie dans la seconde moitié du XVIième siècle* (Paris, 1881), especially pp. 217–33.]

14. [On a slip of paper attached to the Ms of this chapter Trevor-Roper recorded his intention to provide, in revising the book for publication, 'a fuller account' of the *Detectio*, as also of *de Jure Regni*, than that which stands here now.]

15. Sir Nicholas Throckmorton to Queen Elizabeth, 19 July 1567: British Library, Ms Cotton, Caligula. I, 28–31. This letter was missed out from the series of such letters printed in Joseph Bain, ed., *Calendar of the State Papers relating to Scotland and Mary, Queen of Scots, vol. II: 1563–69* (Edinburgh, 1900), where it should have appeared on pp. 356–7.

16. Buchanan, *Opera Omnia*, I, 168. [Bond's translation, *History of Scotland*, I, 405.]

17. Thomas Randolph to William Cecil, 1 March 1570, in William K. Boyd, ed., *Calendar of State Papers relating to Scotland, vol. III: 1569–1571* (Edinburgh, 1903), p. 93.

18. Buchanan, *Opera Omnia*, II, epistle V: Buchanan to Rogers from Leith, 4 Cal. August 1571.

19. Edited by P. Hume Brown as *Vernacular Writings of George Buchanan* (Edinburgh and London, 1892).

20. Hume Brown, *Vernacular Writings of Buchanan*, p. 36.

21. [Ibid., p. xxxviii.]

22. Here in particular, but also at other points in this chapter and part of the next, I draw on evidence, arguments and conclusions which I first presented in greater detail in my essay 'George Buchanan and the Ancient Scottish Constitution', published in the *English Historical Review*, Supplement 3 (1966), pp. 1–53.

23. William Camden, *Annales* (translated as *The History of the most renowned and victorious princess Elizabeth . . .1675*), pp. 154–5, anno 1571.

24. George Mackenzie, *The Lives and Characters of the most Eminent Writers of the Scots Nation*, vol. III (Edinburgh, 1722), pp. 180–1.

## Chapter 3 Buchanan's Nemesis

1. William Salesbury to Archbishop Mathew Parker in 1565, cited by Robin Flower, 'William Salesbury, Richard Davies and Archbishop Parker', in *National Library of Wales Journal*, II (1941), p. 9.
2. H. Lhuyd, *Commentarioli Descriptionis Britannicae Fragmentum* (Cologne, 1572), pp. 24–5, 32–9. [English translation by Thomas Twyne as *The Breviary of Britayne* (London, 1573), pp. 6, 21, 28–9, 33, 36–44, 47.]
3. Innes, *Critical Essay*, p. 195.
4. In the dedication to *de Jure Regni apud Scotos*.
5. On this see Williamson, *Scottish National Consciousness*, pp. 122–5.
6. *Rerum Scoticarum Historia* in Buchanan, *Opera Omnia*, ed. Ruddiman (Edinburgh, 1715), I, 2–3, 5, 44; *[History of Scotland*, trans. William Bond (London, 1722), I, 3, 6, 9, 112].
7. Buchanan, *Opera Omnia*, vol. 1, in the preface, p. xx: Rogers to Buchanan, 28 February 1577.
8. Buchanan, *Opera Omnia*, I, 2–5; [*History of Scotland*, I, 3–9].
9. Ibid., I, 44–5; [*History of Scotland*, I, 112–13].
10. Joseph Scaliger, *Catulli, Tibulli, Propertii nova editio* (Paris, 1577), p. 159.
11. Buchanan, *Opera Omnia*, I, 44–5; [*History of Scotland*, I, 107–109].
12. Ibid., I, 44; [*History of Scotland*, I, 112–13].
13. William Camden, *Britannia* (London, 1586), pp. 40–1.
14. *The Basilikon Doron of King James VI*, ed. James Craigie (Scottish Text Society, Edinburgh, 1944), I, 149.
15. Buchanan, *Opera Omnia*, II, epistle xxxv: Edward Bulkley to Buchanan, 28 November 1580.
16. Buchanan, *Opera Omnia*, II, epistle xxvii: dated 9 November 1579.
17. Hume Brown, *George Buchanan*, p. 298.
18. This treatment of Boece by Buchanan is amply demonstrated by Innes, *Critical Essay*, pp. 209–20.
19. *Basilikon Doron*, I, 149–50.
20. For these bibliographical details see *George Buchanan, Glasgow Quatercentenary Studies* (Glasgow, 1907), pp. 47–52, 221–2, 454, 464–6.
21. See the *Dictionary of National Biography*.
22. Henri Leclerq, *Mabillon*, vol. II (Paris, 1957), pp. 868–70.
23. A. Bellesheim, *History of the Catholic Church of Scotland*, trans. O. Hunter Blair (Edinburgh, 1890), IV, 204–10, 408–13.
24. R. Wodrow, *Analecta: or Materials for a History of Remarkable Providences; mostly relating to Scotch Ministers and Christians* (Maitland Club, Edinburgh, 1842–3), III, 516–17.
25. Recorded in Hearne's diary on 26 February 1721: Philip Bliss, ed., *Reliquiae Hearnianae: the Remains of Thomas Hearne* (London, 1869), II, 126.
26. In a letter dated 1732 he mentioned that he had got a copy made for him thirty years earlier of a Scottish manuscript chronicle in the Bodleian Library at Oxford: *Registrum de Panmure: Records of the Families of Maule, Brechin and Brechin Barclay*, ed. John Stuart (Edinburgh, 1874), I, cxxxvii.
27. *Registrum de Panmure*, I, cxviii.
28. Ibid., I, cxxi.

29. Emmanuel de Broglie, *Mabillon et la Société de l'Abbaye de Saint-Germain des Prés à la fin du dix-septième siècle* (Paris, 1888), II, 290–95; Augustin Joly, *Un Converti de Bossuet: James Drummond, Duc de Perth, 1648–1716* (Lille, 1933), pp. 182–3, 365–7; Leclerq, *Mabillon*, II, 868–70.

30. Innes used in the body of his *Critical Essay*, and printed in five appendices at the end of it (pp. 411–21), documents of great importance for the early history of Scotland which were drawn from Mss in the Colbertine Library.

31. Innes, *Critical Essay*, e.g., p. 285; Edward Gibbon, *Memoirs of my Life*, ed. G.A. Bonnard (London, 1966), p. 147.

32. *Registrum de Panmure*, I, cxxii. An English translation of Fleury's work was published at London in four volumes in 1727–30; and a part of it was reissued in three volumes over a century later in a revised translation by John Henry Newman, who pronounced it still, at that time, the best extended treatment available of the history of the early centuries of the Christian Church. See the preface, pp. iii–viii, to his first volume (Oxford, 1842).

33. The manuscript of the book, as far as he had gone, passed to his great-nephew Alexander Innes and was ultimately published by the Spalding Club, Aberdeen, 1853, as *The Civil and Ecclesiastical History of Scotland, AD 80–818.*

34. *Registrum de Panmure*, I, cxxiii.

35. Wodrow, *Analecta*, III, 516–17. On the hypocritical Lord Grange see H. Grey Graham, *The Social Life of Scotland in the Eighteenth Century* (London, 1901), p. 498. When his wife's random tongue endangered him, he hired a party of Highlanders to kidnap her, and carry her off to the remote island of St Kilda. Then he declared her dead, celebrated her funeral, and wrote pious letters deploring the infidelity of the age.

36. Innes, *Critical Essay*, memoir p. xviii, and p. 330.

37. *Registrum de Panmure*, I, cxvi–cxxiii.

38. 'Papers by Father Innes', *Spalding Club Miscellany*, II (Aberdeen, 1842), pp. 353–6.

39. One who did was the Jacobite scholar and firebrand Francis Atterbury, former bishop of Rochester, subsequently an exile in France. See his comments in letters dated 1730 and 1732 to Daniel Williams, *Spalding Club Miscellany*, II, pp. 357–8.

40. Gibbon shows no sign of having read or even known of Innes' work, which would have saved him from serious error on the origin of the Scots.

41. John Pinkerton, *An Enquiry into the History of Scotland*, I, lv, 314. According to Pinkerton, the neglect of Innes' *Critical Essay* in Britain between 1729 and 1789 was owing to its author's reputation as 'a papist and violent Jacobite' (*Enquiry*, I, 240). But it may also have been a consequence of 'a subject so dry and unpleasant as that of our remote antiquities', as Innes himself admitted, compounded by 'the repetitions and digressions with which it is clogged', as recognised even by Innes' admirer, Atterbury: *Registrum de Panmure*, I, cxxi; *Spalding Club Miscellany*, II, 357.

## Chapter 4 The Search for a Celtic Homer

1. Gibbon, *Memoirs*, p. 84.
2. Henry Grey Graham, *Scottish Men of Letters in the Eighteenth Century* (London, 1901), pp. 321–3.
3. John Gibson Lockhart, *The Life of Sir Walter Scott* (Edinburgh, 1902), I, 88.
4. *The Letters of David Hume*, ed. J.Y.T. Greig (Oxford, 1932), I, 204.
5. Graham, *Scottish Men of Letters*, pp. 62–9.
6. [A slightly different version of this exclamatory appeal is cited in Ernest C. Mossner, *The Life of David Hume* (Oxford, 1970), p. 379.]
7. Pinkerton, *Enquiry into the History of Scotland*, I, xi.
8. Thomas Blackwell, *Enquiry into the Life and Writings of Homer* (London, 1735), pp. 15, 26, 35, 64, 105, 108, 116–19, 133.
9. Ibid., pp. 232, 288.
10. *Rerum Scoticarum Historia* in *Buchanani Opera Omnia*, I, 22–3. [*History of Scotland*, trans. William Bond (London, 1722), I, 63–4.]
11. Innes, *Critical Essay*, pp. 115, 261.
12. Martin Martin, *A Description of the Western Islands of Scotland* (London, 1703), pp. 115–16.
13. [E. Burt], *Letters from a Gentleman in the North of Scotland to his Friend in London* (1754), letter XXI, ed. R. Jamieson (London, 1818), II, 62–4. The worthy Sir John Sinclair, who was not very sensitive to humour or irony, quotes this passage in all seriousness as evidence that the ballad must have been of Homeric or Virgilian quality and part of a Homeric or Virgilian epic, 'and most probably a part of Ossian': *The Poems of Ossian in the Original Gaelic* (London, 1807), I, xxi–xxii.
14. Blackwell, *Enquiry into Homer*, pp. 113–14.
15. John Johnston in the preface to his *Heroes ex omni historia Scotica lectissimi* (Amsterdam, 1602).
16. Lucan's reference to the bards is in his *Bellum Civile*, I, 447–9:

    Vos quoque, qui fortes animos belloque peremptas
    Laudibus in longum vates dimittitis aevum
    Plurima securi fudistis carmina, Bardi.

    [English translation by J.D. Duff in Lucan, *The Civil War*, Loeb Classical Library (London, 1928): 'The Bards also, who by the praises of their verse transmit to distant ages the fame of heroes slain in battle, poured forth at ease their lays in abundance.']
17. J. Toland, 'The History of the Druids', in *A Collection of Several Pieces of Mr John Toland* (London, 1726), I, 24–9.
18. [David Hume], *A True Account of the Behaviour and Conduct of Archibald Stewart, Esq., late Lord Provost of Edinburgh. In a Letter to a Friend* (London, 1748), pp. 11, 41.
19. Voltaire, *Dictionnaire Philosophique* (édition Ménard et Desenne, Paris, 1827), I, 44: 'Epopée: de Virgile': 'Homère n'a jamais fait répandre des pleurs'.
20. Voltaire's notes to his play *Les Lois de Minos* in *Œuvres Complètes de Voltaire* (édition Garnier frères, Paris, 1877), VII, 177.

21. Thomas Gray, 'The Bard, a Pindaric Ode': *The Complete Poems of Thomas Gray*, ed. H.W. Starr and J.R. Hendrickson (Oxford, 1966), p. 19. The parallel with Ossian was pointed out by J.S. Smart, *James Macpherson: an Episode in Literature* (London, 1905), p. 101.

22. The fact was recorded as 'well known' just ten years after James Macpherson's death, and preserved in a note on pp. 563–4 of the third volume of *Poems of Ossian in the Original Gaelic*, issued in 1807 by Sir John Sinclair and other members of the Highland Society of London. This highly significant note was pointed out first, so far as I can see, by Derick S. Thomson in his article 'Bogus Gaelic Literature *c.*1750–*c.*1820' in *Transactions of the Gaelic Society of Glasgow*, vol. V (1958), p. 177. The note occurs in a catalogue of Gaelic books and manuscripts which is placed towards the end of the volume, following John McArthur's translation of Cesarotti's dissertation on the poetry of Ossian (with its own attendant notes); and the information was given in the course of praise for the Gaelic poetry and other talents of Lachlan Macpherson of Strathmashie. The author of the note is not identified in the text of the volume, so far as I can see. But having been written so soon after James Macpherson's death, and having received the *imprimatur* of the committee of the Highland Society of London responsible for promoting the Gaelic version of Ossian, we can almost certainly regard it as reliable evidence. [This catalogue of Gaelic books and Mss was compiled by the Rev. Donald Mackintosh, identified as Gaelic Secretary to the Scottish Antiquarian Society. See National Library of Scotland, Advocates Mss 73. 2. 11, f. 84: Colin Macrae, writing from London on 24 November 1806 to Sir John Sinclair; also Adv. Mss 73. 2. 16, f. 80 verso, and 73. 2. 24, ff. 34–5. Donald Mackintosh had been born in Blair Atholl in 1743. The son of a tenant farmer, he moved to Edinburgh, and became in succession a postman, a clerk and a tutor. In 1785 he published the first printed collection of Gaelic proverbs. Later still, he became the last consecrated priest of the Jacobite, non-juring, episcopal church; and in that capacity he travelled widely in Scotland in order to minister to a very scattered flock. His travels and his interest in collecting the remains of Gaelic literature recommended him to the Highland Society of Edinburgh, which appointed him to be its official 'keeper of manuscripts' in January 1801. In May of that year he inventoried, and subsequently transported to Edinburgh from the house of Major MacLauchlan of Kilbride near Oban, the second most important extant collection of old Gaelic Mss (James Macpherson's own collection being the most important). Donald Mackintosh was one of the two Gaelic experts to serve on the committee of the Highland Society of Scotland which, between 1797 and 1805, worked to produce its famous *Report* on Ossian. His interests and his contacts thus appear to render him a thoroughly trustworthy source for the information given in the text above. On him, see the account given by Ronald I. Black, 'The Gaelic Academy: the Cultural Commitment of the Highland Society of Scotland', in *Scottish Gaelic Studies*, vol. XIV, part 2 (winter, 1986), pp. 11–13].

23. Henry Mackenzie, ed., *Report of the Committee of the Highland Society of Scotland, Appointed to Inquire into the Nature and Authenticity of the Poems of Ossian* (Edinburgh, 1805), Appendix, p. 68: undated note by John Home.

24. John Ramsay of Ochtertyre, *Scotland and Scotsmen in the Eighteenth Century*, ed. Alexander Allardyce (Edinburgh and London, 1888), I, 293.

25. At the beginning of the eighteenth century Ruthven had 'the only school between Speymouth and Lorne'. Alexander Cameron, *Reliquiae Celticae: Texts, Papers and Studies in Gaelic Literature and Philology* (ed. A. Macbain and J. Kennedy, Inverness, 1892), I, xix.

26. A neighbour and slightly older friend of James Macpherson in the 1750s claimed, after the poet's death, to have set him on the Ossianic path to 'genteel bread' in about 1757, after hearing him complain of the tediousness of the schoolmastering profession. This friend, Donald Macpherson, was already acquainted with 'ludicrous poems' composed by James on local events and characters, and now introduced him to more promising material in the traditional recitations of his (Donald's) grandfather. NLS, Advocates Mss 73. 2. 13, f. 47: Donald Macpherson from Laggan, 1 Oct. 1797, to the Rev. John Anderson, the poet's principal executor in Scotland.

27. *Scots Magazine*, xviii (January 1756), p. 15.

28. Highland Society *Report*, pp. 33, 43. On Strathmashie as poet, see the brief account in Nigel Macneill, *The Literature of the Highlanders: a History of Gaelic Literature from the Earliest Times to the Present Day* (Inverness, 1892), pp. 267–8. Ten of his poems were printed in Gaelic, with English translations and notes (not always accurate) by the Rev. Thomas Sinton in *The Poetry of Badenoch* (Inverness, 1906). See below, chapter 6.

29. Highland Society *Report*, Appendix, pp. 157–61.

30. On the manuscript and its history, see the typescript catalogue of Gaelic Mss at the NLS, compiled by Ronald I. Black (Adv. Ms 72. 1. 37).

31. Mss of John Macpherson cited in the unpublished Edinburgh University Ph.D. thesis (1967) by James N.M. Maclean on 'The Political Careers of James (Fingal) Macpherson and Sir John Macpherson'. See below, chapter 5, note 43.

32. Highland Society *Report*, Appendix, p. 66: letter of Alexander Carlyle, dated Musselburgh, 9 Jan. 1802.

33. Robert Heron, *Observations Made in a Journey through the Western Counties of Scotland* (Perth, 1793), II, 495–6. Heron had at one time been Blair's assistant.

34. *The Correspondence of Thomas Gray*, ed. Paget Toynbee and L. Whibley, revised by H.W. Starr (Oxford, 1935), II, 672, 679–80.

35. *Fragments of Ancient Poetry Collected in the Highlands of Scotland* (Edinburgh, 1760), Preface, pp. iii–vii.

36. Highland Society *Report*, Appendix, p. 58: letter of Hugh Blair, Edinburgh, 20 Dec. 1797.

37. Part of Buckle's *History of Civilisation in England*, of which the first two (and only) volumes appeared in 1857 and 1861. Conveniently reprinted with this title by Chicago University Press in 1970, edited by H.J. Hanham.

38. Ludwig Stern, 'Ossianic Heroic Poetry' (trans. J.L. Robertson), in *Transactions of the Gaelic Society of Inverness*, vol. XXII (1890), p. 274; Smart, *James Macpherson*, pp. 90–94.

39. Thomas Hull, ed., *Select Letters between the Late Duchess of Somerset, Lady Luxborough, William Shenstone Esq., and Others* (London, 1778), II, 167–70: letter to Shenstone from Mr M[ac]G[owan], dated Edinburgh, 21 June 1760.

40. See T. Bailey Saunders, *The Life and Letters of James Macpherson* (London, 1894), pp. 229–31; Smart, *James Macpherson*, pp. 157–8.
41. *Letters of David Hume*, I, 330.
42. Ibid., I, 328–31.
43. Adam Smith, *Lectures on Rhetoric and Belles Lettres*, ed. John M. Lothian (Edinburgh, 1963), p. 131.
44. Blair's letter of 23 June 1760 to Sir David Dalrymple, printed on pp. xvi–xvii of the introduction to vol. 1 of Malcolm Laing, ed., *The Poems of Ossian, etc, Containing the Poetical Works of James Macpherson, Esq.* (Edinburgh, 1805).
45. Highland Society *Report*, Appendix, p. 58: Blair's letter of 20 Dec. 1797; *Letters of David Hume*, I, 331.
46. In the discussions that took place around 1800, concerning the circumstances of Macpherson's Ossianic work, Morrison was always referred to as 'Captain', from having been the captain of a corps of loyalist volunteers in the American revolutionary war. What he did before then, I have not discovered.
47. NLS, Adv. Mss 73. 2. 12, ff. 128–9: Ewan Macpherson's undated 'declaration'.
48. Highland Society *Report*, Appendix, p. 10: letter from Dr John Macpherson, Sleat, 27 Nov. 1763, to Blair.
49. Highland Society *Report*, Appendix, p. 4: letter from Sir James Macdonald, Isle of Skye, 10 Oct. 1763, to Blair.
50. On the MacMhuirich family see Derick Thomson, 'The MacMhuirich Bardic Family', *Transactions of the Gaelic Society of Inverness*, XLIII, (1960–63), pp. 276–304.
51. On this subject, see David Stevenson, *Alasdair McColla and the Highland Problem in the Seventeenth Century* (Edinburgh, 1980).
52. Highland Society *Report*, Appendix, pp. 278–9: Declaration of Lachlan MacVuirich, made at Torlum in Barra, 9 Aug. 1800.
53. Highland Society *Report*, Appendix, pp. 31, 36, 80–83; Appendix, pp. 20, 96–7.
54. NLS, Adv. Mss 73. 2. 12, ff. 128–9: Ewan Macpherson's undated 'declaration'. There is a slight conflation of identities here. Thomas Fraser of Boleskin, the current hereditary guardian of the manuscript, from whom it came to Macpherson, was a clergyman of Inverness-shire. The manuscript had come originally, however, from a clergyman of Perthshire: for Sir James MacGregor, whose name was entered in the manuscript as its owner, had been vicar of Fortingall in Perthshire, as well as Dean of Lismore in Argyll; and it was with Fortingall that he and his family had mostly been associated. For more on this famous manuscript, see chapter 6 below.
55. Highland Society *Report*, Appendix, p. 177.
56. Macpherson did, however, visit Mull at some point: presumably in the following year, when better weather permitted it. We are told this by the Rev. Archibald McArthur, minister of the parish of Kilninian and Kilmore on Mull, in a letter to Henry Mackenzie of 2 October 1797: NLS, Adv. Mss 73. 2. 13, ff. 48–9. His letter throws an interesting, rather negative light on Macpherson's proceedings and their effects on his contemporaries. McArthur was a native Gaelic speaker, born in Glen Lyon in about 1734. Educated at the university of St Andrews, he became a scholar: he would be one of the team employed by the SPCK to produce its great translation of the Bible into Gaelic between 1783 and 1801. In his youth McArthur had

enthusiastically memorised, and even written down, many of the Ossianic poems that he had heard recited by old men in different parts of the country. But when *Fingal* was published, he had been persuaded that all the poems which he had ever heard recited were of 'that inferior kind' – i.e. mere ballads – which Macpherson had dismissed in his notes to *Fingal* as 'later imitations of the genuine compositions of Ossian'; and consequently McArthur had lost much of his former 'relish' for them: writing in 1797 that it was now a very long time since he had 'paid any attention' to recitations of Ossianic poetry. In 1765, however, when he had first gone to Mull as minister, he had made enquiries about Macpherson's visit to the island a few years earlier. His informants had formed a strong impression that Macpherson was uninterested in anything that was recited to him on the island. A 'countryman' famous on the island for his recitations was fetched from a considerable distance specifically to perform for Macpherson; but Macpherson did not trouble to commit to paper anything he heard recited then, or elsewhere on Mull. We may wonder whether Macpherson had taken any competent Gaelic transcriber along with him, or whether he had already completed, before this trip, the work that he would shortly publish as *Fingal*, and was just going through the motions of further investigation for appearances' sake. At the conclusion of his letter, we may note, McArthur expressed to Mackenzie his hope that the Highland Society would employ, in the work of transcribing for the press the late James Macpherson's manuscripts, 'some person who understands the orthography of the Gaelic language better than he seems to have done himself'. That McArthur's own interest in collecting Ossianic poetry from contemporary recitation should have been discouraged by Macpherson's publications is particularly regrettable; for his earlier transcripts were passed on, when he stopped collecting, to the Rev. James Maclagan (of Amulrie, and later Blair Atholl), and are described by a modern expert as among the best of that era: Derick Thomson, *The Gaelic Sources of Macpherson's Ossian* (Edinburgh, 1952), pp. 8–9.

57. Highland Society *Report*, Appendix, pp. 176–7, 271: Captain Morrison's answers to queries, Greenock, 7 Jan. 1801; affidavit of Archibald Fletcher, Edinburgh, 19 January 1801.

58. Highland Society *Report*, Appendix, p. 155: letter from James Macpherson, Edinburgh, 16 Jan. 1761, to Rev. Mr Maclagan (in Perthshire).

59. It seems to have been the snuff and tobacco stains which persuaded the willing Ferguson that Macpherson's papers were old. For Ferguson could not, himself, read the old Gaelic script, as he admitted in a letter written thirty years later: Saunders, *Life and Letters of James Macpherson*, p. 151.

60. Highland Society *Report*, Appendix, pp. 59, 63: letters from Blair, 20 Dec. 1797, and Adam Ferguson, dated Hallyards near Peebles, 26 Mar. 1798.

61. *Letters of David Hume*, I, 342–3.

62. The Yale edition of Horace Walpole's Correspondence, ed. W.S. Lewis, vol. 15: *Horace Walpole's Correspondence with Sir David Dalrymple* (London, 1952), p. 72: Walpole to Dalrymple, 14 April 1761.

63. *Boswell's London Journal, 1762–1763*, ed. Frederick A. Pottle (London, 1950), p. 182. Cf. also ibid., p. 83.

64. I have drawn these quotations from Blair's *Lectures on Rhetoric and Belles Lettres*, first published in 1783, and from his *Critical Dissertation on the Poems of Ossian*, the substance of which, he explicitly states (in his Appendix to the third edition of *Fingal*), 'was originally delivered, soon after the first publication of *Fingal*, in the course of my lectures in the university of Edinburgh'.

65. Horace Walpole's Correspondence, vol. 9: *Horace Walpole's Correspondence with George Montagu* (London, 1941), pp. 407–8: Walpole to Montagu, 8 Dec. 1761.

## Chapter 5 James Macpherson and *Fingal*

1. The similarity most often noticed was between the invocation to the sun in Carthon and two passages of *Paradise Lost*; but many other parallels were observed. Cf. *Boswell: The Ominous Years (1774–1776)*, ed. Charles Ryskamp and Frederick A. Pottle (London, 1963), p. 84.

2. Horace Walpole, *Memoirs of the Reign of King George the Third*, ed. Sir Denis Le Marchant, revised G.R.F. Barker (London, 1894), III, 120.

3. E.g. *Three Beautiful and Important Passages omitted by the Translator of Fingal, and restored by Donald Macdonald* (1762); a jovial burlesque, not without wit.

4. See 'Notices of Ancient Gaelic Poems and Historical Fragments in a MS volume called "The Dean of Lismore's Book", in the Advocates Library' by Rev. Thomas McLauchlan, *Proceedings of the Society of Antiquaries of Scotland*, II (1862), pp. 38–41; the estimate of the number of lines of verse contained in the volume comes from Ronald Black's typescript catalogue in the NLS, cited in the notes to the previous chapter (nineteenth-century estimates were of about 11,000 lines).

5. [W.F. Skene's introduction to Thomas McLauchlan's edition of *The Book of the Dean of Lismore* (Edinburgh, 1862), pp. xxxviii–xl; Saunders, *Life and Letters of James Macpherson*, pp. 105–9.]

6. *A Galick and English Vocabulary*, designed to aid missionary teaching in Highland schools, was the product of the Scottish Society for the Propagation of Christian Knowledge.

7. Martin, *Description of the Western Isles*, pp. 152–3. There were several eighteenth-century editions of this work. One of them was evidently read by William Wordsworth, whose account of the cuckoo

> Breaking the silence of the seas
> Beyond the farthest Hebrides

must be based on Martin's account of St Kilda. Only St Kilda could be described as 'beyond the farthest Hebrides'.

8. William Buchanan of Auchmar, *An Historical and Genealogical Essay upon the Family and Surname of Buchanan* (edition of Edinburgh, 1775), p. 16.

9. *Fingal, an Ancient Epic Poem in six books: together with several other Poems, composed by Ossian the son of Fingal* (London, 1762): p. xvi of the

'Dissertation concerning the Antiquity of the Poems'; the penultimate page (unnumbered) of the Preface; note to part I of 'Cath-loda' in *Temora: an Ancient Epic Poem in eight books: together with several other Poems composed by Ossian the son of Fingal* (London, 1763), p. 184.

10. Highland Society *Report*, p. 44: letter of Rev. Andrew Gallie, dated Kincardine, 4 Mar. 1801, to Rev. Dr Kemp.

11. Saunders, *Life and Letters of James Macpherson*, pp. 178–80; Smart, *James Macpherson*, pp. 131–2.

12. *Letters of David Hume*, I, 400.

13. Saunders, *Life and Letters of James Macpherson*, prints on p. 249 the public letter of Becket the bookseller, dated 19 January 1775, confirming, at a time of renewed controversy, that 'the original manuscripts of *Fingal*', etc., had lain in his shop, open to inspection, for 'many months in the year 1762'. Saunders admits, however, on pp. 180–81, that we do not know whether these 'originals' were 'the old manuscripts' which Macpherson and his friends had discovered in the Highlands, or the versions in modern Gaelic which they had produced from their oral sources. Cf. Smart's comments, *James Macpherson*, pp. 140–42.

14. See Paul van Tieghem, *Ossian en France* (Paris, 1917), I, 165–6. Ludwig Stern conjectured that the author of the articles was Abbot Connery: 'Ossianic Heroic Poetry' (trans. J.L. Robertson) in *Transactions of the Gaelic Society of Inverness*, vol. XXII (1897–8), p. 261.

15. *Boswell's Life of Johnson*, I, 396.

16. Ibid., II, 126; V, 183.

17. *Letters of David Hume*, I, 398–401.

18. Ibid., I, 403.

19. Highland Society *Report*, Appendix, p. 60 (Blair to H. Mackenzie, 20 Dec. 1797).

20. The replies to Blair are printed in Highland Society *Report*, Appendix, pp. 3–37: the quotations are taken from pp. 6, 15, 11 (Rev. John Macpherson, 14 Oct. 1763, 27 Nov. 1763); 27 (Rev. Alexander MacAulay, 25 Jan. 1764); 21–2 (Rev. Neil Macleod, 22 Jan. 1764); 10 (Rev. John Macpherson, 27 Nov. 1763).

21. Highland Society *Report*, Appendix, pp. 8–9.

22. Highland Society *Report*, Appendix, p. 60: Blair's letter to Mackenzie of 20 Dec. 1797.

23. *Boswell, the Ominous Years (1774–1776)*, pp. 73, 87.

24. *Temora* (1763), prefatory Dissertation, p. xviii. This passage, and its significance, was noticed and astutely analysed by Smart in *James Macpherson*, pp. 39–40.

25. Thomson, *Gaelic Sources*, pp. 59–67, says that in this first book of *Temora* Macpherson 'conflated' his Gaelic ballad sources; and, 'because he was not sufficiently conversant with the written language', he misunderstood and distorted their meaning: producing a version that was 'certainly unorthodox' and, as Smart had written earlier, hitherto 'unheard of'. The entire remainder of this 'epic' (seven more books) was the product of 'one Graeco-Badenoch source, to wit, Macpherson's own imagination'.

26. For Hume's teasing of Blair and John Home, see *New Letters of David Hume*, ed. Raymond Klibansky and Ernest C. Mossner (Oxford, 1954), pp. 208–10.

27. Blair's 'Appendix' to his *Critical Dissertation*, published in the collected edition of *The Works of Ossian* – described as 'the third edition' – (London, 1765). The *Critical Dissertation* occupies the second half of volume two, and is paginated separately, the Appendix following thereafter. See particularly pp. 117, 119, 130.

28. *The Letters of Sir Walter Scott*, ed. H.J.C. Grierson (London, 1932), I, 322: letter to Anna Seward of Litchfield on the Ossian phenomenon, probably September 1806.

29. Mossner, *Life of David Hume*, p. 417.

30. The evidence concerning this episode (which was ventilated in pamphlets published at the time) has been set out in John Small, 'Biographical Sketch of Adam Ferguson', in *Transactions of the Royal Society of Edinburgh* (1864), pp. 34–41, and in *The Correspondence of James Boswell with Certain Members of the Club*, ed. Charles N. Fifer (London, 1976), pp. 117–21.

31. John Macpherson, *Critical Dissertations on the Origin, Antiquities, Language, Government, Manners and Religion of the Ancient Caledonians* (Dublin, 1768), pp. 83–4, 87, 36–44, 188–9, 197–8, 92.

32. John Whitaker, *The Genuine Origin of the Britons Asserted* (London, 1772), pp. 5–6.

33. John Macpherson wrote to Lachlan Macpherson of Strathmashie on 8 December 1763, asking him, if he should see 'James Macpherson, the poet' to enquire after 'papers belonging to my father in his hands'. NLS, Adv. Ms. 73. 2. 14, f. 109: reported in a letter to Sir John Sinclair from the Rev. Alexander Irvine, dated Dunkeld, 26 Nov. 1808, after searching the remaining Strathmashie papers inherited by Colonel Butter of Fascally, which were then located at Castle Menzies.

34. Charles O'Conor, *Dissertations on the History of Ireland* (Dublin, 1766): preface, pp. iv–v, xiii–xviii; appendix, *passim*, but especially pp. 26–8, 38–42, 44–5, 47–51, 59–62. It is worth noting here that Derick Thomson, the most authoritative modern investigator of Macpherson's epic constructions, made a particular study of his use of Irish sources, and convicts him repeatedly of being 'highly disingenuous': commenting on 'the same curious blend of misreading and wilful misrepresentation which has already been noticed in his handling of some of the ballads'; and concluding: 'Here, as elsewhere in Macpherson's work, it is not easy to assess what is disingenuous and what is written in good faith and bad judgment'. Thomson's chapter on 'Macpherson's Debt to Irish Historians' in *Gaelic Sources*, pp. 69–71.

35. James Macpherson, *An Introduction to the History of Great Britain and Ireland* (Dublin, 1771), p. 54 footnote; third, 'greatly enlarged' edition (London, 1773), p. 102 footnote.

36. Whitaker, *The Genuine Origins of the Britons*, pp. 1–8, 154–5.

37. Macpherson, *Introduction to the History of Great Britain and Ireland*, 1771 edition, pp. 44–5, 156; 1773 edition, pp. 78–9, 206–7.

38. William Shaw, *An Enquiry into the Authenticity of the Poems ascribed to Ossian* (London, 1781), p. 36.

39. His friend and neighbour of the 1750s, Donald Macpherson, meeting James walking about in Ruthven one Sunday, solitary, scowling, and sick of school-

mastering, commented in retrospect that he had seemed even 'more morose, silent and pensive than usual': NLS, Adv. Mss 73. 2. 13, f.47: Donald Macpherson, 1 Oct. 1797, to the Rev. John Anderson.

40. Sir Nathaniel Wraxall, *The Historical and the Posthumous Memoirs 1772–1784*, ed. H.B. Wheatley (London, 1884), IV, 233–8. Wraxall was a colleague of Macpherson not only in Parliament but as agent in London to the Nabob of Arcot.

41. Sydney C. Grier, ed., *The Letters of Warren Hastings to his Wife* (Edinburgh and London, 1905), p. 215.

42. *The Glenbervie Journals*, ed. Walter Sichel (London, 1910), p. 55.

43. The political machinations of the two Macphersons and their Highland mafia in India are illustrated by two sets of documents, viz: (1) the Mss of Sir John Macpherson, which contain John Macpherson's private correspondence with James Macpherson and with his cousin Martin Macpherson, minister of Golspie, and (2) the correspondence of James Macpherson with his cousin Colonel Allan Macpherson of Blairgowrie. Neither of these sources has been used in any published study of James Macpherson. Sir John Macpherson's papers were bequeathed by him to Hugh Macpherson, professor of Greek and Hebrew at the university of Aberdeen, who was the son of the Rev. Martin Macpherson; and they were still in the possession of his descendants in 1927, when they were lent to H.H. Dodwell for his publication *Warren Hastings' Letters to Sir John Macpherson* (London, 1927). Dodwell was director of the School of Oriental and African Studies in London. After Dodwell's death, the papers were described (in P.J. Marshall's *The Impeachment of Warren Hastings*, 1965) as 'Mss of Professor C.H. Philips'. Professor (now Sir Cyril) Philips was Dodwell's successor as director of SOAS. Sir Cyril Philips evidently treats the papers as his private property; and he has refused to allow me to see them. However, many of them are cited in the unpublished Edinburgh Ph.D. thesis of the late James Maclean on 'The Political Careers of James (Fingal) Macpherson and Sir John Macpherson' (1967), and I have quoted them as quoted by him. Maclean's thesis is valuable because he is the only Gaelic scholar to have read the Mss, including the most secret parts of the correspondence which were written in Gaelic. [In 1981 Sir Cyril Philips, professor of Indian History, director of the School of Oriental and African Studies, vice chancellor of the University of London, was finally forced by mounting academic, family, and ultimately legal pressure, to disgorge what was left of the collection of Macpherson papers which he had guarded illegitimately, jealously, and incompetently for thirty-five years. For one more year the collection remained in purdah. Then, in 1982, four boxes of manuscript material, containing 218 items relating to Sir John Macpherson's career, by no means all that had been lent by the Macpherson family to Professor Dodwell in 1926, were passed to the India Office Library: their intended destination, following Dodwell's publication of the letters to Hastings. A long-running academic scandal, damaging to historical scholarship, had finally come to an end. Even so, access to the papers was severely restricted at first. The India Office Library collections were subsequently absorbed into the British Library, where the Macpherson Collection (Mss EUR F291) is on permanent loan and now fully open to use by scholars.]

The correspondence of James Macpherson with Allan Macpherson was produced as evidence in a lawsuit brought by Allan Macpherson against James Macpherson's executors after James Macpherson's death. They seem to have been unknown to James Maclean. They were printed in the records of the court (First Division, 25 February 1813, Lord Armadale, Ordinary: case of Allan Macpherson v. James Macpherson *et al.*). I am grateful to Colonel R.T.S. Macpherson for lending me his copy of these documents.

Unless otherwise specified, the material on the activities of James and John Macpherson in the rest of this chapter comes from one or other of these two sets of sources.

44. Sir Robert Harland to Earl of Rochford, 10 Sept. 1772, India Office Library, H. Misc. S. 110, pp. 495–6, cited in James Maclean's thesis.

45. Dodwell, *Warren Hastings' Letters to Sir John Macpherson*, p. 192: Hastings to Macpherson, 27 Jan. 1784.

46. Keith Feiling, *Warren Hastings* (London, 1954), p. 176.

47. Laing, *The Poems of Ossian/James Macpherson*, I, p. xlvii.

48. *The Last Journals of Horace Walpole during the Reign of George III: from 1771 to 1783*, ed. A Francis Steuart (London, 1910), I, 524, and II, 387.

49. Dodwell, *Warren Hastings' Letters to John Macpherson*, p. 169.

50. Ibid., p. 146: Hasting to Macpherson, July 1782.

51. British Library, Additional Mss 29141, f. 342.

52. Dodwell, *Warren Hastings' Letters to John Macpherson* (letters of 1776–9), pp. xxiv, 54, 60.

53. Charles Ross, ed., *Correspondence of Charles, first Marquis Cornwallis* (London, 1859), I, 383, 430, 454–5: letters from Cornwallis to Henry Dundas, from Calcutta, 1 Nov. 1788, 8 Aug. and 1 Nov. 1789.

54. His successors gaelicised it to 'Balavil', its modern name.

55. James Cameron Lees, *A History of the County of Inverness* (Edinburgh and London, 1897), p. 298.

56. See Voltaire, *Dictionnaire Philosophique*: 'Anciens et Modernes: d'un passage d'Homère' (édition Ménard et Desenne, Paris, 1827), II, 122–32.

57. For Cesarotti see especially his *Epistolario* in *Opere de Melchior Cesarotti* (1817), vols I–III; Vittore Alemanni, *Un filosofo delle lettere, Melchior Cesarotti*, vol. I (all published) (Turin, 1894). Cesarotti was a classical scholar, a philosopher of aesthetics, and a disciple of Rousseau. He knew no English, and relied on an imperfect Italian version by his friend Charles Sackville, an illegitimate son of the Duke of Dorset, who lived in Venice. As a scholar, Cesarotti admitted grave doubts about the authenticity of the poems: doubts which were suggested to him by the Irish scholars Charles O'Conor and Joseph Walker, and which were not dispelled by Macpherson's peremptory dismissal of all Irish objections; but his doubts were overcome by admiration for 'il più gran genio che sia mai comparso sulla scena poetica'.

58. This project is described in the diary of William Blair, minister of Kingussie between 1724 and 1780, cited in Alexander Macpherson, *Glimpses of Church and Social Life in the Highlands in Olden Times* (Edinburgh, 1893), pp. 205–6.

59. *Horace Walpole's Correspondence with William Mason*: Horace Walpole's Correspondence, vol. 29 (London, 1955), p. 300: Walpole to Mason, 11 May

1783; *The Works of James Barry* (London, 1809), II, 371. Barry's splendid painting can still be seen in the Great Room of the Royal Society of Arts.
60. *Horace Walpole's Correspondence with Mason*, vol. 29, pp. 151–2, 157.

## Chapter 6 The Controversy over Ossian

1. *Boswell's Life of Johnson*, II, 296–7; II, 309–10; V, 242.
2. See the evidence and arguments adduced by Smart, *James Macpherson*, pp. 142–50.
3. *Boswell's Life of Johnson*, V, 242.
4. *Letters of Sir Walter Scott*, I, 322.
5. Samuel Johnson, *A Journey to the Western Islands of Scotland*, ed. Mary Lascelles (Yale edition of the Works of Samuel Johnson, vol. IX, London, 1971), pp. 118–19.
6. *Boswell's Life of Johnson*, V, 120–1.
7. Ibid., II, 309.
8. Ibid., II, 298.
9. *The Letters of Edward Gibbon*, ed. J.E. Norton (London, 1956 ), II, 91.
10. Edward Gibbon, T*he History of the Decline and Fall of the Roman Empire*, ed. J.B. Bury, vol. I (Methuen, London, 1909), pp. 141–2.
11. *Letters of David Hume*, II, 310–11.
12. Gibbon, *Decline and Fall of the Roman Empire*, III, 43.
13. M.V. Hay, *A Chain of Error in Scottish History* (London, 1927), especially pp. 32–9.
14. The description is that of Sir John Sinclair in *Poems of Ossian in the Original Gaelic*, I, ccxv.
15. Sir John Sinclair, *An Account of the Highland Society of London, from its Establishment in May 1778 to the Commencement of the Year 1813* (London, 1813), pp. 1–4.
16. Ibid., p. 4.
17. See Robert F. Metzdorf's essay 'M'Nicol, Macpherson, and Johnson' in W.H. Bond, ed., *Eighteenth-Century Studies in Honor of Donald F. Hyde* (Grolier Club, New York, 1970), pp. 45–61; also NLS, Adv. Ms. 73. 2. 15, ff. 11–12: Malcolm Laing to Lord Bannatyne, the judge and Ossianic enthusiast, 8 April 1802.
18. Donald MacNicol, *Remarks on Dr Samuel Johnson's Journey to the Hebrides; in which are contained Observations on the Antiquities, Language, Genius, and Manners of the Highlanders of Scotland* (London, 1779), pp. 78, 303–4.
19. [Quoted, but without indication of source, in Thomson, *Gaelic Sources*, p. 7.]
20. On Shaw, see the following sources: *The Dictionary of National Biography; Boswell's Life of Johnson* (in the Hill-Powell edition); Smart, *James Macpherson*; Shaw's own (anonymous) *Memoirs of the Life and Writings of the late Dr Samuel Johnson* (1785), ed. Arthur Sherbo (London, 1974), especially pp. 42–8; Kenneth D. MacDonald, 'The Rev. William Shaw – Pioneer Gaelic Lexicographer', in *Transactions of the Gaelic Society of Inverness*, vol. 50 (1976–78), pp. 1–26.

21. Published in 1778 under the title *An Analysis of the Galic Language*.

22. Shaw, *Enquiry into the Authenticity of Ossian*, pp. 43–4.

23. Shaw's *Memoirs of Dr Johnson*, p. 44; (also cited on p. 145 of Smart, *James Macpherson*).

24. Shaw, *Enquiry into the Authenticity of Ossian*, pp. 53–60, 84–5.

25. Information given to Shaw by Clark himself, and entered into the second edition (1782) of Shaw's *Enquiry into the Authenticity of Ossian*: in a footnote on p. 75 of an Appendix which systematically rebuts the disingenuous allegations made in Clark's pamphlet, and supplies additional evidence.

26. John Clark, *An Answer to Mr Shaw's Inquiry into the Authenticity of the Poems ascribed to Ossian* (Edinburgh, 1781), pp. 33–4. See also pp. 23–4 for Mackenzie's 'authorisation' of a related statement; but compare these passages with their rebuttals in the second edition of Shaw's pamphlet, cited in the note above, pp. 64–5, 67–72, 81.

27. On Gibbon's relations with Pinkerton, see my essay 'The Other Gibbon', in *The American Scholar*, vol. 46, number 1 (Winter, 1976), pp. 94–103.

28. *The Literary Correspondence of John Pinkerton, Esq.*, ed. Dawson Turner (London, 1830), I, 347. The testimony is conveyed by Pinkerton himself. However, it is confirmed by words which Gibbon employed elsewhere, and is supported by Lord Sheffield: *The Miscellaneous Works of Edward Gibbon* (London, 1814), III, 552, 572–5; II, 494.

29. Pinkerton, *Enquiry into the History of Scotland*, I, xix.

30. Ibid., I, 199–200; II, 53.

31. Ibid., II, 77–9; Pinkerton, ed., *Ancient Scottish Poems* (London, 1786), xlv–lii.

32. Pinkerton, *Enquiry into the History of Scotland*, II, 78–83.

33. W.F. Skene, ed., *John of Fordun's Chronicle of the Scottish Nation* (Edinburgh, 1872), II, lxxi–ii.

34. Pinkerton, *Enquiry into the History of Scotland*, II, 34.

35. Ibid., I, 246–7, 340; II, 12, 35,48.

36. Ibid., I, 341.

37. *Literary Correspondence of John Pinkerton*, I, 235–6.

38. NLS, Adv. Mss 73. 2. 24, ff. 15–16 *et seq.* contains a series of extracts from the minutes of the Highland Society of London, recording their committee's first meeting with Macpherson concerning the publication of the Gaelic 'originals' of Ossian, and their successive encounters with him, and his responses.

39. *Poems of Ossian in the Original Gaelic*, I, ccxvii–ccxix.

40. Ibid., I, ccxxii–ccxxiii; NLS, Deposit 268: Mss of the Highland Society of London, box I (General Correspondence, 1781–1820), ff. 18–19.

41. *Poems of Ossian in the Original Gaelic*, I, ccxx.

42. Saunders, *Life and Letters of James Macpherson*, p. 293.

43. Small, *Biographical Sketch of Ferguson*, p. 54–5; rather inaccurately reprinted in Saunders, *Life and Letters of James Macpherson*, pp. 293–6.

44. *Poems of Ossian in the Original Gaelic*, I, lxxxviii.

45. *Letters of Sir Walter Scott*, VII, 296: to J.W. Croker, 5 Jan. 1823; *The Journal of Sir Walter Scott*, ed. W.E.K. Anderson (Oxford, 1972), p. 257: 26 Dec.1826.

46. Thomas Carlyle, *Reminiscences*, ed. J.A. Froude (London, 1881), I, 282.

47. NLS, Deposit 268: Mss of the Highland Society of London, box 1, ff. 10–11: letters dated London 13 Dec. 1783 from Clanranald's friend Major Alexander Donaldson to John Mackenzie, and Mackenzie's reply.

48. Highland Society *Report*, pp. 33–4: letter of Rev. Andrew Gallie, Kincardine 12 Mar. 1799, to Charles Mackintosh.

49. Highland Society *Report*, Appendix, p. 177: Captain Morrison's Observations, Greenock, 7 June 1801; and p. 96: the Declaration of Ewan Macpherson at Knock in Sleat, 11 Sept. 1800.

50. Highland Society *Report*, Appendix, p. 62: Blair's letter to Mackenzie, 20 Dec. 1797.

51. Highland Society *Report*, pp. 79–80.

52. The letter acknowledging receipt of these manuscripts is in the Mss of the Highland Society of London, NLS, Deposit 268, box I, f. 77: Lewis Gordon, deputy secretary of the Highland Society of Edinburgh, to John Mackenzie, 14 Feb. 1803.

53. Thus in its *Report* the Committee of the Highland Society of Scotland states that 'of the Ms books of which the committee had so often heard' [i.e. those described as given to Macpherson] only one was recovered': a small volume of no importance which it returned to Clanranald (p. 80). And yet, in the Appendix to the Report (p. 300), Dr Donald Smith refers to the 'valuable' Mss supplied by the late Mr John Mackenzie, including the Book of the Dean of Lismore. These Mss were first publicly identified as having come from Macpherson by John McArthur, LL.D., a leading member of the committee of the Highland Society of London, in a note to the 1807 edition of Ossian's poems (III, 347–8). But Malcolm Laing had deduced the connection between the Mss in Mackenzie's hands and Macpherson three years earlier. Preparing a second edition of his dissertation on Ossian's poems, he wrote on 8 April 1802 to Lord Bannatyne, suggesting that the Highland Society of Edinburgh should ask Mackenzie, as Macpherson's executor, to produce in public the Gaelic Mss which had belonged to Macpherson, and which had been referred to in the notorious interpolations in MacNicol's *Remarks on Dr Samuel Johnson's Journey to the Hebrides*: NLS, Adv. Mss 73. 2. 15, ff. 11–12.

54. Highland Society *Report*, pp. 151–2.

55. The committee did, however, hint (very cautiously) that the 'modernisms' which it saw in *Temora* put that poem in a somewhat different category from *Fingal*, as far as authenticity was concerned; and it speculated that the success of *Fingal* might have made Macpherson overconfident and careless in his second epic production: Highland Society *Report*, pp. 153–5.

56. Highland Society *Report*, pp. 59–61. The letters from the Rev. John Smith to the committee are printed in the Appendix to the *Report*, pp. 70–91. The 'profound ingenuity', but also the 'cool impudence', of Smith's Ossianic imitations is noticed on p. 180 of Thomson's article, 'Bogus Gaelic Literature', pp. 172–88.

57. Highland Society *Report*, Appendix, p. 175; *Poems of Ossian in the Original Gaelic*, I, ccxxv. Colin Macrae told Sir John Sinclair on 15 June 1806 that he himself could perfectly well remember seeing Captain Morrison at work, transcribing Macpherson's Gaelic manuscripts 'on his return to

England after the conclusion of the American war': NLS, Adv. Mss 73. 2. 11, ff. 50–51.

58. For Ross see *Fasti Ecclesiae Scoticanae*, ed. Hew Scott, VII (Edinburgh, 1928), pp. 158–9. He was also employed by the SPCK to supervise the publication of the second edition of the Gaelic Bible, and he compiled a Gaelic spelling book.

59. *Poems of Ossian in the Original Gaelic*, I, clxx.

60. Ibid., I, xl–lviii.

61. Rev. John Sinclair, *Memoirs of the Life and Works of the late Rt. Hon. Sir John Sinclair, Bart* (London, 1837), II, 227.

62. Sinclair, *Account of the Highland Society of London*, p. 16; Sinclair, *Memoirs of the Life and Works of Sir John Sinclair*, II, 234–5.

63. Stern, 'Ossianic Heroic Poetry', p. 269.

64. John Campbell Shairp, *Aspects of Poetry* [(1881)], p. 284; cited in Smart, *James Macpherson*, pp. 24–5.

65. It was long supposed that the Ms of Ross's corrected version of the Gaelic text had also been lost. The printer's copy of the whole text of Sinclair's edition was presented by Sinclair to the Advocates Library in 1823. Subsequently it disappeared from sight. However, it re-appeared again in 1965, and is now in the NLS, Adv. Mss 4. 1–6. See *Summary Catalogue of Advocates Mss* (1971), p. 42.

66. Thus the dictionary of William Shaw, of which Dr Johnson had had high hopes, was in the end a failure. Many Scottish subscribers refused to accept the work because Shaw, unable to obtain sufficient evidence in the Highlands (he claimed that the success of Ossian had caused the Highlanders to put a prohibitive price on even the most insignificant pieces of information), had been obliged to gather words and meanings from Irish Gaelic in place of Scottish: *Enquiry into the Authenticity of Ossian*, pp. 53–62.

67. Stern, 'Ossianic Heroic Poetry', pp. 267–71; Smart, *James Macpherson*, pp. 197–203; Thomson, *Gaelic Sources*, p. 85.

68. See Donald T. Mackintosh, 'James Macpherson and the Book of the Dean of Lismore', in *Transactions of the Gaelic Society of Inverness*, XXXVII (1936), 347–65; but also, more recently and reliably, Ronald Black's catalogue of Gaelic manuscripts in the NLS, Adv. Ms 72. 1. 37.

69. Johnson, *Journey to the Western Islands of Scotland*, p. 119.

70. Saunders, *Life and Letters of James Macpherson*, p. 294.

71. The following account, including quotations, is taken from: 1) Thomas McLauchlan's 'Notices of Ancient Gaelic Poems', pp. 35–47; 2) William J. Watson, ed., *Scottish Verse from the Book of the Dean of Lismore* (Scottish Gaelic Texts Society, Edinburgh, 1937); 3) Neil Ross, ed., *Heroic Poetry from the Book of the Dean of Lismore* (Scottish Gaelic Texts Society, Edinburgh, 1939); 4) Ronald Black's 'Description of Gaelic Mss: Advocates 72. 1. 37: the Book of the Dean of Lismore; Description and History of the MS' (typescript in NLS).

72. A facsimile of the Dean's script was reproduced, opposite p. 310, in the Highland Society *Report*.

73. Highland Society *Report*, pp. 93–106, and Appendix, pp. 300–305.

74. Thomson, *Gaelic Sources*, pp. 39–40.

75. Ibid., p. 80.

76. Mossner, *Life of David Hume*, p. 415.

77. Highland Society *Report*, Appendix, p. 78: the declaration of Lachlan MacVuirich, 9 Aug. 1800.

78. Highland Society *Report*, Appendix, pp. 96–7: the declaration of Ewan Macpherson, 11 Sept. 1800.

79. Highland Society *Report*, Appendix, p. 19: letter to Blair from Rev. Angus MacNeill, Hovemore, South Uist, 22 Dec. 1763.

80. Highland Society *Report*, pp. 79–81.

81. By Alexander Cameron in *Reliquiae Celticae* (Inverness, 1894), II, 148–309; but the Ms is wrongly identified in the introduction (pp. 138–47) as the Red Book.

82. Those who believe that the Red Book was not the book published in 1894 describe the latter as the 'Little Book of Clanranald': little, because it is smaller than the Red Book as that has been described. The Little Book has 232 leaves, on paper (not vellum), of five and a half inches by three and a half inches in size. It dates from the latter part of the seventeenth century.

83. On the wild goose chase in Australia see Ronald I. Black, 'In Search of the Red Book of Clanranald', in *Clan Donald Magazine*, no. 8 (Edinburgh, 1979), pp. 43–51.

84. Indeed, Morrison told the Rev. Alexander Irvine of Dunkeld that 'Macpherson understood the Gaelic language very imperfectly': to such an extent that Morrison himself (as he claimed) 'wrote out the Gaelic for him, for the most part, on account of Mr Macpherson's inability to write or spell it properly'. Irvine's testimony is recorded in Patrick Graham, *Essay on the Authenticity of the Poems of Ossian* (Edinburgh, 1807), pp. 283–5.

85. There is evidence that in 1793 James Macpherson had difficulty even in reading the Gaelic 'original' of the second book of *Temora*, written by Strathmashie thirty years earlier. NLS, Adv. Ms. 73. 2. 14, f. 66. See below, p. 179 and note (112).

86. NLS, Adv. Mss 73. 2. 24, ff. 32–3: Macleod to Lord Bannatyne from Glasgow College, 21 Jan. 1801.

87. Saunders, *Life and Letters of James Macpherson*, pp. 152–3.

88. Two very different scholars – the Scottish Celtic scholar W.F. Skene (in his introduction to *The Book of the Dean of Lismore*, pp. lvi–lvii) and the French literary scholar Paul van Tieghem in *Ossian en France*, I, 84–9, have argued that the Gaelic text *must* have preceded the English, and have suggested – what almost necessarily follows – that Strathmashie was the main author of the Gaelic text. So far as I can see, these are separate judgments: van Tieghem does not seem to have known Skene's work, and they came to their conclusions by different routes – Skene on linguistic, Van Tieghem on literary grounds. Van Tieghem deviated here from his usual guide, J.S. Smart, who assumed that Macpherson had written the Gaelic text in the period 1783–92. Skene was mistaken in thinking that Captain Morrison was present during the cooking-up of Ossian at Ruthven.

89. van Tieghem, *Ossian en France*, I, 84.

90. Highland Society *Report*, p. 33.

91. Highland Society *Report*, p. 43.

92. NLS, Adv. Ms. 73. 2. 14, f. 51: Andrew Gallie, from Kincardine on 14 June 1802, to Charles Mackintosh at Edinburgh. Gallie twittered with apprehension on this whole subject: as the *Report* tactfully puts it, there were details which 'his modesty had not allowed him to mention in a correspondence of so public a nature as that with the Committee'. Gallie presumed that Macpherson had refused to divulge his Mss, lest the untutored public should read those 'corrupt' passages which had crept into them, but which the pure judgment of Macpherson had, commendably, excised: Highland Society *Report*, p. 43.

93. Smart, *James Macpherson*, pp. 138–9, 165–70.

94. See p. lvii of Skene's introduction.

95. NLS, Adv. Ms. 73. 2. 14, f. 14. This is all the more significant, since it was the second book of *Temora* which Macpherson had mentioned particularly in 1763 (in his preliminary dissertation, cited above) as having reached him lately from a correspondent in the Highlands.

96. Highland Society *Report*, Appendix, pp. 8–9.

97. There are grounds, however, for suspecting that the reverend editor may not have translated Strathmashie's verses accurately and fully in every instance.

98. Smart, *James Macpherson*, pp. 19–29.

99. Sinton, *Poetry of Badenoch*, pp. 448–50, 454–6, 489.

100. Ibid., pp. 489, 441–3.

101. Ibid., pp. 489–92.

102. *Fingal*, p. xv.

103. Saunders, *Life and Letters of James Macpherson*, p. 146.

104. Highland Society *Report*, Appendix, pp. 8–9.

105. *Temora* (1763), prefatory Dissertation, p. xviii.

106. NLS, Adv. Ms. 73. 2. 24, f. 51: Andrew Gallie to Charles Mackintosh, 14 June 1802.

107. Ibid.

108. NLS, Adv. Mss 73. 2. 14, f. 109: Alexander Irvine to Sir John Sinclair, 26 Nov. 1808.

109. There are interesting reflections on this fact in a letter written to Henry Mackenzie on 1 July 1802 by Anne Grant of Laggan. Mrs Grant's observations were certainly based on what she had been told by Ewan Macpherson, who lived near her in his old age and had taught her Gaelic. They may also have been based on what she had learned from conversations with James Macpherson himself during his latter years at Belleville. (She too was a poet and an admirer of Ossian.) When Macpherson had undertaken to collect and translate the works of Ossian, wrote Mrs Grant, he had found himself 'in the situation of Pope when he set about translating Homer . . . He could enter fully into the spirit of his author, and had powers to do justice to him, but he was not full master of the delicacies and difficulties of his language.' 'Conscious of this defect', James had engaged Ewan to accompany him as he toured around Skye and the other islands, 'hoping to supply it by his assistance'. That tour had been embarked on, Mrs Grant asserted, 'in search of more fragments ostensibly, but in reality to improve in the figurative and elevated language used in those countries where gentlemen still conversed

in Gaelic on topics susceptible of elegance and dignity'. NLS, Adv. Mss 73. 2. 15, ff. 17–20.

110. This story was related by the Rev. John Price, the keeper of the Bodleian Library who showed Macpherson the manuscript, to the Rev. Dr Charles O'Conor, while showing him the same manuscript at a later date. This Charles O'Conor was the grandson of that earlier Charles O'Conor who, as we have seen, published a learned attack on Macpherson's Ossian in 1766. The younger O'Conor had inherited the books and papers and scholarly interests of his grandfather. In about 1800 he moved from Ireland to England to serve as chaplain to the Marchioness of Buckingham and librarian at Stowe house. From Stowe he had easy access to the Bodleian Library, where he did some of the research for his four-volume work, *Rerum Hibernicarum Scriptores Veteres*, of which the first volume appeared at London in 1814, containing much discussion of early Irish Mss. It was in that first volume (preliminary matter, pp. ci, cxxiii) that O'Conor recorded (in Latin) Price's story about Macpherson. The story was then repeated (in English) in prize essays of 1829 on the subject of Macpherson and Ossian by two other notable Irish scholars, William Hamilton Drummond and Edward O'Reilly, published in the *Transactions of the Royal Irish Academy*, vol. 16 (1931), Part II, pp. 106, 245, 334.

The approximate date of Macpherson's visit to the Bodleian Library, when this episode occurred, has to be arrived at by inference. After the publication of his translation of Homer in 1773, Macpherson was commissioned by London booksellers to produce a History of England that would take up the story where Hume's *History* had finished, in 1688. The result was published in 1775 in two volumes as *The History of Great Britain from the Restoration to the Accession of the House of Hannover*, accompanied by two further volumes of *Original Papers containing the Secret History* of that period. In the preface to *Original Papers* (vol. I, p. 9) Macpherson thanked Price warmly for helping him to pick out documents relevant to his research from materials contained in the Bodleian Library (selected from the Ormonde, Tanner and Rawlinson Mss: see vol. I, pp. 42, 152, 296). Price died in 1813, having been the Bodleian's head librarian for forty-five years. He was particularly known, as an obituary notice recorded, for 'his readiness to communicate information from the rich literary stores over which he presided': W.D. Mackray, *Annals of the Bodleian Library, Oxford* (Oxford, 1890), p. 293. The records of the library ought to be able to show when Macpherson consulted those documents. Regrettably, they do not. Macpherson's name is not to be found in either Library Records e. 534, which lists persons formally admitted to the library throughout the eighteenth century, or Library Records e. 561, which shows what rare books and Mss were consulted, and by whom, between 1769 and 1775. The volume of Curators' Minutes covering the years between 1770 and 1786, which might perhaps have shown Macpherson gaining consent to his consultation and publication of Bodleian Library Mss, is missing.

111. It is printed in Highland Society *Report*, pp. 82–3; Macpherson's notes on the process of handing over various parts of the poems are not dated, as Mackenzie's were in his diary as he received them.

112. NLS, Adv. Ms. 73. 2. 14, f. 66 (recto and verso).

113. Andrew Gallie to Charles Mackintosh, 14 June 1802: NLS, Adv. Ms. 73. 2. 24, f. 51.

114. Sinton, *Poetry of Badenoch*, p. 236.

115. Highland Society *Report*, p. 31, and NLS, Adv. Ms. 73. 2. 24, f. 51.

116. Highland Society *Report*, Appendix, p. 60. Cf. also Carlyle's statement, ibid., p. 67.

117. For one of these dinners, see *Letters of Edward Gibbon*, II, 2. On 28 Jan. 1774 Gibbon, still only an aspiring author and keen to make his mark in the literary world, dined at the British Coffee House with Macpherson, John Home, David Garrick, Oliver Goldsmith and George Colman (the play-wright and theatre manager): people who, as he wrote to Lord Sheffield, were 'good company to know but not to live with'.

118. Horace Walpole used the word 'bully' when describing Macpherson's letter to Johnson in 1775. (It should be noted that Walpole was even-handed, for he described Johnson at the same time as 'a brute'.) *The Last Journals of Horace Walpole*, I, 444. John Ramsay, who met Macpherson in 1761, reports that he had shown early (at college) 'that harsh, overbearing spirit which made him so unpopular' in later life. Ramsay, *Scotland and Scotsmen*, I, 545.

119. *Boswell's London Journal*, p. 110.

120. *Private Papers of James Boswell from Malahide Castle*, ed. G. Scott and F.A. Pottle (privately printed, New York), vol. I (1928), pp. 127–8, cited in Mossner, *Life of David Hume*, p. 415. The rest of Hume's report, not quoted by Mossner, illustrates further just how giddy and arrogant Macpherson's meteoric ascent to fame had made him by November 1762.

121. *Boswell's London Journal*, p. 302.

122. *The Autobiography of Dr Alexander Carlyle of Inveresk, 1722–1805*, ed. John Hill Burton (Edinburgh, 1910), p. 417.

123. Ramsay, *Scotland and Scotsmen*, I, 549.

124. Highland Society *Report*, Appendix, pp. 60–61: Blair's letter of 20 Dec. 1797.

125. *Boswell's London Journal*, pp. 264–6, 255, 258–9; *Boswell on the Grand Tour: Italy, Corsica, and France, 1765–6*, ed. Frank Brady and Frederick Pottle (London, 1955), I, 549.

126. See Saunders, *Life and Letters of James Macpherson*, pp. 229–31.

127. Horace Walpole's Correspondence, vol. 33: *Horace Walpole's Correspondence with the Countess of Ossory* (London, 1965), p. 320.

128. Macpherson v. Macpherson, p. 150; also ibid., p. 170: 'having never extended my views farther than a perfect independence, to which I have attained'.

129. Robert Carruthers, *The Highland Note-book: or, Sketches and Anecdotes* (1843; 2nd edn, Inverness, 1887), pp. 360–61.

130. Mrs Anne Grant, *Letters from the Mountains: being the real Correspondence of a Lady between the years 1773 and 1807* (3rd edn, London, 1807), III, 34–5.

131. van Tieghem, *Ossian en France*, I, 87.

132. Cf. the verdict of Derick Thomson (*Gaelic Sources*, p. 83): 'It seems not unlikely that at one time he [Macpherson] was really under the impression that there existed an epic poem, or epic poems, in Gaelic ... But it is not likely that he held such a belief for long, while it is quite certain that he tried to impose it on the public.'

133. See Blair's comments on Macpherson's character in his letter of 20 Dec. 1797: Highland Society *Report*, Appendix, pp. 60–61.
134. Highland Society *Report*, Appendix, pp. 64, 67: the letters of Ferguson and Carlyle.
135. Gallie's letter of 4 Mar. 1801 in Highland Society *Report*, p. 39.
136. J.S. Blackie, *The Language and Literature of the Scottish Highlands* (1876), p. 203 (cited by Smart, *James Macpherson*, p. 171).

## Chapter 7 The Coming of the Kilt

1. *Basilikon Doron*, I, p. 71.
2. Andrew Fletcher, *Two Discourses concerning the Affairs of Scotland* (Edinburgh, 1698), p. 23.
3. I Geo. c. 54; 11 Geo. I c. 26.
4. 19 Geo. II c. 39; 20 Geo. II c. 51; 21 Geo. II c. 34.
5. Martin Martin, *Description of the Western Isles of Scotland* (2nd edn, London, 1716), p. 206.
6. *Literary Correspondence of John Pinkerton*, I, 230: the story, with its authenticating chain of transmission, was passed on to Pinkerton in a letter of 27 September 1789 by George Dempster, MP, of Dunnichen near Forfar.
7. James Gordon, *History of Scots Affairs* (Spalding Club, Aberdeen, 1841), III, Preface, Appendix, pp. xliii–xliv; Wodrow Mss cited in *Blackwoods Magazine*, April 1817, p. 69, and in Donald William Stewart, *Old and Rare Scottish Tartans* (Edinburgh, 1893), pp. 19–20; William Cleland, *A Collection of Several Poems* (1697), pp. 11–13; *The Grameid* (1691) (*Scottish History Society*, 1888).
8. The supporters are printed by Stewart, *Old and Rare Scottish Tartans*, p. 21; the whole coat of arms in *Alexander Nisbet's Heraldic Plates* (1892), p. 77. For other pictorial evidence see H.F. McClintock, *Old Highland Dress and Tartans* (2nd edn, Dundalk, 1949), pp. 12–28.
9. 28 Hen. VIII c. 15.
10. [Edward Burt], *Letter from a gentleman in the North of Scotland to his friend in London*, letter XXII (1818 edn), II, 84–91.
11. On Rawlinson's Scottish venture see Alfred Fell, *The Early Iron Industry of Furness and District* (Ulverston, 1908), pp. 346 *et seq.*; Arthur Raistrick, *Quakers in Science and Industry* (London, 1950), pp. 95–102.
12. John Telfer Dunbar, *History of Highland Dress* (Edinburgh, 1962), pp. 12–14, 69–70.
13. Martin, *A Description of the Western Islands of Scotland* (1716), p. 208.
14. The evidence on this point is set out conclusively by McClintock, *Old Highland Dress and Tartans*, and Dunbar, *History of Highland Dress*.
15. Stewart, *Old and Rare Scottish Tartans*, p. 36.
16. Johnson, *Journey to the Western Islands of Scotland*, pp. 57, 51, 102.
17. David Stewart, *Sketches of the Character, Manners and Present State of the Highlanders of Scotland* (Edinburgh, 1822), I, 112 note.
18. Thus John Hay Allan, in his *Bridal of Caolchairn*, pp. 308–9, remarks that, at Highland weddings, of the unfashionable tartan 'little or nothing is to be

seen'. This was published in 1822, the year when George IV's visit caused tartan to envelop the limbs of the higher classes in Edinburgh.

19. J.G. Herder, *Auch eine Philosophie der Geschichte 3ur Bildung der Menscheit* (1774).

20. Pitt's speech in the House of Commons, 14 January 1766, quoted in Sinclair, *Account of the Highland Society of London*, p. 3.

21. On the Highland regiments see Stewart, *Sketches of . . . the Highlanders of Scotland*; James Browne, *History of the Highlands and the Highland Clans* (1837); corrected by Dunbar, *History of Highland Dress*, pp. 155–87.

22. 'The Highlander wears no breeches, but his plaid belted about his waist, which hangs exactly like the folds of the Roman garment which we see on equestrian statues': *A Short History of the Highland Regiment* (1743), cited in Dunbar, *History of Highland Dress*, pp. 164–5; also in *Remarks on the People and Government of Scotland, particularly the Highlanders* (Edinburgh, 1747), pp. 19–20.

23. Quoted in James Logan and R.R. McIan, *The Clans of the Scottish Highlands* (London, 1843), p. 3.

24. See Sinclair, *Account of the Highland Society of London*.

25. See *Prize Essays and Transactions of the Highland Society of Scotland*, vol. I (Edinburgh, 1799).

26. Quoted in Dunbar, *History of Highland Dress*, pp. 161–2.

27. [John] Pinkerton, *Dissertation on the Origin and Progress of the Scythians or Goths* [(London, 1787)], p. 54.

28. Pinkerton, *Enquiry into the History of Scotland*, II, 73 note.

29. The English scholar Richard Gough, in his 1789 edition of Camden's *Britannia*, described the kilt or philibeg as a 'little plaid or short petticoat reaching to the knees, substituted *of late* to the longer end of the plaid' (vol. III, p. 390); and in 1771 Thomas Pennant, in his *Tour of Scotland*, wrote that 'the *feil beg*, i.e. little plaid, also called *kelt* . . . is a modern substitute for the lower part of the plaid' (3rd edn, Warrington, 1774, p. 191 ). Both writers' information would almost certainly have come from Scottish sources. So much for the 'universal belief of the people' referred to by David Stewart, *Sketches of . . . the Highlanders of Scotland*!

30. *Literary Correspondence of John Pinkerton*, I, 404.

31. Ibid., pp. 405–10; *The Correspondence of the Rt Hon. Sir John Sinclair, bart* (London, 1831), I, 471–3.

32. The phrase is from George Skene's anonymous essay, 'The Heirs of the Stuarts', published in the *Quarterly Review*, vol. lxxxi (1847) (on which, see the next chapter). But George Skene's own brother, W.F. Skene, who was the best nineteenth-century scholar of Celtic Scotland, had a very high opinion of Pinkerton's work, as we saw earlier.

33. *A Historical Account of His Majesty's Visit to Scotland* (2nd edn, Edinburgh, 1822), p. 30; *Letters of Sir Walter Scott*, VI, 338, 343, 452; Lockhart, *Life of Scott* (1850), pp. 443, 481–2.

34. Thus Stewart described the memorandum in the *Edinburgh Magazine* as being 'by a gentleman whose name is not mentioned', although the name of the author, Euan Baillie of Abereachean, is clearly printed there.

35. Stewart, *Sketches of . . . the Highlanders of Scotland*, I, 72–7, 113 note.

36. *Dictionary of National Biography*, under 'Stewart, David (1772–1829)'.
37. *Letters of Sir Walter Scott*, VII, 70, 213.
38. The Wilson correspondence – some twelve thousand letters from correspondents throughout the world – is now mainly in the National Library of Scotland. A few thousand are in the National Museum of Antiquities in Edinburgh; and some two thousand are held in the Museum of Scottish Tartans at Comrie in Perthshire, to whose director, Dr Micheil Macdonald, I am indebted for valuable information.
39. James Logan, *The Scottish Gael* (London, 1831), p. 237. The collection is now, I am told, in the vaults of William Glyn's Bank in Whitehall.
40. *A Historical Account of His Majesty's Visit*, p. 94.
41. Ibid., pp. 30, 74; *Letters of Sir Walter Scott*, VII, 214–15; Lockhart, *Life of Scott*, p. 484; *Letters to Sir W. Scott on the moral and political character and effects of the visit to Scotland . . . of H.M. George IV* (Edinburgh, 1822), p. 74.

## Chapter 8 The Tartan

1. Chapter XIII of Macaulay's *History of England from the Accession of James II*, ed. C.H. Firth, vol. 4 (London, 1914), p. 1591. This was written in the 1850s.
2. See his obituary notice in *Gentleman's Magazine*, 1800, p. 201 (where 'Devonshire' is clearly a misprint for 'Downshire').
3. *The Bridal of Caölchairn and other Poems* by John Hay Allan, Esq. (London, 1822). The volume evidently sold badly, for the pages were afterwards made up with a new title page describing them as by Sir Walter Scott, 'fifth edition', – perhaps the first major imposture of their author.
4. 'Thomas Allan' and 'Allan' were presented to King George IV at Edinburgh, the former by the Earl of Strathmore, the latter by the Earl of Leven. In his *Reply to the Quarterly Review*, in 1848, the elder brother denied that he had been in Scotland at the time of the royal visit, and said that he had not been abroad between 1822 and 1826. Since he would hardly have courted an easy refutation, this may well be true. If so, 'Allan' would probably have been the younger brother, and he would have been the author of the stanzas which are printed in *A Historical Account of His Majesty's Visit*, pp. 62–4.
5. The tradition was circulated in the time of their grandfather, the Admiral (see *Gentleman's Magazine*, 1800, p. 1021). After the death in 1717 of Charles Hay, thirteenth Earl of Errol, the title passed, through his sister and niece, to the Boyd family (earls of Kilmarnock till 1745), who thereupon changed their surname to Hay. Among the poems published in 1822, 'John Hay Allan' included one entitled 'Lines written upon coming in sight of the Coast of Scotland', which invented a remote Celtic origin for the Hay family, taken from 'an Ancient MS History of the Hays' (footnote, p. 336).
6. *Letters of Sir Walter Scott*, XI, 201; Dunbar, *History of Highland Dress*, p. 119.
7. *Journals and Correspondence of Lady Eastlake*, ed. C.E. Smith (London, 1895), I, 54–5.
8. This is shown by the learned notes in their *Lays of the Forest*, published in 1848.

9. Sir Thomas Dick Lauder, who knew them well, wrote of them that, 'though full of knowledge, gobbled up at random, and forming in their brains a *rudis indigestaque moles*, yet, that being bottomed on no education, they are in many respects most woefully ignorant'. Lauder to Scott, cited in Dunbar, *History of Highland Dress*, p. 122.

10. The transcript, which is indeed a beautiful book, is still extant. Sir Thomas Dick Lauder's daughter left it to a friend, whose niece, Miss Greta Morritt, presented it, in 1936, to Queen Mary. It is now in the Library of Windsor Castle.

11. For the correspondence between Lauder and Scott, see *The Journal of Sir Walter Scott* (Edinburgh, 1910), pp. 710–13; *Letters of Sir Walter Scott*, XI, 198–202; Stewart, *Old and Rare Scottish Tartans*; Dunbar, *History of Highland Dress*, pp. 120–23. The account of the episode in [George Skene], 'The Heirs of the Stuarts' (*Quarterly Review*, vol. lxxxi, 1847), is evidently a garbled reminiscence of this correspondence.

12. Henry Jenner, 'The Sobieski Stuarts' (*Genealogical Magazine*, May 1897, p. 27), assumed that the letter from 'J.T. Stuart Hay' was genuine, and written by the father. On all grounds of probability, and from the language of the letter, I assume that it was forged by the two brothers in order to evade Scott's demand that the manuscript be shown. Although it is often said that their father was involved in the brothers' claims, I have not seen any evidence to justify such a statement. The names, titles, opinions, etc., ascribed to their father all rest, so far as I can find, solely on the evidence of the brothers.

13. See the facsimiles printed by Stewart, *Old and Rare Scottish Tartans*, p. 56. Stewart insinuated, without stating, that the signature is genuine.

14. As Jenner pointed out, the brothers prudently waited, before advancing their Stuart claims, till the only person who could have confirmed or denied them – Louise von Stolberg, the legitimate wife of the Young Chevalier and their supposed grandmother – was dead. She died in January 1824.

15. The children were Charles Edward, Marie, Louisa Sobieska, and Clementina: their names recalling the Young Chevalier, his wife, and his mother.

16. Mr Hugh Fraser, MP, the present occupant of Eilean Aigas, has shown me an autograph document written by John Sobieski Stuart, containing rules for the behaviour of the two youngest children of Charles Edward Stuart. The rules are a series of absolute, not to say Mosaic, prohibitions. [Sir Hugh Fraser, knighted in 1980, died in 1984.]

17. 'It was only by the ingenuity of the author, John Sobieski Stuart, that the sets and designs in the *Vestiarium* were created': J.G. Mackay, quoted in Dunbar, *History of Highland Dress*, p. 142.

18. Stewart, *Old and Rare Scottish Tartans*, p. 58.

19. On the chevalier Watson, see the *Dictionary of National Biography* and Alistair and Henrietta Tayler, eds, *The Stuart Papers at Windsor* (London, 1939), pp. 22–30. Jenner suggested (*Genealogical Magazine*, May 1897) that Watson may have been the initiator of the Sobieski Stuarts' fantasies; but there is no reason to suppose that they even knew him. They took care not to cite him till he was conveniently dead.

20. Stewart, *Old and Rare Scottish Tartans*, p. 59.

21. Dunbar, *History of Highland Dress*, p. 111.

22. The attack was published in the *Quarterly Review*, vol. 81 (1847). John Sobieski Stuart's *Reply to the Quarterly* was published separately in 1848. Both attack and reply were afterwards reprinted together under the title *The Genuineness of the Vestiarium Scoticum* (Edinburgh, n.d.). This reprint was evidently published by the brothers, or in their interest (Dunbar, *History of Highland Dress*, p. 128).

23. John Sobieski Stuart assumed – as did many others – that the author of the review was the Scotch historian James Dennistoun. Others again assumed that it was J.W. Croker (e.g. John Ashton, *When William IV was King*, 1896, p. 222). It was also ascribed to J.G. Lockhart. In fact, the review was by George Skene, professor at Glasgow and brother of the Celtic scholar W.F. Skene, assisted by Skene's kinsman, Dr William Forbes.

24. Dunbar, *History of Highland Dress*, p. 140.

25. *Dictionary of National Biography*.

26. The correspondence on this subject is now in the Royal Library, Windsor Castle (PP 1/79).

27. I refer to D.W. Stewart, who, in his erudite work on Scottish tartans, published in 1893, consistently praised the scholarship of the Sobieski Stuart brothers, never allowed any damaging criticism to stick to them, avoided all suggestion of forgery or fantasy, and left his readers unaware of their true character.

28. Stewart, *Old and Rare Scottish Tartans*, p. 58.

29. Dunbar, *History of Highland Dress*, pp. 152–4.

30. Ibid., p. 139.

31. Ibid., p. 140.

32. The Sobieski Stuarts are not known to have had any gainful occupation, or any inherited wealth. Their father inherited only £100 from his father; and he was, anyway, still alive when his two sons were living in some state in Scotland. Their publications must have been costly, but no patron or subscriber is mentioned. They are said to have lost money by these ventures; but how they acquired the money to lose is unknown.

# Further Reading

Jeremy J. Cater

Some readers may wish to compare Trevor-Roper's treatment of the rôle played by myth and myth-makers in the historical development of the Scottish self-image with that offered by other writers since he worked on this book in 1979–81. Only a few suggestions will be made, and those only of books. Specialists will be aware already of the more detailed studies available in learned journals.

There is a general survey of the field by William Ferguson, *The Identity of the Scottish Nation* (Edinburgh, 1998), learned and argumentative. On the early history there is the tough but ultimately rewarding monograph of Dauvit Broun, *The Irish Identity of the Kingdom of the Scots in the Twelfth and Thirteenth Centuries* (Woodbridge, Suffolk, 1999). That can be followed by I.D. McFarlane's magisterial *Buchanan* (London, 1981). Murray Pittock, *The Invention of Scotland: the Stuart Myth and the Scottish Identity, 1638 to the Present* (London, 1991), is lively and stimulating. Colin Kidd, *Subverting Scotland's Past: Scottish Whig Historians and the Creation of an Anglo-British Identity, 1689–c.1830* (Cambridge, 1993), presents a vigorous and interesting analysis, though concentratedly conceptual in expression. Fiona Stafford, *The Sublime Savage: James Macpherson and the Poems of Ossian* (Edinburgh, 1988), is good, but stronger on empathetic understanding than on judgement. Some useful essays are collected in Howard Gaskill, ed., *Ossian Revisited* (Edinburgh, 1991). For those who wish to experience for themselves *The Poems of Ossian and Related Works*, there is an excellent complete edition by Howard Gaskill, introduced by Fiona Stafford (Edinburgh,

1996). On the later stages of Trevor-Roper's story, there is a pair of complementary studies, well researched, well organised and entertainingly different from each other: Peter Womack, *Improvement and Romance: Constructing the Myth of the Highlands* (London, 1989), and Robert Clyde, *From Rebel to Hero: the Image of the Highlander, 1745–1830* (East Linton, East Lothian, 1995). Finally, for an enjoyable account of the climactic events of 1822, when myth and reality were blended spectacularly in Edinburgh, see John Prebble, *The King's Jaunt: George IV in Scotland, 1822* (London, 1988).

# Index

# Index

Pinkerton, John, iconoclastic scholar: ablest antiquary after Innes 3, 146; his verdict on Innes 71; on Blackwell's *Homer* 78; literary beginnings 145; forges second part of *Hardyknute* 76, 184; impertinent about Virgil and Gibbon 145, but redeems himself in relation to Gibbon 3, 146–7, 254; aims to rescue history of Scotland from Highlanders 146, 148; on Macpherson's poetry and history 147–8; his admiration for Goths and scorn for Celts 148–5, his violent language does not persuade many fellow-countrymen 149–50, some of whom copy him in racial slurs 188; viewed as Anglicised traitor 187, and sneered at by successors 210, 233; confirms English origin of modern kilt 200, but condemns it as smelly and indecent 209–10; deplores tasteless vulgarity of most tartans, but allows merit to Sir J. Sinclair's version 210; a believer in breeches 208; despised by Sobieski Stuarts 226–7, though they agree on modern English origin of kilt 228

Pitt, William, the elder, earl of Chatham, prime minister 127, 205

Pitt, William, the younger, prime minister 131

Plutarch, ancient supplier of virtuous models 38, 54

Pope, Alexander, poet, his translation of Homer's *Iliad* 78, 258

Portugal: Inquisition in 37–8; king of 37

Price, Rev. John, keeper of Bodleian Library 259

Psalms, Buchanan's virtuoso translation of 39, 45

Ptolemy II, king of Egypt 25, 56

Pugin, A.W.N., neo-Gothic architect 232

Puritan party at court of Queen Elizabeth 47, 61

Pye, Henry, poet laureate xx

*Quarterly Review*, exposes Sobieski Stuarts 230; kills Keats 231

Ramsay, Allan, poet and bookseller 76

Ramsay, John, of Ochtertyre, describes Macpherson 182, 260

Randolph, Sir Thomas, English diplomat 50, 61

Rawlinson, Thomas, Quaker ironmaster and inventor of modern kilt 198–202

Red Book of Clanranald 139–40, 143, 166–7, 257

*Report* of Highland Society of Scotland (1805) 155–6, 162, 187–8, 255, 258

Reynolds, Sir Joshua, painter and friend of Dr Johnson 114

Riccio, David, murdered musician 45

Robert II, king of Scotland 65

Robert III, king of Scotland 49

Robertson, Rev. William, historian and university principal 91

Rogers, Daniel, humanist and diplomatist 57, 61

Romans, in Britain 4, 18, 56, 58, 60, 83, 123, 141, 164

romanticism 84–5, 134, 203–5, 216–17, 228, 231

Ronsard, Pierre, French poet 33–4

Ross, Rev. Thomas, transcribes Gaelic text of Ossian 156, 158, 256

Rousseau, Jean-Jacques, an instigator of romantic movement 85

Ruinart, Thierry, Benedictine scholar 68

Ryswick, Peace of 66

Sackville, Charles, translates Ossian into Italian for Cesarotti 252

Saint Margaret, Saxon wife of Malcolm Canmore 16

Scaliger, Joseph, classical scholar 34, 59

Scone, capital of Caledonia? 6; location of coronation stone 11, 15, 23

Scota, daughter of Pharaoh, ancestress of Gaels 13, 17, 22

*Scotichronicon*, Scottish chronicle 16, 20

Scots College in Douay 157, 224–5

Scots College in Paris 65–6, 68, 224

*Scots Magazine* 89

Scott, Sir Walter: a dual personality, both enlightened practical unionist and romantic Jacobite poet 210–11; great oracle of Scottish antiquarianism and tradition 221; his historical imagination combines with developing mood of current events 211, to give Scotland a new sense of national identity 212; loves *Hardyknute* 76; detests Sinclair 153; meets Burns 184; is deceived by a fabricated ballad 184; sees Ossian as a national shibboleth 119, 139, but also a false idol 204; presides over Celtic Society of Edinburgh 211; responsible for spread of tartan mania 211, and is blamed by Macaulay 217; is the man in Scotland George IV most wants to meet, and accepts task of orchestrating loyalty of nation as a predominantly Highland affair 213; drills tartan armies in Edinburgh, a Lowlander in charge of Highlanders 214; produces 'celtified pageantry' 214, and a ballooning of the new tartan myth 188; recovers balance after euphoria of 1822